THE IBERIAN AND WATERLOO CAMPAIGNS:

The letters of Lt James Hope

(92nd (Highland) Regiment), 1811-1815

Revised edition by S Monick

ACKNOWLEDGEMENTS

The editor is profoundly indebted to Mr Arnold James Henderson, who provided the former with access to the latter's most invaluable and enlightening research on the life and career of Lt James Hope. The editor also wishes to express his thanks and deep appreciation to Mr John McAra Cruikshank, who acted as a most important liaison agent in the editor's research.

N
&
M
PRESS

CONTENTS

INTRODUCTORY ESSAY

The writer

The family name Hope derives from John de Hope (1500-1560), who probably came to Scotland from France in 1537 in the entourage of Magaden de Valois, Queen of James V, and established himself as a merchant in Edinburgh. In his history of the 92nd Regiment, Lt Col Greenhill Gardyne states [1] that James Hope was a nephew of Sir John Hope, a colonel of the Regiment. However, this lineage is seriously questioned by Mr A J Henderson, a noted authority on the life and career of Hope. Hope's military career commenced as a Volunteer in the 92nd Regiment, and he served in this capacity between 26 July 1809 and 1 November of that year; during which period he accompanied the Regiment in the Walcheren exepedition to Holland. The Volunteer was a peculiar feature of the British Army at that time. He was a member of the battalion who occupied a socially ambivalent role, in so far as, whilst serving in the ranks and thus not possessing the status of a commissioned officer (unlike the midshipman in the Royal Navy) he nevertheless had access to the officers' mess. This lack of official officer status is illustrated by the fact that, on the Chelsea Prize Roll for Walcheren [PRO (Public Records Office): WO/163/200] Hope is recorded as a Private in No 1 Company, and as being entitled to receive prize money to the sum of 18s.6. three-farthings (ie the amount of 5th Class prize money payable to those of the rank of corporal and below).

The regimental history [2] cites the Regimental Order (despatched from Capelle), dated 11 August 1809, which states:

> 'Volunteer Mr James Hope is to do duty as a supernumery officer in the Grenadier Company, and to be obeyed...
> accordingly till further orders.'

The above order is revealing in two respects. The first is the reference to 'supernumery officer': indicating that volunteers were employed in the officer establishment although not in formal possession of a commission. Second, one encounters the term 'Grenadier Company'. The reference to 'grenadier' should not be confused within this context with the Grenadier Guards. In the 18th Century the grenadier companies were the equivalent of today's shock assault troops. Grenadiers were especially trained troops adroit at hurling grenades, or small bombs (the primitive ancestors of the modern hand grenade). Hence the device of a flaming grenade to denote such a unit. In 1686 King James II had introduced grenadier companies into each line regiment. As the duty of this type of soldier was dangerous and demanded special qualities (similar to those required of a modern commando in the Royal Marines or Special Air Service Regiment), the grenadier was regarded as a member of an elite unit. By the latter part of the 18th Century, the grenade had been discontinued, but the term 'grenadier' continued to bestow special distinction. (Thus, the First Regiment of Foot Guards was named Grenadiers as an honour, following their distinguished service at Waterloo). Hope's membership of a grenadier company thus suggests that he was a tenacious and resourceful soldier (and, in addition, was probably a powerfully built individual). His early military promise is further evidenced by a letter written by the OC of the battalion, Lt Col John Cameron, to the commander-in-chief, dated 20 September 1809, in relation to Hope and a Mr McDougall; presumably recommending them for the vacant ensign's commissions [3]:

'I beg leave to do myself the honor [sic] of forwarding the Memorials of two young Gentlemen, for the favourable consideration of the Commander in Chief.
These young Gentlemen have conducted themselves extremely well indeed whilst with the 92nd Regt., so much so that I think very highly of both. Mr. Hope is the senior Volunteer ...'

(It is noteworthy that neither this letter, nor Hope's Memorial, to which it refers, makes no reference whatsoever to his relationship with the colonel of the regiment; surely a telling point, adding considerable leverage to Cameron's recommendation).

However, Hope's subsequent career did not fulfil this early promise; and he never rose above the rank of captain. The details of that career are as follows [4]:

In September 1811 he was sent to Portugal in command of a draft for the 1st Battalion; the intention being that he should return to the 2nd Battalion as soon as he had delivered his draft.

However, as the 1st Battalion suffered from a shortage of officers, he was retained by them until such time as their full establishment was attained. As a result, he served in the Peninsula for a little over two years; being present at the battles of Arroyo del Molinos, Almarez, Alba de Tormes, Vittoria, the Maya Pass (where he was wounded in the head by a musket ball) and Nivelle. On 7 January 1813 he obtained the rank of lieutenant, through purchase. Finally, in December 1813, he was released from duty with the 1st Battalion and returned to the 2nd Battalion in Great Britain. When the 2nd Battalion was disbanded in 1814, Hope was returned to the 1st and accompanied his battalion to Flanders in May 1815. He served at both Quatre Bras and Waterloo. In the latter battle he was wounded by a musket ball in the groin during the latter phase of the engagement. His wound would probably have proved fatal had not the musket ball struck a small comb in his pocket which he had purchased a short time previously as a souvenir [5]. Hope was placed on half-pay in March 1817, and remained without military employment for 15 years. On 3 February 1832 he was awarded a lieutenancy in the 75th Regiment. (Curiously, he is the sole member of the Regiment to have served in both the 75th and 92nd Regiments; the two battalions which comprised the restructured Gordon Highlanders when it was reformed in 1881 on the basis of linked battalions, in accordance with Cardwell's reforms). However, he never actually served with the 75th Regiment, as he transferred to the 29th Regiment on 6 April of the same year (1832). A letter which he wrote, dated 24 March 1840 cites Hope as being an adjutant in the Liverpool recruiting district. On 30 December 1842 he was again placed on half-pay, in the Quartermaster's Department, until circa 1854/1856, at which time he probably sold his commission. He died in Kensington on 18 March 1860. Hope was awarded the *Military General Service Medal* (with clasps for Vittoria, Peninsula and Niville) and the *Waterloo Medal*.

One gains the impression of an officer tenaciously seeking to advance his military career, but being continually frustrated. It is feasible that the wound that he received at Waterloo (for which he received a pension of £70 per year, commencing on 25 December 1821), blighted his prospects of advancement as a regimental officer, resulting in his long periods on half-pay following Waterloo.

On 27 August 1816 he married, at Keith in Banffshire, and sired six children (four sons and two daughters).

James Hope's work was originally entitled *Letters from Portugal, Spain, and France, during the memorable campaigns of 1811, 1812, and*

1813; and from Belgium and France in the year 1815. Published in 1819, the cumbersome 18th Century style title was unaccompanied by any author, the authorship being simply ascribed to 'A British officer'. The work's anonymous character is, perhaps, the reason why it has been omitted from the principal bibliographies relating to the Peninsular and Waterloo campaigns.

Hope authored a second volume, entitled, *The military memoirs of an infantry officer 1809-1816* (1833), also anonymous, and privately printed. This work is essentially a reworking in narrative form of the same material as that contained in the book published in 1819, but with additional matter relating to his service in the Walcheren expedition and Ireland.

Ultimately, we are compelled to address the question: What is the essential value of Hope's work (with specific reference to the volume published in 1819)? The book is but one element in a vast corpus of literature relating to the Peninsular and Waterloo campaigns, as is noted belowl. Nor is the material contained within the letters in dispute. Four battles form the centre stage of the writer's campaign experience; viz Maya Heights, Vittoria, Quatre Bras and Waterloo. The three last named engagements have been extensively documented and Quatre Bras and Waterloo have been the subject of a massive volume of published work. The following introductory essay seeks to resolve this question.

The following introduction has two principal focal points:

— The shaping influences underlying the work.
— The central features of the text.

1 Shaping influences

The major shaping influences in Hope's work are the literary antecedents of the form which he adopted. These antecedents are the traditions of the letter; and the vogue for travel literature (reflected in the widespread popularity of the picaresque novel).

(i) *The letter*

Hope's text features the letter as the medium of communication with his audience. The letters are the receptacle of his experiences in the Peninsula, France and Belgium during the period 1811-1815.

The letter in the 18th Century: The letter had enjoyed a particularly wide vogue with the Augustans of the 18th Century. It is hardly surprising that the intellectual elite of the 18th Century, with their urbane values and the conviction that 'the proper study of mankind is man' (to quote Pope) should have found the mediums of the letter and diary particularly congenial. The letters were, in the main, exchanges of a public nature (in terms of their subject), concerned with political or diplomatic affairs. The 18th Century witnessed the apotheosis of this particular form of letter writing. There are numerous illustrations of the process whereby the Augustans cultivated the art of letter writing to a highly sophisticated literary form. An important illlustration is contained in the works of 1st Viscount Henry St John Bolingroke. His work, *A letter to Sir William Wyndham* (written in 1717 but published only in 1753), concerning the Jacobite question, is persuasively written and of interest with regard to Bolingbroke's comments upon his former colleagues, as well as his descriptions of the court of the Old Pretender (ie James Edward Stuart, the son of the exiled King James II). Bolingbroke's *Letters on the study and use of history* (written in 1735 and published in 1752) argues that Britain should follow the example of her European neighbours and produce written histories. The book was widely read, and not only in England, for Voltaire acknowledged its influence. In 1736 Bolingbroke also wrote *A letter on the spirit of patriotism* (published in 1749), regarding his future conception of the Tory Party. An especially famous series of 18th Century letters was compiled by Philip Dormer Stanhope, 4th Earl of Chesterfield, whose *Letters to his son, Philip Stanhope* was published in 1774. An important contributor to the Augustan development of this genre was Jonathan Swift, in his *Journal to Stella*; a collection of private letters which he despatched from London between September 1710 and 1713, to his close friend, Esther Johnson and her companion, Rebecca Dingley, residing in Dublin. ('Stella' was Swift's later nickname for Esther Thompson (although not at the time of the compilation of the letters, the name being superimposed upon the much later publication of the work; cf below). Swift was in London on an official commission to plead a case for the Irish clergy, and the letters afford an intriguing inside view of the metropolitan world of political intrigue, party wrangling and gossip (of both a literary and political character). Already a man of some reputation, Swift had many powerful acquaintances, and the early letters reveal him as being eagerly involved in public affairs. But gradually he becomes anxious and disillusioned, as his health deteriorates and he voices his ambiguous feelings for Esther; he yearns for the subdued and docile company of

Ireland (as he envisaged it). Although the letters were never designed for publication, a selection appeared in 1766, and an edition was prepared by his cousin, Deane Swift, in 1768.

There is a curious paradox implicit in the letters of the 18th Century. Although primarily concerned with the public world, they were essentially private in so far as, in the main, they were not intended for publication. The publication of Boligbroke's letters was delayed by a quarter of a century; Swift's *Journal to Stella*, never intended for publication, waited for some half-century before its appearance in published form. This marked reticence with regard to publication is clearly symptomatic of the highly confined audience for which the diarists and letter writers of the 18th Century compiled their missives; a readership comprising a socially close-knit and exclusive social elite. There is thus a curious paradox implicit in such works; although dealing primarily with public affairs, they were intended for perusal by only an extremely limited audience.

The tradition of the letter as a medium for the record of public affairs received a fresh impetus from the Napoleonic Wars. Of the vast extent of this literature there can be no doubt. The most significant of these letters included those written by: Brig Gen Catlin Craufurd; Lt Gen Thomas Dyneley (covering the period 1806-1815); Sir Augustus Frazer; Maj Edward Griffith; Commissary General Haviland le Mesurier and his son, Col Havilland le Mesurier (covering the French Revolutionary and Napoleonic Wars); Robert Bullard (a general of cavalry); the Pakenham family (spanning the period 1806-1815); Maj Gen Sir F P Robinson; Lt Rice Jones, RE; Ralph Heathcote (entitled *Letters of a young diplomat and soldier during the time of Napoleon*); Arthur Shakespeare; William Warre; the Duke of Wellington (letters written to his brother, William Wellesley); the brothers Henry and Charles Booth; William Bell, 89th Foot (covering the period 1808-1810); Marshal Beresford (letters written to his wife, Lady Anne Beresford); Lt and Capt George Bowles; Lt William Brereton, RHA; Rev Samuel Briscall; and Lt John Carss.

(ii) *The vogue for travel literature*
As will be discussed below, Hope was an acute observer of the peoples and environments of the various countries through which he travelled (ie Spain, Portugal, France and Belgium); and his work bears the distinct stamp of the travelogue. In this respect, he was responding to the continuing vogue for travel literature, which was a marked feature

of the 18th Century reading public. Especially noteworthy works in this genre were James Cook's *A voyage towards the South Pole and round the world*, published in 1777; and *A voyage to the Pacific Ocean*, by the same author, published in 1784. Both works enjoyed a continuing appeal in the succeeding century. (Indeed this interest greatly captured the Romantic imagination, and pervaded the poetry of the period (eg as in Coleridge's *Rime of the Ancient Mariner* (1798)). A major contributor to this literature was Henry Fielding, whose work, *The journal of a voyage to Lisbon* (1755), is a sharply observed but unavoidably depressing account of his final travels. Probably one of the finest achievements of 18th Century travel literature is Samuel Johnson's *Journey to the western islands of Scotland* (published in 1775), the record of a journey which he undertook to this region in conjunction with James Boswell in 1773. The latter's separate account of the tour (*Journal of a tour to the Hebrides with Samuel Johnson* (1785)) is casual and anecdotal. Johnson, in contrast, offers to the reader a formal survey. He journeys to Scotland with the hope of exploring the variety and extent of nature, particularly human nature (a recurrent theme in Hope's narrative). Johnson's aim was to record local differences in a scientific spirit and universal truths in a philosophical tone. Daniel Defoe's *A tour thro' the whole island of Great Britain* (3 vols, 1724-1727) is an outstanding evocative guide.

The picaresque novel: The keen interest in travel during the 18th Century was reflected in, and counterpointed by, the widespread popularity of the picaresque novel, with its central motif of the journey. The tradition of the picaresque novel enjoys a long lineage. Its origins reside in what might be termed the literature of roguery. The Spanish *picaro*, whence the term derives, was a disreputable character of the lowest socio-economic levels of society, living on his wits and often a scoundrel; but the term can eventually to be applied to any individual in conflict with society. The *picaro* first appeared in fiction in the anonymous *Lazarillo de Tormes* (1554). *Guzman de Alfarache* (1559), by Mateo Alemain, was widely read and translated, and the picaro was eventually to appear in the literature of western Europe. The picaresque novel is characterized by an episodic narrative describing the progress of the *picaro*. Its most well known manifestation is probably Don Quixote, in Cervantes' novel of that title (1605, 1615), which is related in the picaresque form, whilst being a satirical romance. Further important illustrations are *Gil Blas of Santillane* (1715-1735), by Le Sage, and Hans Jacob Christoph von

Grimmelshausen's *Der Abentheurliche Simplcissimus Teutsch* (1669). The former work was familiar to English readers through the translation (or possibly revised translation) by Tobias Smollett, published in 1749. In English literature the tradition begins with Thomas Nash's *The unfortunate traveller* (1594). The novel is an account of the adventures of Jack Wilton, an English page, and his nerve wracking experiences and narrow escapes from death in France and Italy. Daniel Defoe's *Moll Flanders* (1722) continues the tradition, as do the novels of Tobias Smollett, Laurence Sterne and Charles Dickens. (With regard to the last named writer, the *Pickwick Papers* (1837) owes much to the picaresque tradition). The picaresque novel gradually discarded the literature of roguery and was normally an episodic story involving a journey. Sterne's *Sentimental journey* (1768) is a classic example of the picaresque genre. In the novel he records some of his impressions of a seven month tour of Italy and France that he undertook in 1765, related in a fragmentary and fictionalised narrative. (It should also be noted that Sterne was a writer of non-fiction travel. He edited *A compendium of authentic voyages, digested in a chronological series*, which appeared in seven volumes (1756)).

2 Central characteristics of Hope's text

The foregoing discussion of the literary antecedents of Hope's work has furnished a framework within which to analyse the central features of *The Iberian and Waterloo campaigns*.

Hope's record is contained in a series of letters which are addressed to a fellow officer who had left the theatre of operations and returned home. The document was thus not compiled restrospectively, but immediately following the events which they describe. This pattern of narration undoubtedly lends a strong sense of freshness and spontaneity to the narration; often lacking in carefully considered memoirs (frequently subject to constant revision prior to publication) and shaped by reflective musings. [It should also be noted that the letter form adopted by Hope generates certain enigmas which it is impossible to resolve at this distance in time. For example, if the letters were despatched to his respondent, were they reclaimed by the writer subsequently, with a view to publication? Alternatively, were they published under the auspices of the respondent? A third scenario is feasible; viz that the writer retained duplicates of the letters. This argument is extremely dubious, however; in the light of the absence of any mechanical methods of reproduction at that point in time, combined with the limited time afforded him due to the pressure of his regimental duties. If, indeed, the letters were reclaimed by the writer, are any original missives absent? (This would not appear to be the case, as they appear to follow one another in a continuous stream of narrative, with no apparent lapses in the time sequence)].

(i) *A highly restricted audience but a transition in readership*
The highly confined readership assumed by Hope is an obvious feature of the work. To reiterate, Hope addresses his remarks to a fellow officer is serving in other theatres of the Peninsular campaign. (Reference to such service is made on pages 59 (in which the respondent is stated to be serving before the siege of Badajoz) and 71, where his comrade is cited as serving in the force despatched to Almarez). In this respect, the writer's approach exemplifies the Augustan concept of the letter as a medium of communication within the confines of 'polite society', a socially exclusive elite. The important common denominator between this tradition and Hope's work is the highly confined readership.

However, an important qualification must be applied to this argument, in the light of the fact that the work was published within a comparatively short time after its completion. In other words, a mass audience was subsequently sought. In this respect, the *Iberian and Waterloo campaigns* reflect an important transition in the development of the 19th Century approach towards the communication of information; viz the emergence of a mass readership. The publication of the journals and letters relating to the Napoleonic Wars obviously represents a departure from the approach of such writers as Swift, Lord Bolingbroke and Lord Chesterfield. In other words, the publication of Hope's letters exemplifies the absorption of the general public into the mainstream of history. Within this context, George Steiner, in his highly perceptive work, *The death of tragedy*, writes:

> 'The audience of Racine [the famous classical 17th Century French tragedian] were, in the main, a closed society to which the lower orders of the social and economic life had little entry. Throughout the eighteenth century the centre of social gravity shifted towards the middle classes. The French Revolution, essentially a triumph of the militant *bourgeoisie*, accelerated this shift...
> This is a crucial point. The French Revolution and the

Napoleonic Wars plunged ordinary men into the stream of history. They laid them open to pressures of experience and feeling which had, in earlier times, been the dangerous prerogative of princes, statesmen and professional soldiers. Once the great levies had marched and retreated across Europe, the ancient balance between public and private life had altered. An increasing part of private life now lay open to the claims of history. And that part grew with the expansion of the means of communication...

The nineteenth century is the classic age of low cost mass printing, of serialisation, and the public reading room. The novelist, the populariser of humane and scientific knowledge, the satirist, or the historian, now had far readier access to the public...A man could stay by his warm fire with the latest part-issue of a novel, with the newest number of the *Edinburgh Review*, or the *Revue des deux mondes*. The spectator had become the reader.'

[Steiner, George. *The death of tragedy*. London: Faber, 1961, pp 116-118].

Two highly significant points emerge from the above extract. The first is the central role of the Napoleonic Wars in facilitating this profound transition from an enclosed and exclusive audience to a mass readership. In this respect, the literature of the Revolutionary and Napoleonic Wars embodies an essential response to ther new and universalist interest in public affairs and was instrumental in effecting this transition. (Hope was undoubtedly aware of the public interest generated by the Peninsular and Waterloo campaigns. The book, *Campaign in Portugal and Spain* (published anonymously) had appeared in 1810; Lt Col (later Maj Gen) Henry Mackinnon had written *A journal of the campaign in Portugal and Spain* (published in 1812); the work, *Journal of a soldier of the 71st or Glasgow Regiment, Highland Light Infantry, from 1806 to 1815*, was published in 1819; *Journal of the sieges undertaken by the Allies in Spain*, by Lt Col J T Jones, had been published in 1814; C Kelly had produced the work, *The memorable battle of Waterloo*, published in 1817; and F C F von Muffling had authored *History of the campaign of 1815* (edited by J Sinclair), published in 1816). The second significant point indicated by George Steiner is the role of the novel, the mass circulation journal and popular history in catering to this new popular interest. These media superseded the letter and private journal as communicators of experience.

(ii) *External reportage*

Hope's account exemplifies an approach to recorded experience which might be termed 'external reportage'. In other words, the writer's predominant concern is the record of the movement and development of external events in which, in many instances, he is both observer and participant. The element of subjective impression or emotional response is minimalised. In this respect, Hope's work is far removed from the succeeding Romantic tradition (cf below). The writer's narrative is informed by a predominant degree of objectivity. It is, for example, characteristic of Hope's approach that, his participation in the battle of Waterloo having been terminated by a serious wound, he concludes his account, not by a series of reflections and impressions, but by a letter relating the last phase of the battle, which he had received from a friend (6). To cite but one example of this factual, objective reportage, one may quote his report of the battle waged on the Maya Heights (25 July 1813) (pp 166-167):

'The picquets and light companies of the 2d Brigade sustained the first onset of the enemy with great gallantry, but their efforts in defence of the post were rendered unavailing, from the overwhelming numbers which the enemy brought against them. The 34th was the first regiment that got up to their assistance, and which, in an attempt to arrest the torrent, was nearly cut off. The 50th having arrived on the heights, that regiment, in conjunction with the 34th, charged the enemy, and gave a temporary check to their career.

The enemy, availing himself of his great numerical superiority, charged these two battalions in front, and at the same time sent large bodies of infantry round their flanks, to surround them. At this crisis the right wing of the 92d Regiment was brought into action, and in a few minutes began one of the most severe actions recorded in modern history, if the numbers engaged are taken into account.

From the camp the 92d Regiment had moved along the ridge in open column of companies, right in front, but when close to the enemy, the rear companies moved quickly to the front and formed on the grenadiers. Scarcely had the

Highlanders formed line when their Colonel ordered them to prepare to charge. On perceiving their intentions, the enemy halted, which gave the 34th and 50th time to form anew.

The right wing of the 92d Regiment had now for some time to sustain the brunt of the conflict. Their numbers did not exceed 370 men, whilst that of their enemies could not be fewer than 3 000 veterans. Col Cameron, on seeing the enemy halt, withdrew his little band about 30 paces, in order to draw them forward, that he might have an opportunity of charging them. They greedily swallowed the bait - they advanced, but as soon as the 92d halted, the enemy did the same. The French now opened a terrible fire of musketry on the Highlanders, which they returned with admirable effect. For a quarter of an hour the French officers used every means in their power to induce their men to charge us, but their utmost efforts were unavailing. Not one of them could they prevail on to advance in front of their line of slain, which in a few minutes not only covered the field, but in many places lay piled in heaps.'

The same admirable clarity in capturing the tempo and pace of the battle, anchored in the stance of the detached observer, is clearly apparent in Hope's graphic description of the battle of Vittoria (21 June 1813), as is illustrated by the following extract:

'During these operations, the 50th and 92nd regiments were ordered to support the attack on the heights. These troops had nearly gained the summit, when they received an order to return. We had descended about half-way, when a third order arrived, for the 50th Regiment to proceed to their first destination, and the 92d to attack a French battalion of infantry, posted on a ridge a little to their front, and which acted as a corps of communication between the troops of the left wing and those in the wood to the left of the centre.

Through fields of wheat, which rose above many of the men - over ditches thickly lined on each side with thorns and briers, the 92d Regiment marched to meet their foes. Having arrived at the foot of the ridge on which the enemy had been posted, the Highlanders were ordered to load, and prepare to charge. With a firm pace they ascended, every moment expecting to be met by their enemies:- conceive, then, their surprise, when, on arriving at the top of the ridge, they found that the enemy had precipitately retired to another during their advance.'

As in the earlier quoted extract, the reader is presented with an admirably lucid account of the movement of his battalion, pervaded with a strong visual quality with which the topography is impressed upon the mind's eye ('fields of wheat, which rose above many of the men – over ditches thickly lined on each side with thorns and briers...'

Hope's accounts of the battles in which he was engaged maintain an uninterrupted and accelerating momentum. There are virtually no intercessions or interludes occasioned by the description of individual incidents or subjective impressions, facilitating an emotional response. A striking illustration of this approach occurs on p 231. Hope records the death of his OC, Lt Col Cameron, in the battle of Quatre Bras, in the following unadorned terms:

'Our brave Colonel, Cameron, was mortally wounded close to the garden, and retired from the field, regretted by the whole corps.'

In the close knit social world of the regiment at that time, the OC would undoubtedly have been a close acquaintance of Hope. Yet the former's death does not present the occasion for detailed reflections upon Cameron's loss, or impressions of his personality, such as abound, for example, in the memoirs of Frederick Hope Pattison, who also fought at Waterloo as a junior battalion officer (cf below). Hope is primarily concerned with recounting the factual detail of Cameron's death within the context of the overall movement and development of the battle scenario.

These features are highlighted by comparing Hope's account with that of another writer, who had fully absorbed the Romantic tradition; viz Frederick Hope Pattison, whose account of Waterloo, in which he served in the 33rd Regiment, was privately printed in Glasgow in 1870, and bears the title, *Personal recollections of the Waterloo campaign, in a series of letters to his grandchildren* [7]. Pattison's narrative of Waterloo is deeply coloured by a highly subjective, impressionistic approach. One may quote as an illustration the following passage in Letter I, in which the writer records his reactions to the battle of Quatre Bras:

'The multitudinous thoughts which arose and passed through my mind in quick succession, after the termination of this bloody conflict, were so complex and anomalous, that to attempt an analysis of them were altogether vain. The most prominent of these throughts, however, was a deep sense of gratitude and thankfulness to the God of battles, who gives the victory to whom He pleases for shielding me from those winged messengers of death that cut down so many of my comrades on my right hand and on my left, summoning them with all their imperfections to his dread tribunal; and for vouschafing to me the composure and presence of mind to enable me, I trust, to fulfil my duty on that trying occasion.'

In a similar vein of emotional release, he writes in Letter II, in relation to Quatre Bras:

'Now that the fierce and cruel passions engendered by war had been softened down, the heart must have been hard indeed which would contemplate without deep emotion and poignant regret, those foul deeds of blood and devastation perpetrated the day before, and forced on our attention by the all-revealing light of another morning. Wives made widows, children fatherless, plighted vows broken, maidens' hearts desolated, these were the remoter associations of the scene. The immediate ghastly and revolting picture that lay before our eyes was made up of a beautiful country, bearing in its bosom the rich garments of an approaching harvest, trodden under foot with the blood of our bretheren and strewn with their corpses; cuirassiers dead, still cased in their armour; wounded sufferers fevered; war-horses, artillery - carriages, muskets, pistols, swords, innumerable refuse of cartridges and other impediments of war, promiscuously mingled together. O, War!, War! offspring of hell and sin, disguise and mingle the cup, as thou wilt, thou art yet indeed a bitter draught.'

The sense of profound pathos which the author thus evokes is perhaps most powerfully realised in Pattison's heart rending evocation of the mutilated cavalry mount, standing on only three legs (his fourth having been shattered) standing in mute suffering on the battlefield (Letter V). We instantly share with him the deep sense of regret felt at having no recourse to a pistol with which to terminate the poor creature's suffering.

In marked contrast, Hope's vantage point is powerfully externalised. He submerges personal impressions and emotive responses beneath the skein of objective observation. His vantage point in this respect is explicitly stated in the opening paragraph of his book:

'I shall transmit to you a detailed account of every movement made by this corps - every little anecdote, whether of regiments or of individuals, with all the information regarding the movements of the Northern Army, which I may procure from authentic sources'.

In the succinctness and precision of these observations, Hope was indisputably a talented journalist who, in a later age, would have rendered good service as a war correspondent. Thus, one has the stark contrast between a highly personalised, subjective memoir (Pattison) and a highly objective, eye witness record of events compiled immediately after their occurrence.

It should be noted, within this context, that Hope does not seek to expand his narrative beyond the scope of his own observations and impressions. Thus, he does describe in detail the overall movement of the armies in the Peninsular campaign, nor does he make comment upon the strategy and tactics of the commanders. (For example, Hope does not voice the oft expressed British execration of the corrupt Spanish general Cuesta (although he refers to this general on several occasions), which recurs in the memoirs of the period. Thus, his work is singularly lacking in what might be termed value judgements. In this respect Hope's account is markedly different from the memoirs of John Douglas, of the 1st Regiment (Royal Scots). [Douglas, John. *Douglas's tale of the Peninsula and Waterloo*; ed by S Monick. London: Leo Cooper, 1997 (Pen and Sword)].

This high degree of detachment on Hope's part certainly does not imply insensitivity or callous indifference to the human drama which was constantly unfolding about him. For example, he is clearly moved to compassion by the great sufferings of the civilian population of Portual resulting from the depredations of the French. We read on p 38:

> 'Should the enemy ever attempt another invasion of this country, the result will prove far more disastrous than any that has preceded it. The atrocities committed by them since the first invasion of these realms, has wound up to the highest pitch the people's detestation of the French name. Their atrocities will ever live in the remembrance of the present, and by them be handed down to generations yet unborn. The name of a Junot, a Loison, a Soult, a Massena, and a long list of inferior agents of French tyranny and oppression, will ever be pronounced in this country with execration and horror.'

However, it is characteristic of Hope's literary technique that he does not seek to work upon his readers' emotions by accumulating visual details of the French pillage, accompanied by a long series of abstract epithets and adjectives; but, rather, expresses his outrage through the medium of factual reportage, as in the following extract (pp 5-6), which relate the disasters that befall a family living in the French village of Valada:

> 'When Lord Wellington found it necessary to retire from Almeida to his famed position at Torres Vedras, the inhabitants were invited, by his Lordship, to remove to a place of safety in the rear, taking with them all their movables. The proffered protection was eagerly embraced by the majority; but some, deaf to all entreaty, remained in their dwellings, and became an easy prey to the enemy's troops. Among the latter was an old man, who, at this time, occupied a small house at Valada: his family consisting of a wife and an only child, a beautiful daughter; every other person in the village removed, either to Lisbon, or crossed over to the province of Alentejo. The progress of the French general [Massena] having been arrested at Torres-Vedras, the whole country, for many miles around, was immediately

covered by the numerous legions of which his army was composed, seeking to shelter them from the inclemency of the weather. Valada was occupied, and a party from the detachment ordered to take possession of the old man's house. The sparkling eyes of the beautiful Maria soon attracted the attention of the foreign inmates. First one, and then a second, paid their addresses to her, but their proffered hands were rejected with marked disdain. Irritated by her refusal, these two villains planned the ruin of the poor girl. Day after day, insult was heaped on insult to every member of the family. The eyes of the old man were at length opened. He beheld the precipice on which he stood, and fervently prayed for forgiveness from her for whom, for the first time, he now saw on the brink of inevitable destruction. It was a considerable time before they could find an opportunity for carrying into execution the dreadful act which they meditated. At length an order arrived for the detachment in Valencia to retire to Santarem. On the evening of the day that they received the order of recal [sic], one of them again solicited her hand, which she, as before, refused; this refusal was conclusive – they dragged the unfortunate girl from under her father's roof, while he, in attempting to protect his daughter, received a stab from one of their bayonets, of which he soon after died – Maria was robbed of the brightest jewel that ever adorned her sex. Her mother was ill-treated, and the house was plundered. In fact, nothing was left but the bleeding trunk of the once happy father, the wretched widow, and the once beautiful, virtuous, and happy, but now the miserable and unhappy Maria. The former now lies hid from the sight of men, but the other two are still to be seen in Valeda: the widowed mother mourning over the loss of a beloved husband, and the misfortunes of her only daughter; and poor Maria, deprived of a parent's fostering hand, sits brooding over her misfortune, with misery staring her in the face, being, at this moment, unable to walk, from the cruel treatment she received from the hands of these vile miscreants.'

The above tale is a cameo of the sufferings eternally inflicted upon the civilian population by marauding armies in an apparently endless cycle through time. The indictment of such atrocities is compressed within a single brief but powerful narrative. There is only a minimal concession to melodramatic effect through the medium of metaphor ('He beheld the precipice…brink of veritable destruction'/'brightest jewel …adorned her sex'/'misery staring her in the face') or visual detail ('bleeding trunk of the once happy father'). The principal effect is achieved through the escalating tension of the narrative. The above extract is further characteristic of Hope's technique in so far as he relates the sack of Valeda to the overall movement of Massena's armies.

There are two central factors which separate the approaches and treatment displayed by Hope and Pattison. First, one has the important dimension of time. Pattison's letters were compiled in 1869, more than half-a-century after the events which they describe. In this respect, they correspond to memoirs. It is a feature of such works that reflection and detailed impressions are often integrated with - and indeed frequently overshadow - the purely narrative facet. Hence, digression is often a feature of memoirs (a noticeable aspect of Pattison's work). Conversely, as stated above, Hope's letters were compiled immediately following the events described, and thus the writer was fettered by the pressure of his regimental duties, often disallowing the time and scope for such reflection. He was thus the captive of the immediate pressures and demands of the external world. In the light of such pressures, Hope's facility to form an objective, detached view of battle scenarios in which his own role - that of a junior officer in a line regiment - was of an essentially minor character in the overall development of the engagement, is especially creditable. (In this respect, one has a certain parallel with the literature of the First World War - and specifically that of the Western Front - in which a decade elapsed after the end of the War before the detailed exploration of interior states of mind and emotional responses appeared in the form of autobiographies and novels. The immediate response to battlefield scenarios was encapsulated, in published form, in brief poems reminiscent of lyrics). Precisely because Hope was committed to detailed factual reportage - in which personalised impressions play a minimal role - the record of events is tightly ordered; there are no digressive excursions which intervene and disrupt the narrative of the record. Indeed, this point is underscored by Hope himself, through the medium of the second volume which he published in 1833. This later work lacks the tightly ordered narrative structure of the earlier volume, and suffers from irritating and prolonged manifestations of a highly self-opinionated personality. For example, his narrative is plagued with tortuous digressions on the 'moral fibre' of officers (pp 49-51); religion (pp 51-53); the duties of officers (pp 212-232). Clearly, the disciplined narrative structure which characterizes the first volume has been shattered by these turgid digressions, and the spontaneity and vividness of the earlier work submerged. (The latter work, possibly, reflects an embittered personality, the fruit of disappointment generated, perhaps, by a frustrated military career, which frequently manifests itself in an argumentative and aggressive habit of mind, as if the author were seeking to compensate for a felt sense of inadequacy. It is, perhaps, significant, that the second volume was published after he had renewed his service for one year, following 15 years unemployment in a military capacity. This impression of his personality is confirmed by a highly acerbic letter which he wrote regarding his entry in *Hart's Army List*; ie that dated 24 March 1840, referred to above). Hope's later work thus graphically illustrates a consistent and besetting flaw in retrospectively compiled memoirs; viz egocentricity, eradicating much of the charm and lucidity - manifesting itself in spontaneity and freshness - of the author's earlier work.

The second major source of the distinction between Pattison and Hope is the intervention of the Romantic movement. This movement profoundly shaped the form of the letter (and journal) as a literary medium. Nineteenth century Romanticism profoundly differed from the Augustan literary tradition of the preceding century, and this break centred on the dimension of subjectivity; the letter and journal emerging as an emotional liberating force. This expression of emotion was synonymous with a process that may be termed the femininisation of society, not in the sense that there were to be far more women writers in the 19th Century but - of far greater significance - the concept that the release of feminine modes of feeling and expression were essential components of general human experience. The emotional responses were thus enormously heightened in Romantic literature, in contrast with the Augustan ideal of the narrowly reasoned and tightly imposed control of emotional life. (We note, for example, that Swift was anxious to conceal his affection for 'Stella'). The freedom of emotional expression is a distinctive trait of the Romantic 'sensibility'. The regular, patient recording of events (such as we find in Hope's text) as the foundation of the writer's thoughts and reflections become rarer; often to be replaced by long soliloquies unrelated to - or only tenuously so - to any particular occasion, by confessions of varying degrees of candour. This approach has been defined by one critic as the 'pleasure of recollection'. Thus, the heavily classical orientation of the 18th Century letter - with its preponderant emphasis upon correct form and highly polished style - yielded during the 19th Century to a far more subjective and personal approach; attaining its apotheosis in the letters of Byron and especially those of Keats, whose 200 letters were composed within a span of only four years. One has, of course, to acknowledge that the Romantic movement - represented by Wordsworth, Keats, Shelly and other writers - had reached its height in the 1830s, a generation before the letters of Pattison were completed; and, during the last quarter of the 19th Century, had entered upon a phase of decadence. Nevertheless, the Romantic movement had attained its apotheosis at a point in time which coincided with Pattison's youth and middle age and, in this respect, were formative influences in his reading.

(iii) *A restrained style*
Whilst Hope admirably captures the atmosphere and tempo of combat, he projects these facets of the battlefield scenario in a sober, judicious style, very far removed from the excessive hyperbole and striving for metaphorical effect which is such a marked feature of Pattison's text (and which is most clearly apparent in the extracts from his work quoted above). For example, in Hope's account of the struggle for Hugomont, at the battle of Waterloo, we read (pp 246-247):

'At half past eleven, Jerome Bonaparte moved down his division from the heights on the left of La Belle Alliance, and attacked our light troops in front of the Chateau of Hougomont. On descending the heights, the French troops were stopped two or three times by our artillery, almost the first shot from which having killed or wounded several of them. The whole extent of the ridge was at the same time occupied by numerous and well appointed cavalry, who, proud of their own strength, advanced towards us by the half-way, with all the audacity of soldiers careless of danger. Our cavalry having moved forward to meet them, a terrible conflict appeared inevitable, when the greater part of both was called to another part of the field.

The fire of their artillery was truly terrible. - Their attacks were made with the greatest impetuosity; - these were met, and repelled by the determined bravery of the British garrison. Every tree was contended for, as if it had been a kingdom. No neutral walls or hedgerows were allowed; either the one party or the other behoved to be the absolute possessor; every avenue to the ancient mansion was contested for with an obstinacy seldom equalled. The gates of the palace were assailed by the enemy with a bravery bordering on frenzy; - numbers, in an attempt to force them, fell, pierced with wounds. Our troops having loopholed the court wall, fired thence on their fierce antagonists, whose bodies in a short time covered the ground around the chateau. The enemy continued their attacks for an hour and a half, and every time with increased force. - The furious Napoleon, enraged at this obstinate defence, by the handful of British guards at Hugomont, and seeing that the Field-Marshal [Wellington] was determined to keep possession of it, at whatever cost, turned his attention to the left wing and centre.'

This factual reportage succinctly and powerfully evokes the frenzied desperation energising both attackers and defenders. Yet this powerful and dramatic capture of the pace and tempo of the conflict involves only the minimal use of metaphor (eg 'Every tree was contended for, as if it had been a kingdom. No neutral walls or hedges were allowed'), the impact of which is enhanced by its very selectivity. It is this economy of style which so greatly contributes to the evocative description of the battle scenario.

(iv) *The influence of the vogue for travel narrative*
The foregoing discussion has influenced upon the description of battles in which Hope was involved. However, it is most important to note that the letters encompass an extremely variegated canvas. The writer is deeply interested in the social and political panorama of the theatres of war through which he journeys, and carefully details the impressions gained in the course of such journeys. Thus, at the very outset of the work, the reader is presented with the graphic (and far

from flattering) portrait of Lisbon:

> 'The streets of Lisbon are, in general, very narrow, ill
> paved, and, in many places, covered, to the depth of several
> inches, with nastiness of every description. None of the
> inhabitants ever contribute, either by personal service or
> pecuniary aid [ie financial assistance], to remove the nuisance
> now complained of. The present system of police, I believe,
> allows of no scavengers, but those only known in Britain as
> house or watch dogs. These poor creatures are starved all the
> day, and in the evening, are turned out to the streets, to find
> food for the ensuing day. Hundreds of these dogs nightly
> parade the streets, who, having got nothing to satsify the
> cravings of hunger, in the morning, are seen to be supporting
> themselves against the walls, unable to walk from weakness.
> The piteous howling of these animals, as they crawl along the
> streets, would wring a tear of sympathy from the most
> hardened savage that ever trod the African dersert, yet it
> produces no effect on the heart of the Portuguese, except so
> far as to excite a laugh at the expense of the person
> commiserating with the cruel fate of the four-footed
> scavenger.'

The middle class English reader (who formed the bulk of Hope's
audience) is at startlingly presented with a social ethos quite alien to
that of the English; featuring a cruel indifference to the fate of
innocent dumb creatures. We are plunged into the totally different
world of the Iberian Peninsula, the culture and value system of the
peoples completely distinct from that of the British. As is characteristic
of his style, the impact of Hope's narrative centres upon factual detail;
viz the layers of nauseaus human and animal detritus on the street, the
pathetic starving dogs used as scavengers, the citizens cruelly
indifferent to their sufferings. We are also treated with (far more
amenable) descriptions of Ghent (pp 208-209), Brussels (pp 212-213)
and Mons (p 282).

The extract quoted above points to the considerable interest that
Hope expresses with regard to the social characteristics of the
inhabitants of the various countries through which he journeys.

For example, we are treated to an amusing practical joke played
upon the citizens of Lisbon; in which the writer humorously details

their massive response to a handbill advertising that a British officer, in cork boots, was to walk across the Tagus (pp 38-40). His interest in local customs extends to the bull fight (pp 82-85) and even to the methods employed by the Spanish ladies in extracting vermin from their hair (pp 69-70). In the same journalistic fashion, Hope is anxious to relate the 'political temperature' of the peoples and environments in which he found himself. He thus faithfully recounts the attitudes towards Napoleon of the residents in Belgium, through the medium of his landlord in Brussels (pp 221-222).

Such detailed descriptions of the impressions that Hope gained, and scenes that he witnessed, clearly reflects the response to the widespread contemporary taste for travel narrative, discussed in the first section of this essay.

The value of Hope's work

We are now in a position to answer the question addressed at the outset of this essay; viz the essential value of Hope's work. First, as an account of the Peninsular and Waterloo campaigns, it forms part of a corpus of literature which has exercised a deep impression upon the cultural landscape of the British national consciousness; generating a value system which has had a most ambiguous impact upon the nation's subsequent military history. Second, the reader is alerted to the various forms by which history may be recorded. More specifically, we are informed of the variations that occur within the context of personalised narrative; exemplified by the comparison with Pattison's memoirs.

Third, and most interestingly, we are made aware of the manner in which style may embody character. The factual reportage which has been analysed in some depth as a distinctive feature of Hope's approach, integral to which is economy of style and a tightly ordered and disciplined narrative, is seen as being symptomatic of a personality closely interwoven with the mainstream of the historical events he is recording. With reference to the campaign which is the focal point of Hope's account, the pressure of events afforded virtually no scope for the exploration of emotional responses (in marked contrast to Pattison's memoirs). In this respect, Hope was undoubtedly compelled to repress the private dimension of the emotional life. Hence, a disciplined style and narrative structure may well reflect the imposition of discipline upon one's natural human instincts. Once again, an interesting analogy with the Western Front of World War I presents itself. The poetic sensitivity of writers such as Wilfred Owen, Isaac Rosenberg, Siegfried Sassoon, Edmund Blunden, etc, was very far from being typical of the troops of the Western Front. Indeed, the characters portrayed by Bruce Bairnsfather, the famed cartoonist of that conflict (creator of the immensely popular 'Old Bill') exhibit a cheerful callousness and apparent indifference to the horrific scenario of the Western Front. Such an attitude - centred upon the repression of the imaginative life - is, in such circumstances, conducive to mental health and the facility to continue in one's duty (ie fealty to the public world). It is, perhaps, for this reason that the reader of Hope's work is not presented with the images of battlefield carnage, which feature so extensively in Pattison's memoirs. Superficially, Hope may present the appearance of the public schoolboy adventurer reminiscent of the works of John Buchan, G A Henty, etc. However, such a conception fails to do justice to the pressures upon the emotional life with which he had to contend. In the same vein, the reader may discern in the second volume of Hope's memoirs, published in 1833, a personality which has, to a certain extent, developed a marked egocentric complexion, the fruit of a frustrated career; embodied in the highly opinionated cast of the narrative.

Fourth, the reader is made aware of the manner in which historical writing may be shaped by the prevailing influence of literary traditions. In this context, Pattison's work owes a profound debt to the Romantic tradition; whilst the style of Hope's account is clearly rooted in the Augustan heritage.

Ultimately, we are compelled to address the central question: why do the Peninsular War and Waterloo campaigns continue to exercise so consistent and enduring an impact upon the collective consciousness of the British public? Few – if any – conflicts have matched these campaigns in terms of the vast literature that they have generated; with regard to both contemporary commentators and the writers of subsequent generations. Wellington's career, similarly, has enjoyed an unblemished reputation to the present day (certainly merited). In this respect, commentators have reached a universal consensus; in marked contrast to the Duke of Marlborough, whose reputation has been 'rehabilitated' only in the 20th century. The unmitigated prestige enjoyed by Wellington and the armies that he commanded is especially remarkable in the light of the iconoclastic character which marks the military-historical writing of the present century. There can, for example, be no greater contrast between the treatment of Wellington's command in the Peninsular and Waterloo campaigns and the judgement of the senior Allied commanders in World War I.

There are a number of obvious answers to this question. First, one has the clearly apparent factor of Wellington's undisputed military genius, and the calibre of the armies he commanded. Second, with specific regard to Waterloo, the battle is characterised by several features which immediately capture the popular image. First, it assumes a highly dramatic aspect, in the light of the finely balanced powers of the opposing forces; in terms of numbers, prowess and, not least, courage and tenacity. (As Wellington observed, it was 'a near run thing'). The outcome remained in doubt until the final phase. Secondly, the battle conforms to the defensive posture characteristic of the most notable victories in British military history; Agincourt (in 1415) being an obvious parallel in this respect. Thirdly, one has the political significance of the victory. It irrefutably and irrevocably destroyed Napoleon's power. Commentators of the period (including Hope and Pattison) remarked on the extreme vulnerability of the former Austrian Netherlands to the revival of French control; in the light of the frustration of Belgian national aspirations at the Congress of Vienna. It was almost universally acknowledged that Brussels would have fallen unopposed to the French had Napoleon gained the victory at Waterloo. In this respect, such a triumph might well have resulted in the genesis of a revived Napoleonic Empire within the context of frustrated nationalist aspirations in Poland and elsewhere. Nor could the stability of the European confederacy have been guaranteed in the face of such a victory; the European coalitions being notoriously short-lived in the history of the Napoleonic Wars. In the event, Wellington's victory involved the final and irrefutable termination of Napoleon's power; following which the Continent of Europe avoided a collective conflagration for a century (the peace only being broken by the Crimean War of 1854-1856 and the wars waged against Denmark, Austria and France by Germany, culminating in the creation of the German Empire in 1871). Third, it should be borne in mind that the Peninsula and Waterloo exemplified Britain's outstanding contribution to the Napoleon's defeat. Prior to Britain's entry into the Peninsular War in 1808, her role in the conflict with France had been confined – in the sphere of land warfare – to several futile campaigns in Holland and Flanders, during the 1790s.

There is, however, perhaps another, and far less apparent source, for the enduring impress of the Peninsular and Waterloo campaigns upon the collective consciousness. That source is rooted in the military-social context. The essential culture of the British Army during the Napoleonic Wars, to reiterate, was shaped by the paramountcy of the landowning classes. It bears reiteration that that ascendancy could not survive the vast impact of science and technology during the second half of the 19th Century. The Napoleonic Wars represented the very last major military conflict in which the dynamics of an aristocratically controlled society operated. The Peninsular and Waterloo campaigns embodied the apotheosis of an army controlled by the traditional leadership of society. In a very real sense, the senior officer establishment of the British Army during the Napoleonic Wars exemplified the service of the last heirs of the military aristocracy founded by the Norman invaders of 1066; an integral feature of the feudal system, which pivoted upon the concept of land tenure in reward for military service. Reference has been made above to Agincourt, and the 15th Century battle reinforces the editor's argument. For it may feasibly be argued that the enduring impress of the conflict upon the popular imagination - pivotal to which is, of course, Shakespeare's play, *Henry V*, central to which is the personality of the king -is similarly the final great efforescence of an ideal and image of society which was clearly dying by the dawn of the 15th Century. Within this context, the enemy of the British at Waterloo are highly germane to this hypothesis. For the Napoleonic armies were the embodiment of the forces created by the French Revolution of 1789. Hence, Waterloo is an embodiment of the final great conflict between the *ancien regime* and Revolutionary France.

Henceforth, these social sectors - the aristocracy and gentry - were to suffer an irreversible decline in their prestige; within the political as well as the military spheres. The source of that decline, to reiterate, was the process of bureaucratisation inevitably attendant upon the shaping power of science and technology; which demands the overriding criteria of merit in place of patronage and social prestige. Wellington's military genius ensured that the traditional social fabric of the British armed forces, which he personified, could be welded to a highly efficient military organism. However, the absence of that influence, in the next major war, the Crimean conflict of 1854-1856, dramatically illustrated the poverty of that culture - anchored in patronage - when wedded to a military organism. Essentially, therefore, the enduring impress of the Peninsula and Waterloo campaigns is rooted in nostalgia for a social and cultural fabric which was, even then, dying under the corrosive impact of industrialisation, with its profound attendant consequences of urbanisation and the rise of the new industrial classes.

However, it is a feature of cultural fabrics that the values and attitudes inculcated by a formerly ascendant social class outlive the decline of that class. The tragically incompetent leadership of the senior British military commanders in the Anglo-Boer War of 1899-1902, attaining its climax in World War I, may indeed be construed in this light; viz the anachronistic belief in tactics founded upon the qualities of courage and tenacity exemplified by the officer establishment of the Peninsular and Waterloo campaigns. It may with justice be argued, therefore, that the root of the tragedy of the Western Front is the archaic image of a sacrificial aristocratic officer establishment leading a blindly obedient soldiery, modelled upon the Peninsular and Waterloo experiences. (The dangerous implications of this persistence of archaic attitudes was also apparent in World War II, within the context of armoured warfare. The armoured regiments that were the successors of the heavy cavalry (Household Cavalry and Dragooon Guards/Dragoons) adopted tactics shaped by their horsed predecessors (notably the massed charge and personal duels); which proved disastrous in the face of the far superior German deployment of armour and artillery). One is reminded of George Orwell's acerbic comment in *The Lion and the Unicorn* that, whilst the battle of Waterloo was won on the playing fields of Eton, all subsequent wars have been lost there.

Concluding observations

Hope's work has, in the present century, been a comparatively obscure text, known mainly only to researchers and antiquarian booksellers. The editor hopes that the present edition (the first revised version for 180 years, and the sole edition possessing an attributed authorship and annotations) will re-establish the worth of Hope's original text and assure it of an honoured and permanent place in the canon of literature relating to the Iberian and Waterloo campaigns, culminating in the battle of Waterloo.

S Monick
September 2000

Endnotes

(1) Gardyne, Greenhill. *The life a regiment: the history of the Gordon Highlanders.* London: The Medici Society, 1901. 2 Vols. Vol I: 1794-1816, p 174.

(2) Ibid item [1] above.

(3) The editor is indebted to Mr A J Henderson for facilitating the former's access to this letter.

(4) The editor is greatly indebted to Mr A J Henderson for enabling the former to gain access to the latter's detailed research into the life and career of Lt Hope.

(5) Hope makes no reference to this fact in either of his volumes of memoirs. However, the comb itself is in the possession of Mr A J Henderson, who purchased it together with Hope's medal group.

(6) It is noteworthy that historical documents feature extensively in Hope's work. He reproduces: the Duke of Wellington's Proclamation, dated 21 June 1815 (pp 280-281); the General Orders issued by the Headquarters in Paris in November 1815 (pp 303-307); the Brigade Orders of November 1815 (p 299); a newspaper containing a letter from a French officer, providing details of Napoleon's surrender (p 289); the decree issued by Louis XVIII (pp 287-288); the Order of Battle of the British contingent within the Army of the Netherlands (pp 214-217); and an extract from the Order of the Day, dated 20 June 1815 (p 281). It is clearly apparent that Hope placed great value upon historical accuracy, in accordance with his externalised approach.

(7) Pattison, Frederick Hope. *Horror recollected in tranquillity: memories of the Waterloo campaign.* Rev. ed. by S Monick, Dallington, Sussex: The Naval and Military Press, 2000.

LETTERS,

FROM

PORTUGAL, SPAIN, AND FRANCE,

DURING

THE MEMORABLE CAMPAIGNS

OF

1811, 1812, & 1813;

AND FROM

BELGIUM AND FRANCE,

IN THE YEAR

1815.

———

BY

A BRITISH OFFICER.

———

EDINBURGH:

Printed by Michael Anderson;

AND SOLD BY BELL AND BRADFUTE, PARLIAMENT SQUARE;
MACREDIE, SKELLY, AND CO., AND W. AND
C. TAIT, PRINCE'S STREET.

1819.

LETTERS,

&c. &c.

MY DEAR FRIEND,

You have imposed on me an arduous task, and appear quite determined to exact a due performance of it. Well, be it so—to the utmost of my abilities I shall endeavour to comply with the rules you have laid down. I shall transmit to you a detailed account of every movement made by this corps—every little anecdote, whether of regiments or of individuals, with all the information regarding the movements of the Northern Army, which I may procure from authentic sources.

I must now give you some account of myself, since I wrote you from Fermoy.

We embarked at Monkstown, on the 31st of August, on board the Minerva transport, in all eight officers, six non-commissioned officers, and two hundred rank and file. On the morning of

A

the 7th September we sailed from Cove; and, upon the evening of the 19th, came to anchor in the Tagus, immediately opposite Belem Fort. At three o'clock on the 20th the whole were landed, at the Black Horse Square, in Lisbon :—the soldiers were quartered in a convent, and the officers billetted on the inhabitants.

The city of Lisbon, when viewed from the river, is extremely beautiful. The stranger ought, first of all, to fix his eyes on the houses along the banks of the river, and, when sufficiently feasted, raise them gradually to those above, which, from the northern bank of the Tagus, rise, with a kind of awful majesty, to the lofty summits of the seven hills on which the city stands.

But I must here inform you, that Lisbon visited, and Lisbon viewed at a distance, are not the same. The latter is as superior to the former as the rays of the sun are to the glimmering of a farthing rush-light.—The latter vies in splendour with the finest city in Europe, while the former falls beneath the rank of the very lowest.

The streets of Lisbon are, in general, very narrow, ill paved, and, in many places, covered, to the depth of several inches, with nastiness of every description. None of the inhabitants ever contribute, either by personal service or pecuniary aid, to remove the nuisance now complained of. The present system of police, I believe, allows of no scavengers, but those only known in Britain as house or watch dogs. These poor creatures are starved all the day, and, in the evening, are turned out to the streets, to find food for the ensuing day. Hundreds of these dogs nightly parade the streets, who, having got nothing to satisfy the cravings of hunger, in the morning, are to be seen supporting themselves against the walls, unable to walk from weakness. The piteous howling of these animals, as they crawl along the streets, would wring a tear of sympathy from the most hardened savage that ever trod the African desert; yet it produces no effect on the heart of a Portuguese, except so far as to excite a laugh at the expence of the person commiserating the cruel fate of the four-footed scavenger. If the inhabitants of Lisbon do not take a speedy method of getting rid of such a barbarous custom, it will be difficult to say whether the progression of two hundred years has, alone, had no influence in ameliorating the manners of the inhabitants of the capital of Portugal.

From the immense number of British officers and soldiers continually parading the streets of the city, a stranger, not knowing the cause, would, naturally enough, conclude that Portugal had become a colony of Great Britain. The Adjutant-General, Quarter-Master-General, and Town-Major's offices are filled with British officers from morning till night. Some are reporting their arrival from England, others from the army ;—some are applying for a conveyance to England, others for a route to join the army on the frontiers;—some are copying extracts from the general orders of this army, regarding the conduct and marching of detachments to and from the army, others are in search of billets, and the whole are in pursuit of the commissary.

Having got a week allowed us to furnish the detachment with necessaries and camp-equipment, we made preparations for marching on the 28th.

About five o'clock in the morning of the 28th, the bugle's shrill sound called us from our drowsy pillows to Neptune's cold embrace. Boats having been provided to carry the detachment to the small village of Valada; on board of these we embarked, about six o'clock, and immediately set sail, with a fine breeze, which, in seven hours, carried us into port.

Valada is a very small village, situated on the right bank of the Tagus, forty miles above Lisbon, and twelve below Santarem.

The hand of the ruthless invader is apparent in every corner of the village. There is scarcely one house standing which does not, in some shape or other, bear testimony to the genuine friendship which these locusts had for their possessors. In the evening, when visiting the cantonments, (a duty which every officer is called on to perform, three times a-day, when on a march), the following very melancholy tale was related to me by a person employed in the commissariat department, at that place.—When Lord Wellington found it necessary to retire from Almeida to his famed position at Torres-Vedras, the inhabitants were invited, by his Lordship, to remove to a place of safety in his rear, taking with them all their moveables. The proffered protection was eagerly embraced by the majority; but some, deaf to all entreaty, remained in their dwellings, and became an easy prey to the enemy's troops. Among the latter was an old man, who, at this time, occupied a small house at Valada; his family consisting of a wife and an only child, a beautiful daughter; every other person in the village removed, either to Lisbon, or crossed over to the province of Alentejo. The progress of the French General having been arrested at Torres-Vedras, the whole country, for many miles round, was immediately covered by the numerous legions of which his army was composed, seeking for houses to shelter them from the inclemency of the weather. Valada was occupied, and a party from the detachment ordered to take possession of the old man's house. The sparkling eyes of the beautiful Maria soon attracted the attention of his foreign inmates. First one, and then a second, paid their addresses to her, but their proffered hands were rejected with marked disdain. Irritated at her refusal, these two villains planned the ruin of the poor girl. Day after day, insult was heapd on insult to every

member of the family. The eyes of the old man
were at length opened : He beheld the precipice
on which he stood, and fervently prayed for forgiveness from her whom, for the first time, he now saw
on the brink of inevitable destruction. It was a
considerable time before they could find an opportunity of carrying into execution the dreadful
act which they meditated. At length an order
arrived for the detachment in Valada to retire to
Santarem. On the evening of the day that they
received the order of recal, one of them again solicited her hand, which she, as before, refused;
this refusal was conclusive—they dragged the unfortunate girl from under her father's roof, while
he, in attempting to protect his daughter, received
a stab from one of their bayonets, of which he
soon after died.—Maria was robbed of the brightest jewel that ever adorned the sex. Her mother
was ill-treated, and the house was plundered. In
fact, nothing was left but the bleeding trunk of
the once happy father, the wretched widow, and
the once beautiful, virtuous, and happy, but now
the miserable and unhappy Maria. The former
now lies hid from the sight of man, but the other
two are still to be seen in Valada : the widowed
mother mourning over the loss of a beloved husband, and the misfortunes of an only daughter;
and poor Maria, deprived of a parent's fostering
hand, sits brooding over her misfortunes, with
misery staring her in the face, being, at this mo-

ment, unable to walk, from the cruel treatment she received from the hands of these vile miscreants.

The modern system of war, as adopted and carried on by Frenchmen, in the peninsula, is worthy of him who planned it, and of those now employed in carrying it into execution. How long such a system will be permitted to scourge the human race no man can tell; but let us hope that the day is not far distant when the numerous legions of Napoleon's licentious soldiery (now scattered over the greater part of Europe), will be driven within the ancient boundaries of France, and leave the inhabitants of other nations to reap the fruits of their own soil in peace.

Early on the morning of the 29th, we quitted the wretched Valada, and marched to the once-beautiful city of Santarem. There is scarcely a house in the whole town but what has had some distinguishing mark given it, to shew the proprietor, when he returns, the great regard Marshal Massena had for the people over whom he was destined to reign, had he succeeded in driving the " Leopard" into the sea, at Lisbon.

The doors of almost every house in Santarem were removed to the French bivouac in its vicinity, when those which were not wanted by the officers to sleep on, were converted into fire-wood for the use of the privates. Many of the houses were totally destroyed; and, out of thirteen convents, I believe three only remain. The nuns were compelled to leave these sanctuaries, and follow their armies to the frontier, whence many of them have returned in a most deplorable state off wretchedness.

It was in this town that Marshal Massena established his head-quarters after quitting his position in front of Torres-Vedras. It stands on the summit of a considerable hill, and commands an extensive view of the surrounding country. The Tagus washes the eastern base of the hill, along the bank of which the Old Town, as it is called, is built. The position chosen, on this occasion, by the French Marshal, was excellent. The industry of the occupants, added to the natural strength of the place, had rendered it, long before the 5th of March, almost impregnable. The left of his army rested on Santarem, and his right extended, in a westerly direction, to a considerable distance, There was only one road, of any note, by which the allied army could have advanced against the left of the enemy's position, and that road was so exposed to the fire of numerous breast-works, with which the whole face of the hill was thickly planted, that the assailants must, in the attack, have lost a vast number of men, before they could have got to close quarters with their opponents. The British General, at the head of the allied army, was much censured, at that time, for not attacking the enemy in this position; but I should like to have some of those gentlemen with me just now, when I think I should be able to convince them that Lord Wellington acted with consummate prudence on that occasion, in not attacking the crafty Marshal in his strong-hold, defended as that position was, by a numerous and veteran army, and headed by a general who, from the number of his victories, had acquired for himself the name of the Child of Fortune. I am clearly of opinion, that Lord Wellington's conduct, from the day he commenced his retreat from Almeida, last year, down to the battle of Fuentes de Honor, deserves the unbounded applause of every well-wisher to the cause in which we are engaged.

On the 30th, we marched from Santarem to the village of Gallegao, which, like the other towns on our route, has suffered dreadfully during the late campaign. A great many of the houses were first plundered and then burnt, or razed to the ground. The inhabitants were turned adrift on the world, without money, and without friends. In too many instances, it is to be feared, these lawless freebooters were not satisfied with the *property* of individuals, but that, when it suited their convenience, murder was added to their long catalogue of crimes.

In Gallegao, just now, there is a young man, keeping a small coffee-house, whose father and elder brother were tried by the enemy, on suspicion of corresponding with the English, and condemned and executed. Not content with the lives of these two, they dragged the female part of the family out of doors, and compelled them to go along with them ;—as none of them have yet returned, the young gentleman, (his father was a man of considerable property,) suspects either that they have been murdered by the enemy, or, not inclined to survive their honour, have put an end to their existence.—Such acts of atrocity call loudly for vengeance.

On the 1st of October, we marched to Punhete, once a tolerable village, but now almost a heap of ruins. The pale countenances of the inhabitants were to us a sufficient assurance of their extreme poverty. It is scarcely possible to convey to you the most distant notion of the destruction of property here. Houses have, as usual, been sacked and burnt, or unroofed, and the wood, together with the doors, windows, tables and chairs, carried to the bivouac, and given to the soldiers to cook with—even the churches have not been respected : every thing has been removed from under their sacred roofs, and the building converted into a place of repose for horses, mules, and asses.

On the 2d October we marched to Abrantes. This ancient city is situated on the summit of a hill, two sides of which are nearly inaccessible. The Tagus washes the base of the hill on the east and south, and also the west, but at the distance of from one to two miles. The road from

Lisbon communicates with the city on the north side.

The streets of the town are extremely narrow, ill paved, and very dirty. In the summer season, I should imagine it to be almost impossible for any one to walk the streets, the smell being extremely offensive even now.

The 3d having been allowed us as a day of rest, I embraced the opportunity of making an inspection of the defences of the city, ancient and modern. Previous to the memorable year 1808, the works of Abrantes had been greatly neglected; many parts of them were little better than a heap of ruins, and by far the greater part were in a state of decay: since that period, however, they have undergone a thorough repair, which, with the new works erected, and marked out to be raised, Abrantes, I think, bids fair to rise to that rank in the scale of fortresses, to which she is entitled from her situation.

Early in the morning of the 4th we quitted Abrantes, with little regret, and marched to Gavao, a village situated at the distance of two miles from the *left* bank of the Tagus, four and a half leagues from Abrantes, and eight from this town.

We crossed the Tagus by the bridge of boats, about half a mile from Abrantes; marched for two leagues over a sandy plain, studded with cork trees, and the remainder of the journey, we

marched over a barren heath, the road extremely
bad. Gavao has suffered greatly during the last
campaign.

On the morning of the 5th, we marched to
Alpalhao, a village which has suffered but little
in comparison to those through which we have
marched on our route. If the French had committed their usual ravages in Alpalhao, we should
have seen some trace of them : as there are no
ruins in the village, I consider the apparent poverty of the inhabitants as a convenient pretext at the
present time, and that, upon the whole, it is
more feigned than real.

We had now almost approached within call of
our brethren in arms. The hoarse murmur of the
bagpipe already, as it were, sounded in our ears,—
we beheld officers and privates stretching out
their hands, bidding us welcome to share in their
dangers, and their glory. Our hearts beat high
with native pride at the brilliant prospects before
us—in short, we were all mirth and gladness.

At day-light on the 6th, we quitted Alpalhao,
and about one o'clock marched in here. At a little
distance from the town, we were met by a number of officers, a great many privates, and the
music ;—each officer and soldier greeted their
respective friends, on their safe arrival in the
country, and the band played a few of their favourite airs before us into the town. I am positive, that there was not a private in the detach-

ment, who was not greeted, on his arrival here, by some relation or other, from the nearest of kin to a ninety-ninth cousin.

The regiment has been in quarters here since the 3d September; having got their new clothing a few days since, they make a fine appearance on parade.

When Lord Wellington withdrew the greater part of the allied army from this neighbourhood, the under-mentioned brigades of artillery, cavalry, and infantry, were ordered to remain as a corps of observation, under the command of Lieutenant-General Hill.

ARTILLERY :
Three brigades, British and Portuguese.

ALLIED CAVALRY,
Under the command of Lieutenant-General Sir William Erskine :

Major-General Long's Brigade.
9th and 13th Light Dragoons; 2d Hussars, King's German Legion.

Colonel Campbell's Portuguese Brigade.
4th and 10th Light Dragoons.

2D DIVISION ALLIED INFANTRY,
Under the command of Major-General Howard.

1st, or Major-General Howard's Brigade. *
50th, 71st, and 92d Regiments; 1 company
5th rifle battalion, 60th Regiment.

2d, or Colonel Byng's Brigade.
3d, 31st, 57th, and 66th Regiments; 1 company 5th rifle battalion, 60th Regiment.

3d, or Colonel Wilson's Brigade.
28th, 34th, and 39th Regiments; 1 company
5th rifle battalion, 60th Regiment.

4th, or Colonel Ashworth's Brigade.
6th and 18th Regiments of Portuguese Infantry; 6th Regiment Portuguese Caçadores.

Major-General Hamilton's Division of Portuguese.
1st, or Brig.-General Campbell's Brigade.
2d and 14th Regiments of the Line.

2d, or Brig.-General De Costa's Brigade.
4th and 10th Regiments of the Line.

Adieu.

---

* Major-General Howard being at present in command of
the division, Lieutenant-Colonel Stewart, of the 50th regiment,
has the temporary command of the brigade.

PORTALEGRE, *November* 5, 1811.

I EMBRACE the earliest opportunity afforded me of sending you a detailed account of our late operations in the Spanish province of Estramadura.

About the middle of last month, Brigadier-General Morillo, with the 5th Spanish army under his command, advanced from the frontiers of Portugal, towards the town of Caçares, in the ' province above named, in order to procure supplies for his army, of which they were in want ; and also with the view of increasing his numbers from amongst the spirited youths in those towns and villages through which his route might lead him.

The French General Girard having received correct information regarding these movements of General Morillo, collected about 6000 men of his corps, and advanced from the banks of the Guadiana to meet him. The two armies came in sight of each other in the vicinity of Caçares, when a slight skirmish took place ; at the close of which, Morillo very prudently withdrew his troops to Malpartida. Girard continuing to advance, Morillo retreated to Aliseda, whence he was also compelled to retire towards his old quarters on the frontier.

Lord Wellington having satisfied himself of the accuracy of the statement transmitted to him by the Spanish General, ordered General Hill to advance with all possible celerity to the assistance of our allies, and drive the enemy back to the place from whence he came.

In pursuance of the instructions he had received, General Hill caused an order to be issued on the morning of the 21st November, for the Commissary to have ten days bread, and fourteen days beef, ready to move with the troops, at a moment's notice ; and in the evening of the same day, a second order called on every regiment in the division to hold themselves in readiness to move on the following morning, the officers in light marching order.

Agreeably to the instructions issued to the troops the evening before, every regiment, quartered in this city, was under arms on the general alarm post, a little before day-light in the morning of the 22d, and soon after were put in motion by Major-General Howard, commanding the division.

We had advanced about two leagues on the road to Badajoz, when the bugle with the leading battalion sounded the halt. At this time we were totally ignorant of our ultimate destination ; conjecture, therefore, you may be assured, was extremely busy to find it out. Every one hazarded his opinion on the occasion. According to some, the following morning would show us the lofty turrets of Badajoz ;—others insisted that we were about to take up a position on the frontier, and there await the assault of General Drouet, who, with the corps under his command, was advancing to give us battle : But there was a third class, who considered the idea of a movement on Badajoz as chimerical—and the other as improbable ; and who, in opposition to the opinion of their friends, considered that the sole object of the expedition was to relieve the Spanish General from the unpleasant situation in which he had been placed, by the recent movements of his enemies.

In half an hour, the division was again ordered to advance, when, instead of pursuing our route in the direction of Badajoz, we received orders to turn to the left. In less than an hour, we passed under the village of Alegreta, the last on this road belonging to Portugal, a league in front of which, we crossed the Spanish frontier, and at three o'clock, passed through the village of Codeceira, in the vicinity of which the division went into bivouac.

When about half-way between Portalegre and Codeceira, we were attacked by a terrible storm of wind and rain, which, for several hours, poured its fury with merciless violence on our unsheltered heads. Long ere we arrived at our bivouac, we were all as thoroughly drenched, as if we had been soaked a year in the Bay of Biscay.

The arms of our poor fellows were no sooner in pile, than they set about felling trees, constructing huts, and making fires in several parts of our gloomy and cheerless encampment. Frost having succeeded the rain during the night, our situation had become, by the dawn, one of the most miserable you can possibly imagine. Never, while I breathe, shall I forget the miserable night I spent in the bivouac at Codeceira, where, wet and weary, I laid myself down to sleep,—the cold clay earth my bed, and the canopy of heaven my only covering.

Never did I listen with so much pleasure to the hoarse murmurs of the bagpipes, as on the morning of the 23d, when they called us to arms. At their sound I attempted to rise, but my limbs were stiff, and for some time refused to perform their ordinary functions ; having, after many attempts, succeeded in rising, I prepared to march to where I knew not, but fondly hoped we were going to a more comfortable quarter.

About seven o'clock, we took leave of our wretched bivouac, and at one, arrived at Albuquerque. This ancient city is situated on the northern slope of a ridge of mountains, called the Sierra de Montanches. The streets of Albuquerque are much cleaner in general than those of the other towns and villages which I have vi-

sited since my arrival in this country. This may
be attributed, in some measure, to the declivity
of the ground on which the city stands, and
which is in many places very considerable. Having no scavengers, the inhabitants are under the
necessity of committing the cleaning of their
streets to the rain, which, in the performance of
the arduous duties assigned to it, derives no small
assistance from the rapid descent of many of the
streets, in removing the accumulated heaps of
filth, which every where present their hideous
forms, to the great annoyance of every individual, who, from necessity, is compelled to pace
their streets, lanes, and alleys.

On a rock, a little above the town, there stands
an ancient castle, which, for ages past, has braved the buffetting of the storm. From its antiquat-
ed appearance, there cannot be a doubt, but that
it was built long before the use of gunpowder.
An attempt was lately made to modernize it; but
the engineer might as well have attempted to turn
an old woman of eighty into a girl of six-
teen. The repairs made on it, have added nothing to its strength; indeed, it is much to be
doubted, whether all the engineers in Europe
could, in one hundred years, make it stronger
than it is at this period, unless they could fall on
some method of giving a plentiful supply of
good water, of which it is now deficient.

At an early hour in the morning of the 24th, the division quitted the city, and at four in the afternoon, encamped on a small height which skirts the forest of Albuquerque on the north, at the distance of five leagues from the city of Albuquerque, and two from Aliseda.

The enemy's position having been previously reconnoitred, at ten o'clock we marched from our bivouac on the confines of the forest, and at one, arrived at Aliseda, where we found the Spanish infantry of Morillo, the cavalry of the Conde de Penne Villamur, and Colonel Downie's legion of lancers, in bivouac outside the village. About two miles from this place, our artillery had nearly been stopped, owing to the broken state of the roads. A party of infantry, from our brigade, was ordered to assist the artillerymen in getting the guns forward, in which, after a great deal of trouble, they happily succeeded.

In a small field, on the left of the road leading to Malpartida, our brigade was ordered into bivouac, with orders to cook with all possible dispatch. The beef, not half an hour killed, was put into the camp-kettles about two o'clock; soup was announced at four;—at half-past four, the bugle sounded to arms, and at a quarter from five, the division began to move off towards the enemy, who, at that time, were revelling in Malpartida, unconscious of danger.

On the commencement of our march, the

evening, for the season, was rather mild; but we had scarcely proceeded three miles ere the clouds began to lower, and the rain to fall in torrents—nor did it cease for one moment, till long after day-light on the following morning.

Even in the finest summer weather, night marching is far from being pleasant; but in a dark stormy night, such as the 25th of October, the situation of the poor unpitied soldier becomes one of such affecting misery, that no language can describe it. Too often, indeed, the pale and haggard countenance of the warrior betrays what he wishes most to conceal,—a constitution shattered to atoms by fatigue, hunger and cold.

Our march on the night alluded to, was one of a very trying kind; the bad state of the roads, added to the darkness of the night, and inclemency of the weather, was extremely hard on those of weakly constitutions; had the French been at a greater distance, many of our men, I am positive, would have laid themselves down, and waited the coming of the morning light, to guide them on their cheerless course.

Morning at length broke in upon our gloomy thoughts, and shewed us the village of Malpartida immediately in our front. Whether the enemy had fled, or were waiting for us in the town, we had yet to learn; to be in readiness, however, the arms of the men were inspected, their flints adjusted, and their bayonets kept in readiness to perform their duty when called on. For a quarter of an hour, we were kept in the most anxious suspense—aides-de-camp were flying from one part of the field to another, with orders from the commander of the corps to officers in command of brigades. Every moment we expected the signal for battle would be made to us—we looked for it, but we looked in vain. The enemy having received intelligence of our march from Aliseda, had decamped from Malpartida, about two hours before our arrival.

The Spaniards, and a portion of our light cavalry, were sent in pursuit of the fugitives, with whom they had a very slight skirmish, neither party sustaining any material loss.

From Caceres, General Girard retired in the evening, and on the following day, established his head-quarters in the village of Arroya del Molino. General Hill, with the troops under his command, remained in Malpartida till the morning of the 27th, when, a little after day-light, the pursuit of the enemy was resumed. Our march was directed on Arroya del Molino, by the villages of Aldea del Cano and Alcuesca; at the former, we arrived about one o'clock, whence, after a short halt, we continued our route for the latter, where we arrived about six, and encamped in rear of the village.

On crossing the extensive plain which lies between Malpartida and Aldea del Cano, the division had a rare treat given them by the officers belonging to the corps. Those officers who were mounted, having started a *hare*, all the greyhounds in the division were put in requisition to give chace to poor puss, which, after an excellent run of several minutes, was killed. The officers, perceiving that the soldiers enjoyed the sport equally with themselves, continued it for a considerable time. The effect produced on the spirits of our men, by this little piece of attention on the part of the officers, was much greater than could have been expected from such a cause. I am fully convinced, that during the time the sport lasted, few, if any of the soldiers knew that they were marching at all. Time was wonderfully beguiled—so much so, that after taking up our ground, in the evening, in rear of the village of Alcuesca, numbers of them could not believe that they had marched above one half of the distance they really had done.—To sport of a different kind I must now call your attention.

General Hill having received information, that the enemy intended to remain at Arroya del Molino, ordered the necessary arrangements to be made for an attack, on their position, at day-light on the following morning.

Every measure of precaution was adopted to prevent the enemy from gaining information from our camp, either as it regarded our numbers or intentions. No fires were allowed in our bivouac for the night—we were told to make ourselves as comfortable as we could without them. When this order was communicated to the soldiers, they laid themselves down with the greatest composure, and, without a murmur, wrapt in their blankets, consigned themselves to rest : The rain, at this time, was falling copiously, but every man resigned himself to his fate, and bore his allotted share of misery with a fortitude becoming at once the man and the soldier.

Exposed to the inclemency of the angry elements, for eight long hours we lay, wet and weary, anxiously awaiting the call to " fall in," which at length, about two o'clock in the morning of the 28th, was whispered into our ears by the orderly serjeants. The summons was obeyed with alacrity ; in a few minutes we were on our march, and a few more brought us in sight of the enemy's fires, at the very sight of which, the hearts of our men leapt with joy ;—to them they were the sacred guarantee that Girard was still in Arroya :—to our poor fellows a sight of their fires was more cheering than words can adequately express, as, from whispers, which dropt from them during the march, every man looked forward to the termination of his own sufferings with that of the *first* battle they should fight with General Girard.

The distance between the two armies in the morning was about three miles : To march this short way occupied us fully four hours, the narrow and broken state of the road having caused the files of the column to open out to an unusual length.

It was nearly seven o'clock before the whole of the troops had defiled from the mountains and formed by brigades in close column of companies, under cover of a small height, about half a mile from Arroya del Molino. The final arrangements for the attack having been made, and instructions given to commanding officers of corps, the army moved forward in the following order of battle :

The 71st and 92d regiments, supported by the 50th and two pieces of Portuguese artillery, under the command of Lieutenant-Colonel Stewart, 50th regiment, were directed to carry the village of Arroya del Molino at the point of the bayonet. The right and centre columns, consisting of the second brigade, and Colonel Ashworth's Portuguese, under the command of Major-General Howard, were directed to move to their right, cut off the retreat of the enemy towards Medellin, and, finally, attack their left and rear. The cavalry, under Sir William Erskine, were stationed at every point where their services might be useful ; and, during the action, made several very brilliant charges. The Spanish cavalry of the Conde de Penne Villamur, were also in the field, as were the lancers of Colonel Downie.

The Spanish infantry were at hand, but took no part in the action.

The 71st and 92d regiments moved forward to the village at a quick pace, and, in a few minutes, cleared it of the enemy, who were very far from being prepared for such an unceremonious visit. General Girard, driven from the village, formed his infantry in two squares ; and, at the distance of two hundred yards from it, threw a very destructive fire towards the 71st and 92d regiments. The first lined a wall outside the village, and the latter, quite unprotected, were formed at the entrance of the village, in column of sections. The 92d regiment having orders to reserve their fire, beheld their companions fall around them, without being able to avenge their death. But they were not long in this situation. An order soon arrived for the regiment to form line, and prepare to charge. In a few minutes the line was formed, and the Highlanders only waited for the order to advance. All this time the enemy appeared extremely uncomfortable—something like hesitation was observed in their squares. At this interesting period, the two Portuguese guns, attached to the left wing, were ordered forward, whose fire carried death into the thickest of their ranks. The Highlanders had received orders, and were about to present the enemy with a little of their steel, when they, with that politeness for which Frenchmen are so remarkable, declined the honour we intended them, wheeled to the right-about, and, with rather a hasty step, retired to a steep mountain in their rear, over whose summit the French General, no doubt, fancied he should be able to conduct them to more hospitable quarters.

During these operations on the left, the column under Major-General Howard had cut off the enemy's retreat on Medellin, and was endeavouring to get between them and the mountain, at the time they retired from before the left wing. Failing in this object, the next which presented itself to the Major-General, was, by a rapid movement round the base of the hill, to endeavour to cut off their retreat across the summit of it. By ascending at a point immediately opposite to the one which the enemy had secured to effect a safe retreat, he was aware must bring the two hostile columns in contact with each other; the issue of any conflict, however, could not be doubtful. The two columns met on the shoulder of the hill—a warm skirmish was the consequence; but the enemy, perceiving himself completely hemmed in, on all sides, hoisted a white flag in token of submission.

Our loss, during this action, was very inconsiderable—that of the enemy was great. General Girard was severely wounded, but effected his escape. The second in command, General Brune,

Colonel the Prince of D'Aremberg, the chief of the staff, forty inferior officers, and about eleven hundred non-commissioned officers and privates were made prisoners. All his cannon, (three pieces), baggage, money, and provisions fell into our hands. The enemy had three thousand men in action, of whom, it is said, three hundred only escaped. That enterprising young officer, Lieutenant Strenuwitz, aide-de-camp to Lieutenant-General Sir William Erskine, in charging, at the commencement of the battle, at the head of the Spanish cavalry, was made prisoner by the enemy.

Having collected the wounded, and secured the prisoners, we quitted the field, marched about two leagues on the road to Medellin, and went into bivouac near to the small village of San Pedro.

As soon as we had taken up our ground, cavalry picquets were posted around our camp, in various directions, in order to watch the motions of those French stragglers who were known to have escaped from us in the morning. One of those picquets, perceiving a party of French dragoons making across the plain for Medellin, mounted their horses, and gave chase to them. Our party consisted of a Lieutenant and seventeen privates; that of the enemy of a captain and twenty-three privates. The superiority of the enemy, however, did not deter our party from attacking them. After a slight resistance, the whole were taken prisoners, and brought into our camp, fully equipped, armed, and mounted.

About two o'clock in the morning of the 29th, we marched from our camp near San Pedro, and, at five in the afternoon, arrived in Merida. Throughout the whole of this day's fatiguing march, the rain fell in torrents, which, forming itself into currents, assumed the appearance of small rivers.—After a march of fifteen hours, in such circumstances, without any thing to eat, it is unnecessary for me to inform you that we were fatigued, wet, and hungry.

Merida, once the capital of a province of the same name, is seated on the right bank of the river Guadiana, eight leagues above Badajoz, and five below Medellin. Roman grandeur still rears its head amidst the ruins of this ancient city. The amphitheatre has fallen into complete decay. The triumphal arch has suffered considerably at the hand of Time. The aqueduct is still entire; but many of the people in Merida do not hold it in the same estimation as they do the other works of antiquity; as they allege a part of it was rebuilt about one hundred years ago. The castle, once a place of great importance, is now one heap of ruins. It stands on the left of the street leading from the great square to the river, over which there is a truly magnificent Roman bridge, of 58 arches, and 870 paces in length. The town is surrounded by a wall of considerable height, which is fast hastening to decay.

On the 30th, the division having been allowed a halt, the horses, mules, and asses, captured on the 28th, were sold by public auction in the square of Merida ; the produce of which, together with the money found in the military chest, will, it is said, be divided amongst the troops employed in the expedition.

The division marched on the 31st to Montejo, a large village, lying about three leagues above Badajoz.

About an hour before day-light, on the 1st November, we marched from Montejo for Campo-Major. The distance between these two places being fully seven leagues, General Hill ordered the troops to get two hours rest on some convenient spot. Between twelve and one o'clock, we crossed a very deep, rapid river. Many of us were above the middle in mud and water, and some of the lower in stature were absolutely swimming. The scene was truly a laughable one : The Highlander has greatly the advantage over his brethren, when crossing a river, as the former can at all times tuck up his kilt in a moment to his middle, whilst the latter are forced to cross over in their pantaloons or trowsers ; where, should the water be fully knee-deep, it is obvious, that the Highlander, on getting to the other side of the river, must be quite dry, whilst the latter must be wet through every stitch of his small clothes, and trudge away to the place of destination in this uncomfortable state.

As soon as the whole had crossed over, the bugle sounded the halt. Soon after we got an allowance of grog; and about two o'clock we were again under arms, and, considering every thing, tolerably comfortable. The want of a thorough knowledge of this part of the country caused some one to commit a very singular, yet to us serious mistake, being still at a considerable distance from Campo-Major.—In tolerable spirits we moved off for that town, but had scarcely proceeded three hundred yards before another river, broader, deeper, and more rapid than the first, made its appearance. We were now wet to the arm-pits, night was fast approaching, and eight long miles still between us and the fortress. I will not attempt a description of our situation at that moment; it will, I doubt not, be sufficiently apparent to you from what I have already stated. Whoever the author was of this cruel mistake, I know not; but it is to be hoped that a similar one will never occur again, as the health and comfort of the soldier ought not to be trifled with.

Campo-Major has, by the defence it made in the spring of the present year, forever immortalized itself. The walls of the place are commanded, in several parts, within point-blank shot. The streets of this town are, like those of almost every other which I have seen in this conntry, extremely dirty, and ill paved.

In Campo-Major we halted on the 22d. At an early hour on the following day, we marched from that town for Arronches, where we arrived about mid-day. This is a fortress of the old school ; it is surrounded by a high wall, which, before the use of gunpowder, must have rendered it a place of considerable importance. Many of the houses appear to be as old as the kingdom itself.

Yesterday morning we marched from Arronches at an early hour, and arrived here about one. On our march through the various streets to our former quarters, we were every where greeted with the loud acclamations of a grateful populace. The old, young, and middle aged— all vied with each other in their expressions of gratitude for the services we had rendered them : conscious that these spontaneous effusions of their gratitude flowed from the heart, untainted by hypocrisy, we received them as a *people's thanks*, the *noblest reward* a soldier can receive.

The expedition, I have been told, has succeeded in its object, far beyond the expectations of the Noble Lord who planned it, or the gallant and amiable General who carried it into execution. Throughout the whole of the late operations, it is but justice to the soldiers to add, that by their valour and firmness, (qualities peculiarly their own.) their General was enabled to surmount every obstacle that attempted to arrest his progress.

PORTALEGRE, *December* 17, 1811.

EVER since the 5th of November, all has remained tranquil on the frontier. No movement of any kind has taken place in this corps ; and I believe that the army under Lord Wellington has made none of consequence. The sickly season having now gone by, we may safely calculate on a considerable accession to our present numbers, before the end of the month.

A few days after the division returned to this city from Arroya del Molino, Colonel C. applied to Lord Wellington, to have all the supernumerary officers of the 1st battalion sent home to the second battalion of the regiment, now quartered in Scotland. To this application, an answer was received about the 19th November, granting leave to the officers, named therein, to proceed to Lisbon, and thence embark on board such vessel as should be provided by the proper authorities, to carry them to England. Those officers were six in number, and your friend one of them.

C.

Having taken leave of our friends, we quitted Portalegre on the 22d ultimo, and that night slept in the large but miserable village of Gaffeta. On the following morning, we resumed our journey, and arrived in Gavao about one, where, finding some officers taking quarters for the whole of the 39th regiment, (then on their march from Lisbon), we decamped, and made the best of our way to the village of Villa Franca. On our arrival, we went to the house of the chief magistrate, to get billets for one night's quarters. The worthy man had barred his door, as soon as he had seen us approach his house. We knocked again and again, but no one answered : Perfectly aware that he was at home, and justly enraged at his conduct, it is possible we might have adopted a summary mode of getting into the house, but for the interference of a most respectable looking woman, who stepped forward at the moment, and, in the kindest manner. offered us an asylum in her house for the night. We most gladly accepted of her offer, and, after bestowing a few good names on the worthy patriotic magistrate, followed our hostess to her abode. Dinner was soon got ready, which she served up in her best style ; and in the evening, she favoured us with good mattresses and clean bed-clothes—a great treat in this country.

On the following morning, having returned thanks to our patrona, and invoked a blessing on her and her family, we left the house of this truly good woman, and marched to Abrantes, where a very different reception awaited us. The people on whom Major M. was billetted, were two of the most uncivil creatures that this or any other country ever produced. In order that we might have the benefit of one another's society, it was unanimously agreed on, to have the provision, when received from the Commissary, carried to this house, and cooked. Orders were given to the servants, to have dinner ready by a certain hour; the interval we resolved to pass in walking round the ramparts. At the appointed time, we returned to the house; but had scarcely entered it, before one of the servants, with a visage as long as my arm, informed us, that the people of the caza would not give them one culinary article. This information was not very agreeable; but what could we do, but exercise our patience for a few hours longer. Partly by threats, and partly by entreaty, we at length got two small pans, with which the servants contrived to give us a little soup and a stew, much sooner than we expected. When every thing was ready, these accommodating people would not give us a single dish of any kind to put it in. Had you but seen the infernal couple standing sentry over the stoneware, I am sure you would agree with me, that a finer subject for the caricaturist was never afforded. They had more the appearance of the inhabitants of Pandemonium, than of this world.

Having disposed of our baggage-animals, we, on the morning of the 26th, embarked in a small commissariat boat, on the river, bound to Lisbon. With a gentle breeze, we glided down the surface of the river, till after sun-set, when we disembarked on its left bank, and walked about half a mile, to the clean, neat, little village of Chamusca. In this village, we met with genuine hospitality. Every individual in the houses, where we were billetted, vied with each other in personal acts of kindness and attention.— They spoke to us of some British regiments, which had been quartered there, during the period that Massena lay at Santarem, in the most flattering manner : With those people, the British stand high indeed.

Early next morning, we re-embarked, and proceeded down the river to Valada, where we slept that night. About three o'clock in the afternoon of the 28th, we embarked on board of a larger vessel ; and next morning, at six, landed at the Black Horse Square, in Lisbon.

On the first of December I received a letter of recall from the regiment, to my no small joy. The other five proceeded to Scotland ; they started the same day I left Lisbon on my return hither. A detachment for the regiment having arrived in Lisbon on the 30th of November, I received permission to attach myself to, and return with it, to this place. On the 5th we embarked in boats at Belem, and next day about one arrived at Valada. I paid Maria a visit—she appeared more cheerful than the first time I saw her. On the 7th we marched to Santarem ;—on the 8th to Gallegao ; —on the 9th to Punhete ;—on the 10th to Abrantes, where we halted on the 11th and 12th ;— on the 13th marched to Gavao ;—on the 14th to Gaffeta ; and in the afternoon of the 15th arrived in safety here. Every where on our route from Lisbon, I could easily perceive a manifest improvement in the condition of the inhabitants. Many of the houses that were standing empty in October are now inhabited ; plenty seems to have occupied the place of poverty ; joy beams in the eyes of many whose miseries at that period seemed ready to overwhelm them. At Punhete, the churches continue in the same state as when we passed through the place before ;—almost nothing remains of these structures, which can point them out to the stranger as places of public worship. Having, from my early years, been taught to look on the church, and every thing connected with it, as sacred, you may easily imagine with what feelings I contemplated the sacred ruins ; and devoutly offered up my prayers to the all-wise Disposer of events, that he, in his goodness, would be pleased to avert a similar calamity from our happy isle.

On the whole, I am of opinion, that the inhabitants, in general, are still in possession of considerable pecuniary resources, which, if properly
applied, would in a very few years of peace banish
every trace of the invader from their land.

Should the enemy ever attempt another invasion of this country, the result will prove far more
disastrous to them than any that has yet preceded
it. The atrocities committed by them since
the first invasion of these realms, has wound up
to the highest pitch the people's detestation of the
French name. Their atrocities will ever live in
the remembrance of the present, and by them be
handed down to generations yet unborn. The
name of a Junot, a Loison, a Soult, a Massena,
and a long list of inferior agents of French tyranny and oppression, will ever be pronounced in
this country with execration and with horror.

During the present scarcity of military details,
permit me to give you some account of a Lisbon
hoax, to which I was an eye-witness.

On the 2d instant, hand-bills, printed in the
British and Portuguese languages, were posted and
distributed through every part of the metropolis,
intimating to the inhabitants, that a British officer, accoutred in cork boots, was, for a considerable bet, to start at Fort Belem, and walk a-
cross the Tagus on the following day at one
o'clock. As early as nine o'clock in the morning of the 3d instant, the streets leading to Belem

were crowded with people of all nations, hastening
to the starting-post as fast as their respective modes
of conveyance would allow them.   A considerable
number were in carriages, many on mules and
asses, and thousands of men, women, and children, running as fast as their legs would carry
them.   A company of Portuguese militia, properly officered, kept a clear passage for the hero
to get to the river.   About half-past twelve the
beach was completely covered; I counted, at one
time, of coaches, and other vehicles of a similar
description, upwards of 400, drawn up in three
lines on the beach.   The river was literally covered with boats, in which the naval and military
uniforms of Great Britain and her allies were conspicuous.   The castle and fort were entirely
occupied by the principal nobility and gentry at
that time in Lisbon.   In the latter, with much
difficulty, I got a place.   Six, eight, and even
ten dollars were given for the use of small boats,
the ordinary fare of which does not exceed 1s. 6d.
or 2s.   About one o'clock the scene was at its
height.   As the clock announced the hour, one
jostled another in order to get closer to the spot
where the cork-accoutred hero was to make his
appearance, previous to starting on his perilous
pedestrian voyage.   A few minutes after one, a
voice from the crowd announced his approach, to
get a sight of whom, the eyes of the all-anxious
crowd were bent towards the spot whence

the sound proceeded—He was not there: Two
o'clock struck—still he was absent; the hour of
three was announced—there was no appearance of
an officer with cork boots. About this time the
people, whose appetites were getting a little keen,
whetted, no doubt, by the fresh breeze from the
river, began to steal slily away, fully satisfied that
they had been completely hoaxed. Before four
o'clock the greater part had retired to their respective places of abode, all the way home vowing
vengeance on the British officer and his cork
boots. The number of all ranks assembled on
this occasion, on shore, and in the boats on the
river, have been variously estimated at from
40,000 to 50,000.

Such is but a very poor and imperfect account of
the attempt at the ridiculous on the 3d instant.
The sport of that day, I have been assured, will
furnish *tea-table talk* to the ladies of Lisbon for at
least six months to come. Adieu.

MERIDA, *January* 11, 1812.

BY the mail for England, which leaves this place to-morrow morning at nine o'clock, I send you this letter, in which you will find a detailed account of the operations in this quarter since the 25th ultimo.

About eight o'clock on Christmas evening General Hill issued an order for the troops to hold themselves in readiness to march at a moment's notice. A little before day-light, on the 26th, the bugle called us to arms. In less than an hour the whole division had assembled at the alarm-post, and put in motion towards our old quarters, the village of Codeceira, which we occupied in the afternoon. Next morning we continued our route to Albuquerque, where we were joined by the third brigade, which, ever since the battle of Arroya, has been stationed in that city. At an early hour on the 28th we quitted Albuquerque, and directed our march on Merida. Two leagues from the former place, we passed to the right of the ancient castle of Zagala, beautifully situated on the summit of a high hill, from which you have a fine view of the country to the south, nearly as far as the eye can reach. Three leagues further, we passed through the small village of La Rocka, in front of which, on the western slop of a small height, we went into bivouac. Officers commanding corps were requested to have their fires as much under the hill as circumstances would permit.

Soon after the memorable 25th of October, General Dombrousky, with a mixed force of from 1200 to 1500 men, was ordered into Merida. To take the Pole napping was now the object our General had in view; and to guard against surprise, the French General had raised redoubts on the heights above the town, barricadoed the streets, and loop-holed many of the houses in the suburbs:—decorated with these French trappings, Merida had become a considerable military station. But notwithstanding the formidable preparations which had been made to receive him, General Hill was determined to put in execution a plan of operation similar to that which, on the field of Arroya del Molino, had been crowned with decisive success.

At day-light on the 29th the troops quitted their bivuoac, and, with the cavalry in front, directed their march on Merida. The column had marched a considerable distance when General Hill received information that a body of 500 French troops were in La Nava, (a village at no great distance, and about three leagues from Merida), sent out, the preceding evening, by General Dombrousky, on a plundering excursion.— Intelligence to this effect was sent to Major-General Long, commanding the cavalry in advance; but

which, I believe, did not reach him till the advanced
file of our cavalry had taken the advanced vidette
of the enemy prisoner, close to the village. The
report of the sentinel's pistol gave the enemy intimation of their danger. As every thing depend-
ed on the capture of this party, Major-General
Long made the necessary dispositions to attack
them with the cavalry alone ; but these could not
be made without knowing something of the enemy's strength, which the thickness of the fog,
at the time, rendered it difficult to ascertain.
Before the Major-General was prepared to attack
them, the infantry had formed in square on the
rising ground behind the village. After some
firing, our cavalry charged them, but were repulsed with loss. The enemy began to retire with
our cavalry hovering on their flanks, ready to
take advantage of any opening that might appear
as favourable to the renewal of the charge. The
enemy appeared as cool as if on parade in the
court of the Thuilleries ; again and again their
square was charged by our brave fellows, but were
as often repulsed with loss. Two pieces of artillery
were also sent to their assistance ; but not all the
shot they could pour into the enemy's square,
made the least impression on them. For a league
and a half they retired in square, and bravely disputed every inch of ground with their assailants.
At length, being reinforced by a part of the gar-

rison from Merida, our cavalry gave over the pursuit.

I have been told that the French infantry, throughout the whole of the day, behaved with great coolness and gallantry—not a man of them ever appeared to shrink from the terrible conflict. A gap was no sooner made in one of the faces of the square, than it was instantly filled by others. But the soldiers of this party were no ordinary soldiers, nor was the officer who commanded them a man of common courage or abilities; he was every way qualified to command such men, and they were, from their firmness and courage, worthy of being placed under his command.

The exertions of our own troops were highly meritorious, although victory did not crown them with success. No effort was spared on their part, in order to compel the enemy to surrender. When ordered to give over the pursuit, they retired from the field with regret, satisfied, however, in their own minds, that a body of brave infantry has nothing to fear from the utmost efforts of a cavalry force of double their numbers.

Thus was a victory snatched from us by a trivial occurrence, and that, too, at the very moment when one and all of us were buoyed up with the fond hope of again exalting our own and our country's character.

The whole corps went into bivouac, on a barren

heath, half a league in front of La Nava; and on the following morning, we marched into Merida, without opposition, the enemy having retired from it during the night, to the town of Almendralejo, leaving in our possession a quantity of grain, &c.

The 31st was occupied in making preparations for an attack on the position of the Count D'Erlon at Almendralejo.

A little after day-light, on the 1st January, the division got under arms, crossed the Guadiana by the bridge of Merida, and, in order of battle, advanced towards the enemy.

The enemy having some picquets in front of the town, these were attacked about one o'clock by our cavalry, and driven in, with the loss of a few horses. The French infantry, in the town, on hearing the firing, got under arms, and retired under cover of a thick fog, which, for a length of time, prevented us from ascertaining their precise numbers; but which, when the fog dissipated, was found to consist of a strong rear-guard only, the Count having made off, with the greater part of his family, the previous night. The cavalry, and some rifle troops, followed them for a little distance, but neither party suffered much in the business. Strong picquets having been posted on the roads leading to Fuento del Maestre and Villa-Franca, the division marched into Almendralejo.

In the house in which I was quartered, I found

the dinner of some French soldiers at the side of
the fire. The people offered it to me, saying,
" This is your's; you have driven the French from
" our village : this is the dinner of some of them,
" that have been with us since the 30th." Having some tea and sugar in my haversack, and pre-
ferring a little of that delicious and refreshing beverage to the dinner of my enemies, I begged the
family would make use of the meat. In five minutes it was placed on the table, and in as many
more, such was their liking to the food, or hatred
to their enemies, not a vestige of it was to be
seen.

General Hill, finding that the enemy still held
the villages of Villa Franca and Fuento del Maestre, ordered two detachments from the division,
on the morning of the 3d, to march, and take
possession of them. The 9th and 13th light dragoons, with the first brigade and two pieces of
artillery, under General Howard, marched to the
former place; and the 2d German hussars, 4th
and 10th Portuguese cavalry, and 28th regiment
of British infantry, under the command of the
Honourable Lieutenant-Colonel Abercromby, of
the 28th regiment, marched to the latter.

The French in Villa-Franca were evidently
prepared to retire the moment we came near
them, as they were formed on a piece of rising
ground to the right of the village, and on the
road leading to Los Santos. About a mile from

the village, the detachment was formed into two columns; the right column, consisting of the 92d regiment, and a rifle company of the 6Cth, with one piece of artillery, moved up a valley, in order to attack the enemy in front. The remaining part of the detachment formed the left column, under General Howard, and advanced directly on the village, in order to attack their right, or get to their rear. For some time after these preparations were made to attack them, the enemy walked about, with their arms in pile, as much at their ease as if there had not been a British soldier within a hundred miles of them. But, I dare say, you are perfectly aware, that a Frenchman never appears in better humour than when he is most out of it.—Their numbers not warranting the officer commanding to risk a skirmish with us, he withdrew his troops, when we were quite close to them, on the road to Los Santos. Picquets of companies were ordered to be posted on the different roads around the village, and the remainder marched into it.

The detachment was under arms an hour before day-light, on the morning of the 4th. For two hours, the wind blew, and the rain and the hail fell with such violence, that, in five minutes after we went out of our quarters, we were most completely drenched. Never, in my life, did I witness such a tempest. Those officers and men, who braved the fury of the merciless elements during the night, were, when morning dawned, in a helpless and most deplorable situation; indeed, some of them appeared in a state of temporary insanity. Let those, who imagine that a soldier's life is one of ease and comfort, make but one short campaign in this country; and whenever they may chuse to return again to their native country—to that happy land, they will carry with them a faint recollection, I dare say, of a soldier's life, and a soldier's comforts, in this. Cold as ice, hungry as hawks, and draggled like ducks getting out of the mud, we retraced our steps to Almendralejo; and, on the following day, returned to our present quarters.

On the march from Almendralejo to Merida, on the 5th instant, a soldier, belonging to a regiment in our division, having drunk rather freely of the juice of the grape, quitted the ranks. He had scarcely done so, ere he fell into a sound sleep, from which he did not awake till very late in the evening. Alone, and in an uninhabited part of the country, the poor fellow knew not whither to turn himself. His thoughts uncomposed, he often upbraided himself for his misconduct. He fancied he saw his name handed in to the Adjutant-General as a deserter to the enemy; himself about to be tried for the offence before a General Court-Martial; the sentence of death passed; and the platoon, headed by the Provost-Marshal, ready to carry the sentence into execution. What a situation to be placed in! Yet it is to be feared, that there are too many often similarly situated. Well would it be for the British soldier, if he could bring himself to reflect a little on the consequences that generally follow dissipation, before he seats himself down to taste of the cheering beverage. Thousands of crimes would never be heard of, which now fill the character-rolls of almost every regiment in the service.—On the morning of the 6th, the soldier bent his way towards Merida; but into that town he was afraid to enter. To a village, on his left, he directed his steps, to see if some friendly individual would plead for him at head-quarters. In this village, he was informed, there were two French soldiers concealed. A thought started across his mind, that if he could get them secured, he would be able to carry them into Merida as prisoners, and thereby procure his pardon. Having communicated this idea to some of the inhabitants, they agreed to assist him. In an instant, he loaded his musket; proceeded to the house where they lay—disarmed them; and, in two hours after, marched them off in triumph. Some officers of the 71st regiment, seeing a British soldier, with two Frenchmen as prisoners, coming from the opposite side of the river, where none of the allied troops were at that time quartered, asked the soldier, " What men are these " you have got?" Pat replied, " By J.—s,

" your Honours, I cannot tell: I believe they are
" Frenchmen!"

It is impossible for me to convey to you the
smallest idea of the horrible state of the roads in
this part of the country. Numbers of our men,
on the first of the month, sunk so deep into the
mire, that they were glad to get themselves extricated with only the loss of their shoes. During
the marches of the 1st, 3d, 4th, and 5th of this
month, I am positive that I never had a less quantity of clay at my heels than three or four pounds
weight; and really, at times I could scarcely drag
my feet after me. In the evening of every one of
these days, I was completely knocked up—I did
not require the assistance of any one to put me
asleep. When this was my situation, who had
neither musket, ammunition, knapsack, canteen,
or haversack, what must the poor soldier have suffered, who had to march encumbered with all these
—a weight very little under three stone?

I had almost forgot to mention, that the detachment, sent against Fuento del Maestre, had a
very brilliant affair with some of the enemy's cavalry, in the vicinity of that village; in which, I
have been assured, the 2d German hussars greatly distinguished themselves. The killed and wounded, I believe, amounted to 20, and the prisoners to
31. Our loss was very trifling.

January 12, 8 *o'Clock*, A. M.

P. S.—About an hour ago, General Hill received an order from Lord Wellington, desiring him to retrace his steps to Portalegre. By the courier who brought the above order, advices have been received from his Lordship's army, which state, that Ciudad Rodrigo was invested on the 8th instant; and that in a few days, it was expected, the besiegers' batteries would be carried within a short distance of the body of the place.

The bugles have sounded the warning call. We will all be off in a few minutes. Adieu.

CASTELLO BRANCO, *January* 31, 1812.

On the 12th instant, about nine in the morning, General Hill's corps broke up from Merida, and the same day retired behind La Nava. On the 13th, the troops encamped at a little distance from the Castle of Zagala; and, on the 14th, marched into Albuquerque; thence continued their route, on the 16th, to Codeceira; and on the 17th, marched into Portalegre. Our men were occupied, during the whole of the 18th, in cleaning themselves, washing their linen, and mending their shoes. Early in the morning of the 19th, we quitted that city; and in the after-

D 2

noon, occupied Alpalhao; and, next morning, marched into Niza; where, on the 22d, we received the first intelligence of the fall of Ciudad Rodrigo, which happened on the 19th. All the information we have received, on this heart-stirring subject, states, that our brave fellows mounted the breaches in gallant style; and, throughout the assault, which lasted about half an hour, displayed the greatest coolness, and unconquerable courage. The loss of the allied army I have not been able to ascertain; but I believe that of the French, in killed, wounded, and prisoners, amounts to about 3000 of all ranks.

The British army has sustained a severe loss in the fall of the Major-Generals Crawford and Mackinnon, both of whom stood very high in the list of officers of merit.

It is currently reported in this army, and believed to be a fact, that Marshal Marmont calculated on Ciudad Rodrigo holding out to the 28th or 29th of the month; and that on one or other of these days, he intended to have offered battle. The report is strengthened by this fact, that, so late as the 25th, troops were still hurrying forward, to reinforce the army under Lord Wellington's command; so that it not only clearly appears, that the French Marshal intended to fight before, but had some idea of fighting us after the fall of the place. On the 25th, our brigade left Niza, and on the following day marched into this town. On our arrival, we were informed that an order had been received to stop all the troops advancing from the south, as Marmont had withdrawn his troops to Salamanca, waiting an opportunity for acting on the offensive, when the chance of victory might appear to him more certain. His retreat having rendered our presence in this part of the country no longer necessary, we have received orders to return to Portalegre, by the same route by which we advanced.

Castello Branco is situated on a little rugged hill, five leagues north from the Tagus, and at a short distance from the Spanish frontiers. In former times, it was a place of considerable importance. From its situation, naturally strong and commanding, it might, at the present day, be rendered a fortress of the second rank, and one of the most useful to Portugal.

No opportunity could have been better selected for the siege of Ciudad Rodrigo, than that made choice of by Lord Wellington. Every thing favoured him, in carrying on his operations before the place. Marshal Suchet, anxious to get possession of all the fortresses on the eastern coast of Spain, had, sometime before, applied to Marshal Marmont for a portion of his army to assist him. The required assistance was granted ; the troops were selected, and sent. In the absence of those troops, Marmont was not a match for Lord Wellington. His Lordship knew it; and, taking advantage of this circumstance, (he having every thing ready), carried the place in ten days.

I have just been informed, that our late movement into Estremadura has been of considerable service to the common cause. Our march to Merida, and thence to Villa Franca, gave great uneasiness to Marshal Soult, for the safety of his rear, under Count Drouet. He collected troops from every corner of Andalusia, to march to the Count's assistance. The siege of Tariffa, undertaken by General Laval, with a corps of 10,000 men, was raised, and the battering cannon left in the hands of the garrison; and all this was done after several practicable breaches had been made in the walls of the fortress. This is to us a reward sufficient for all the hardships and miseries we have suffered during the last month. Adieu.

ALBUQUERQUE, *March* 13, 1812.

THE only movements that have been made by
this corps since the fall of Ciudad Rodrigo, are
those from Castello Branco to Portalegre, on the
1st, 2d, 3d, and 4th days of February, and from
the latter city to this place, on the 3d and 4th instant.

By their good conduct our soldiers have endeared
themselves to the kind people of Portalegre.—
Long before we quitted the city, the people looked upon our poor fellows as part of their families,
in whose welfare and happiness they invariably
appeared much interested.

Colonel D., an officer in the Spanish service,
dined at our mess in Portalegre, a few days before we marched from it. After dinner he related a number of anecdotes of French Generals,
which had been procured from sources on which
he cold rely. Speaking of our late movement on
Merida, he mentioned that General Drouet, on
hearing of General Hill's advance on Merida,
caused a courier to be sent every third or fourth
hour to Marshal Soult, with a repetition of the
intelligence — General Hill's unexpected advance,—and in every one of them urging an immediate reinforcement, or the Arroya del Molino devils, (the General's name for our corps),
then at his heels, would devour him in a few days.

I happened lately to be standing near a church in this city, when my ears were saluted with the uncouth melody of a funeral dirge. Being anxious to observe the ceremony, I stepped in.— Around the bier stood a goodly assemblage of priests and friars, chiefly of the lower class, who, for a considerable time, chaunted their hymns for the soul of the deceased. When they had finished, I advanced to take a look of the coffin, when, to my astonishment I found it open, and the face of the lady about to be interred still uncovered. She was clothed in a fine muslin dress, and her countenance, though now in ruins, still exhibited marks of striking beauty. The junior priests proceeded to carry the corpse to a grave prepared in the church, whither, when they had come, the graver-digger drew away the bottom of the coffin, when, of consequence, the body descended, in a manner the most revolting to the feelings, into her place of rest. A very little earth being scattered over the body, the personage before mentioned, with a thick log of wood, began literally to *pound* the body, and continued to do so till it was beat into so little space, as to admit all the earth which had been dug from the hole. During this process, I had remained very near the grave, gazing in silent wonder on the scene before me ; but from my reverie I was soon roused, by a most offensive smell, proceeding from the grave, caused by the exertions of the grave-digger to flatten the body. Feeling a little squeamish, I made the best of my way towards the door, least, by remaining, I should have imposed on the clerical gentlemen the unpleasant duty of carrying me to my lodgings.

The affairs of this country are very evidently hastening to an important crisis. The capture of Ciudad Rodrigo has put us in possession of the key of Spain, and gives additional security to Portugal. The whole of the French heavy train having been taken in that fortress ; Marmont will not find it an easy matter to procure another equally efficient. I look upon the capture of the train as equal to a reinforcement of 5000 men from England ; because, if the French General were in possession of it, he might at this moment, when the greater part of our force is about to be di- rected against Badajoz, lay siege to Rodrigo, and compel Lord Wellington to withdraw from this part of the country to its relief. But now that the latter is safe in our custody, should Marmont attempt its siege, he will not cause so much uneasiness in the breast of our illustrious General, as a similar movement would have done, had the train still been Marmont's. A much stronger force than what is in that neigh- bourhood just now, would also have been requir- ed to watch the motions of the enemy, a d strengthen the fortresses of Almeida and Rodrigo. Upon the whole, therefore, the capture of Rodrigo, with the battering cannon of Marmont's army, forms one of the most glorious achievements of the present war, whilst it adds additional strength to our army, and security to the territory of our allies, the Portuguese.

Preparations of a formidable description have been making for the siege of Badajoz, ever since the fall of Rodrigo. These measures being brought to an end, the trenches will be opened in a few days. The destination of the army has been made known : Our corps, under Sir Rowland Hill, is to form the left of the covering army ; the Hero of Barrosa is to command the right, having under him the greater part of the cavalry, and the 1st, 2d, and 7th divisions of infantry. One brigade of General Hamilton's division of Portuguese is to be employed in the siege, the other brigade is to move with Sir Rowland Hill.

We are all in good health and spirits. Adieu.

CAMP, NEAR TALAVERA LA REAL, *April* 7, 1812.

WITH unfeigned pleasure I congratulate you on the successful termination of the laborious duties of our army before Badajoz, over whose lofty turrets the British flag now waves triumphant.

Lord Wellington crossed the Guadiana on the 16th of March, invested Badajoz the same evening, and on the following day broke ground before the place.

Sir Thomas Graham, with the divisions under his command, also crossed the river on the 16th of March, and directed his march on Santo Martha, Zafra, and Llerena.

Sir Rowland Hill, with the troops under his command, marched from Albuquerque on the 15th of March, and that evening encamped near the castle of Zagala, and on the 16th at La Nava. On the morning of the 17th, the division moved forward on Merida, at that time occupied by a party of the enemy's cavalry—their infantry, to the amount of about 700, were in bivouac in an olive grove on the opposite side of the river, and at the distance of a mile from the town. General Hill, conceiving that a dash at this handful of our enemies might serve to lessen the courage of those, whom, at a future period, we might have to contend with, resolved to attempt their capture before they could be succoured by their friends in the neighbouring villages. The cavalry, under Major-General Long, received orders to cross the river at a ford below the bridge, and the first brigade of infantry to move directly on Merida.

The French cavalry in the town, on perceiving our's cross the river, mounted their steeds, and fled, some by the bridge, others, thinking themselves in danger of being taken on that road, crossed by a ford a little above it, the former firing their carabines all the way, to warn their friends in the wood of their danger. When at a short distance from the town, the 1st brigade got orders to move forward in double-quick time. At this step we run through Merida, crossed the bridge, and for nearly two miles up the left bank of the river. The enemy retired so rapidly, that we never once got within sight of them after they quitted their bivouac. Farther pursuit appearing hopeless, we retraced our steps to Merida. Some prisoners were made in the town, but the exact number I have not learned.

On the morning of the 18th, the division again crossed the river, and marched to Almendralejo. During the morning, and at intervals throughout the day, the thundering of the cannon on the ramparts of Badajoz announced the commencement of operations against that place.

On the 21st, the division returned to Merida. At one o'clock on the afternoon of the 26th, we once more crossed the river and marched to La

Zarza, a village situated at a little distance from the left bank of the Guadiana, and three leagues from Merida. In the morning of the following day we occupied the village of Querena; and on the 28th, the cavalry, several pieces of artillery, and first brigade of infantry, were ordered to drive the enemy from Medellin and Don Benito.

When rather more than half way, the detachment was formed into two columns; the right was placed under the orders of Major-General Howard, and the left under Lieutenant-Colonel Cameron of the 92d regiment.

The left column, consisting of the 92d regiment, a few cavalry, and two pieces of artillery, took possession of Medellin without opposition.

The right column, consisting of the remainder of the cavalry and artillery, with the 50th and 71st regiments, arrived in the vicinity of Don Benito about sunset. Captain Blacier, commanding the rifle company attached to this brigade, was sent with his men into the town to see if all was quiet, and to bring out the alcalde, to provide accommodation for the troops. Capt. Blacier had proceeded a little way down the second street he had come to, when he was attacked by a party of French cavalry, sword in hand. A sharp brush took place, but it was soon ended, by the enemy making the best of their way out of the town, with the loss of a few men wounded. Some of the rifle company received severe sabre cuts about their heads and arms.

Major-General Howard did not expect that such a rencontre would have happened, when he sent Captain Blacier into the village, as, from the reports made to that officer, he was led to believe that the enemy had retired from it in the morning. Our cavalry, at the time the skirmish began, were dismounted, and the infantry had their arms in pile; but in the course of a minute, the whole were at their posts, ready to act as circumstances might require. The extent of the danger was soon ascertained, and the troops marched in and occupied the village.

Medellin is situated on the left bank of the Guadiana, over which there is a very handsome bridge. On a hill above the town stands the castle, an ancient edifice, whose mouldering turrets command an extensive view of the surrounding country. The ascent of the hill being in most places very abrupt, a little trouble and expence would render it a place of no small importance.

The famous battle, between Marshal Victor and the Spanish General Cuesta, was fought between Medellin and Don Benito. The ground is almost level. If there was any advantage of position, it rested with the Spaniards. Cuesta is still much blamed for giving battle to Victor on that occasion. The general opinion here seems to be, that had Cuesta delayed his attack a few days only, the French soldiery, who often can brook no delay, would have compelled their General to attack the Spaniards in their strong position, when Victor's ruin would have been as inevitable as Cuesta's appeared to be, to every one but himself, on the morning of that fatal but memorable day.

During these movements of Sir Rowland Hill's corps, Lieutenant-General Sir Thomas Graham pushed forward the troops under his command to Llerena, where he had intended to surprise the enemy on the 26th; but they having been informed of his approach, retired in the night on the road to Seville.

Sir Thomas Graham having notified to Sir Rowland Hill, his intention of retiring from Llerena, in consequence of Soult's advance towards that town, Sir Rowland Hill made a corresponding movement, in order to concentrate their forces, and prepare to repel any effort the enemy might make to raise the siege of Badajoz.

On the 31st, the troops were withdrawn from Don Benito to La Querena; on the 1st April to La Zarza; and on the 2d, to Merida.

On the 5th, Sir Rowland Hill, with his corps, again crossed the Guadiana, and marched to St Servan; in the vicinity of which we went into camp. In the afternoon of the 6th, we marched towards Badajoz; passed through the village of

Lobon a little after it became dark; and on a
height, in front of which, we went into bivouac.

Sir Thomas Graham retired gradually before
Soult towards the position of Albuera, so famed
for the victory gained over that General the preceding year by Sir William Beresford.

A very short time after taking up our ground,
on the evening of the 6th, we could distinctly
perceive the flashes of the enemy's muskets on
the ramparts of Badajoz. Having received information, the truth of which we could not doubt,
that the place would be stormed that evening,
the greatest anxiety pervaded the allied army for
the issue of the mighty conflict. The flashes turning more vivid, convinced us that our companions
had marched to the assault, and were warmly opposed by the besieged. Prayers were offered up
to the God of Battles, to cover the heads of our
brave friends in the hour of danger, and crown
with success the glorious efforts they were making,
to rescue a suffering people from the iron grasp of
hateful tyranny.

The columns formed for the attack of the different breaches, advanced to the assault with much
spirit, but were beat back with great loss. Again
they tried to effect a passage, but were once more
repulsed. Again, and again, they renewed the
sanguinary conflict, with renovated courage, but

were as repeatedly beat back. For three hours
the issue was doubtful. Our brave soldiers had
done every thing that could be expected of them,
without making any serious impression on the enemy. The ditches, particularly at the breaches,
were literally filled with the dead, dying, and
wounded. The ranks of the attacking columns
were rapidly diminishing. The troops were all
withdrawn from the breaches about midnight,
to form on the ground from which they had
marched to the assault, in order to make another
effort; but the shout of victory from the Castle
happily reached them before they were ready
for a second attack, Lieutenant-General Picton, with the third division, having established
himself in that place about 12 o'clock, which
commands the whole of the works, and the town
of Badajoz. General Phillipon fled to Fort St
Christoval, but at day-light, yesterday morning,
surrendered himself and the garrison prisoners
of war.

Every individual, from the General to the private, fought with a bravery never surpassed.—
Their heroic deeds are worthy of the combatants, and of that happy country which, this
day, should feel proud to claim them as her
sons. May their services be appreciated, and
rewarded as they deserve to be, by that country, for whom they have braved death in ten thousand shapes. Many of them are now in the hos-

F.

pital, helpless as the babe at the mother's breast, without one friendly hand to help them, or a voice of comfort from a wife, mother, or sister, to soothe them in their affliction. Brave companions! you have nobly and faithfully performed your duties —it only remains for your country to perform hers.

Our loss, I have been informed, is between 3000 and 4000 killed and wounded; amongst which there is a large proportion of officers. The enemy's loss is supposed to exceed 5000 men, in killed, wounded, and prisoners.

Marshal Soult had arrived in the vicinity of Zafra on that day, with a mixed force of 38,000 men.

Yesterday morning, Badajoz had all the appearance of a large slaughter-house—many of the bodies of our soldiers being mangled in a manner too shocking to describe. The cries of the wounded were hideous, particularly those, who, lying maimed beneath the clay-cold corpses of their comrades, were unable to extricate themselves. The scene altogether was one of horror.

Mere necessity compelled Lord Wellington to deface the beautiful bridge of Merida; two arches of which were blown up during the latter days of the siege.

ALMENDRALEJO, *April* 30, 1812.

WE marched, on the morning of the 13th instant, from our camp, near Talavera-la-Real, and in the afternoon arrived at this place. Since that period, the division has made no movement whatever.

A detachment was sent, about a week ago, under an officer of engineers, to repair the bridge of Merida.

By letters received from the army under Lord Wellington, we learn that Marshal Marmont, who had advanced to Ciudad Rodrigo, with the greater part of his army, at the commencement of the siege of Badajoz, and subsequently to Sabugal and Castello Branco, has retired to Ciudad Rodrigo, pursued by our light troops.

On the 9th instant, Marshal Soult retired from Villa Franca, with the whole of his army, in the direction of Llerena. At Villa Garcia, his rear-guard was rather roughly handled by our heavy dragoons, under Sir Stapleton Cotton, who attacked and defeated them, with the loss of 300 men killed, wounded, and prisoners. The Marshal now occupies his old quarters in Andalusia.

The Conde de Penne Villamur having been sent by Lord Wellington, with a portion of the 5th Spanish army, into the province of Andalusia, with the view of distracting the operations

F 2

of Soult during the siege, arrived before Seville
on the 4th; and, on the following day, had a severe skirmish with the garrison, which he compelled to retire within the works of the place;
but the smallness of his force prevented him from
undertaking any thing serious.

The capture of Badajoz has given a severe blow
to the interests of Bonaparte in this part of Spain
—every day furnishes us with fresh proofs of it.
Before that important event, the inhabitants were
reserved in their deportment to us; and although
they never were uncivil, yet they seldom did us
an act of kindness. Every little favour we received from them, appeared rather forced than
otherwise. This we never failed to attribute to
their total want of principle—to a hatred of the
British, and regard for the French name. But
already have they convinced us, that our opinions
were too hastily formed. They are now cheerful and easy in their conversation, and extremely attentive and kind in their houses. Some of
the more intelligent part of the community tell
us, that the sacrifices we have made to get possession of the two fortresses, Ciudad Rodrigo and
Badajoz, and the placing of a Spanish governor
in the former, has convinced those (who had
doubts before), that Great Britain has all along
been sincere in her professions of friendship for
them; and that they fully perceive, that she will
lend every assistance in her power, to procure

them emancipation from the dominion of the French.

My present quarters are really the most miserable I have yet been in since I arrived in this country. I have only one small apartment, without a window—a small stool for a seat, and another of the same description for a table, a bed, if such it can be called, well stored with fleas and musquitos, constitute its furniture. The floor is of earth, some parts of which are fully a foot higher than the rest. In short, I wish you saw it, you would then be better able to judge of the comforts of a Spanish campaign.

Those animals which infest the hair of little children in your country, seem to abound on the people here, without excepting age or sex. The method of extracting them from the roots of the hair of the fair donnas, possesses considerable novelty. However, of this you will judge—A rendezvous having been appointed, four, six, or eight females assemble together, to partake in the sports of the chase. The object of the meeting being made known by the senior member of the hunt, the whole proceed to the hall, lobby, kitchen, or street, where they take their places in the following order :—The oldest member usually seats herself first; the second takes her station in the lap of the first; the third in the lap of the second, till every member has been accommodated with a seat. The lady in front, having

nothing else to do, begins to chaunt some favourite
air, whilst the others, with nervous paws, set all
the ten fingers to trace their game through the
almost impenetrable forests before them. Now
and then they may possibly join their friend in
the chorus ; but rather than lose their game, they
would see all the music in Spain burnt before
their eyes. Spain being abundantly supplied with
this particular species of game, the quantity killed
in one day is often immense. None of those fair
creatures can think of giving over the chace, till each
joint of the fingers is quite stiff, from extraordinary
exertion. The manner in which those little captives
are put to death, says very little for the cleanly
disposition of the Spanish fair.

MERIDA, *May* 27, 1812.

LONG before this letter can possibly reach you, Sir Rowland Hill's dispatch, detailing the operations of his corps on the Tagus, will have been made public in England.

Notwithstanding, I cannot deny myself the pleasure which this opportunity affords, of congratulating you and my friends in Scotland, on the glorious result of the expedition to Almarez.

On the 11th instant, the 2d division of infantry was reviewed in the plain near Almendralejo, by Sir Rowland Hill, who expressed himself highly pleased with the appearance of every regiment of which it is composed.

Late in the evening, the under-mentioned regiments received an order to move at a moment's notice, viz. 13th light dragoons, one brigade of British and Portuguese artillery, the 1st brigade of infantry, the 28th and 34th regiments from the second brigade, and the 4th, or Colonel Ashworth's Portuguese brigade. The remainder of the corps were placed under the orders of Lieutenant-General Sir William Erskine, to watch the motions of Count D'Erlon, in the absence of Sir Rowland Hill.

A little before day-light, on the morning of the 12th, those regiments, who had received orders the preceding night, marched from Almendralejo, and in the afternoon, bivouacked in an olive grove, at the distance of a mile from Merida, on the opposite bank of the river Guadiana.

On the following morning, the detachment crossed the river by the bridge, marched about five leagues on the road to Madrid, and went into bivouac. On the 14th, we bivouacked behind the village called Villa Macia, and, on the 15th, marched into Truxillo.

The object of the expedition could now no longer be kept a secret, as it was obvious, even to the most superficial observer, that we could not proceed much farther in this direction, without destroying the enemy's works at the pass of Mirabete and bridge of Almarez.

In order to have the detachment concealed in a wood near Jarceijo, the troops were marched from Truxillo about half past twelve o'clock, on the morning of the 16th, and before the morning light could point out their numbers to the enemy, had arrived at their destination. In this wood we cooked, and made every preparation to march the same evening, to attempt the capture of the enemy's strong places by surprise.

The troops were divided into three columns : The left, consisting of the 28th and 34th British regiments, and 6th Portuguese caçadores, under the command of Lieutenant-General Chowne, was directed to carry the castle of Mirabete by escalade ; for which purpose, the column moved with scaling-ladders. The centre column, consisting of the 13th light dragoons, all the artillery, and the 6th and 18th Portuguese regiments of the line, was placed under the command of Major-General Long, and was directed to move on the works erected on the high road to Madrid, which runs through the pass of Mirabete, and is commanded, at every point within range, by these works, and the Castle of Mirabete, which stands on the summit of a high, rugged mountain, immediately above the former.

The right column, consisting of the 50th, 71st, and 92d regiments, under the command of Major-General Howard, was directed to move by a mountain path, to the bridge of Almarez, and carry the defences of the place at the point of the bayonet. This column was also provided with scaling-ladders.

Before eight o'clock, the different columns had quitted their bivouac to perform the task allotted to them by their General.

A body of troops, when marching in the night, often meet with obstacles which no human foresight can provide against. On this occasion, the badness of the roads, added to the darkness of the night, rendered it impossible for the troops to arrive at their respective points before day-break. Sir Rowland Hill, who moved with the right column, finding that he was still five miles from the bridge at day-light, and aware, that he could not surprise such a wily enemy at that hour of the day, gave orders for the whole to halt. The left and centre columns being within range of the guns of Mirabete, were withdrawn. The right bivouacked on the summit of a ridge of mountains, called the Lina, which, at that place, runs parallel with the Tagus.

The 17th and 18th were spent in making preparations for the meditated assault of the enemy's works at the bridge.

On the left bank of the river, the bridge was defended by a tete-du-pont, strongly entrenched, and on the height above it, by a strong fort, called Napoleon, in which were nine pieces of artillery, and a garrison of 500 men. On the right bank, and on the height immediately above the bridge, there was another fort, called Ragusa, lately erected, which, being a very complete work of the kind, added greatly to the strength of the place.

To carry these, the 1st brigade and 6th Portuguese regiment of the line moved from the bivouac on the mountains, about ten o'clock on the evening of the 18th, and descended into the plain by a narrow foot-path, which, in many places, admitted one file only at a time. This circumstance proved fatal to the plan of our General, which was, to attack the place before break of day.

Notwithstanding the many disadvantages under

which Sir Rowland now laboured, without artillery, and an enemy fully prepared for him, he
resolved to storm Fort Napoleon, resting his hopes
of success on the valour of his troops. The detachment was formed into three columns. The
first, consisting of the 50th and one wing of the
71st regiment, was directed to carry Fort Napoleon; the 92d, and the other wing of the 71st,
formed the second column, which was directed
to storm the tete-du-pont and Fort Ragusa. The
third column consisted of the 6th Portuguese regiment of the line, and two companies of the 60th,
rifle battalion, which formed the corps of reserve.

The arrangements for the attack having been
completed, the 1st column, under Major-General Howard, moved forward to the assault of
Fort Napoleon, and the second occupied the
ground which it had left, in order to be at hand
to lend their assistance, should it be required.
The enemy for some minutes poured a most destructive fire on the 1st column as it advanced;
but as soon as our brave fellows had their ladders
planted, they began to shew some symptoms
of disorder, which were soon encreased by the
advance of our soldiers to their entrench-
ment. In 10 minutes the fort was our own—the
struggle was short, but bloody for its duration; never was a fort carried in a more gallant
style than this was.

Driven from Napoleon, the enemy attempted

to escape across the river, but their *friends* on the other side having cut the bridge, they were under the necessity of submitting to us as prisoners of war. A number of them, in making an attempt to escape by swimming, were drowned.

Fort Napoleon being in our possession, the 2d column was ordered to cross the river, and storm Fort Ragusa; but the enemy perceiving our intention, retired from it with great precipitation, firing a few random shots at the 2d column, and the troops in Fort Napoleon.—Their retreat was not a little hastened by the artillery officer turning the guns in Napoleon against Ragusa.

The whole of the brigade having assembled at the tete-du-pont, Sir Rowland Hill returned thanks to the troops, for their great gallantry in the attack and capture of the place, and assured them, that the object of the expedition had been, by their good conduct, accomplished in a manner that exceeded his expectation.

The enemy had a very large stock of provisions in their different stores, particularly at the tete-du-pont: wine, rum, and brandy were to be had in great abundance; hams and pieces of pickled beef and pork were, in a few minutes, seen suspended from those very bayonets, which, not long before, were dyed with the blood of the enemy. The troops were marched back about half a mile, and put into bivouac, having regaled themselves with a little of the juice of the grape.

Measures were immediately taken to get all the wounded removed to the rear, and to destroy the forts, bridge and cannon, and all the stores which we could not carry away with us. The number of cannon found in the forts amounted to 18. The enemy's loss amounted to about 450 killed, wounded, and prisoners; the latter consisted of 259 of all ranks. Our loss was 177 killed and wounded.

The wounded having been removed to the rear, and the works destroyed, we quitted our bivouac on the morning of the 20th, and marched to the ground we left on the evening of the 18th, and thence the same evening to our former bivouac near to Jarceijo; and on the 21st we marched back to Truxillo.

Truxillo is situated on a rock, and is surrounded by a wall of considerable height, which, in former times, would cause it to be considered a place of strength. Its situation being commanding, I am of opinion, that Spain, whenever circumstances will permit her, ought to bestow a little attention on this place, as, in whatever light we view it as a fortress, it will appear to be one of the first importance to the interests of this country. This town is famed for having given birth to the great Pizzaro; his tomb was shewn to me in what they call the New Church,

but which, I presume, was built before that war‑
rior was born.

On the 24th we marched from Truxillo, and
bivouacked on our former camp ground, near
Villa Macia; on the 25th, near San Pedro;
yesterday, about half way between this town and
Medellin; and early this morning we arrived here.

An act of greater ingratitude, or a display of more
cowardly baseness than the following, stands not on
record. Soon after the 50th regiment got possession
of part of Fort Napoleon, several of the French
soldiers asked for mercy from the conquerors.
Of a British soldier of the 50th, one of these
men begged his life, just as the bayonet was
about to perform its office. With cheerfulness
the honest Briton granted the boon of the peti‑
tioner; but no sooner had he done so, and was
about to follow his comrades, than the ungrate‑
ful Frenchman attempted to plunge his bayonet
into the heart of his preserver! Seeing his dan‑
ger, the poor fellow wheeled about, but received
the bayonet of his antagonist in his arm. Ir‑
ritated at such baseness, the soldier, without fur‑
ther ceremony, plunged his, in return, into the
body of the Frenchman, who instantly ex‑
pired. Now that you have the fact before you,
as related to me, I will leave you to judge, whe‑
ther the summary punishment inflicted by the
one party, was not called for by the unparalleled
treachery, baseness, and ingratitude of the other.

Lieutenant Thiele, of the German artillery, whilst employed in destroying the tower in the Fort Ragusa, was unfortunately blown up. The cause of this melancholy catastrophe, I believe to be as follows :—Lieutenant Thiele was sent with a party to destroy the whole of the enemy's works at Ragusa. In the execution of his orders, he mined the fort, and having fired the train that was to communicate with the powder, he retired to some little distance, to await the explosion. The fire having been much longer in taking effect than he had calculated on, he went forward to ascertain the cause of the delay;—but had scarcely arrived at the entrance of the fort, when the mine exploded, and carried him into the air.

About an hour after the taking of Fort Napoleon, I observed a soldier of the 50th regiment, immediately under its walls, occasionally bending over the lifeless trunk of one of his comrades, and now and then wiping away the salt tear as it trickled down his furrowed cheek. I stepped up to him, and ventured to divert his attention, by inquiring the name of the deceased. Till then he had imagined that he was pouring out his grief in secret; for when I spoke, he looked abashed, and began to dry up the water then in his eyes. In answer to my question, he told me that the name of the deceased was Paddy Carey, and his own brother; that he was the third

of the family that had given their lives for
their country; and that he was now left alone
to mourn the loss of those who had gone before him. He regretted much, that circumstances
prevented him from bestowing decent burial on
the deceased; and when I left him, the noble
fellow had begun to dig a hole with his bayonet,
to receive the mangled remains of his beloved
relative.

A very unfortunate circumstance occurred during the assault of Fort Napoleon. The French
commandant, as soon as resistance appeared useless, immediately surrendered, with permission to
retain his sword. A British officer soon after entered the fort, who, not knowing the terms on
which the French officer had been permitted to
wear his sabre, and, totally ignorant of the French
language, made a cut at the commandant, which,
he not being prepared to parry, unfortunately took
effect on his head. The wound is considered mortal. It is the more to be lamented, as the Colonel has ever been held in the highest estimation
by all who have served under him—being a good
man, and a brave soldier.

ALMENDRALEJO, *June* 10, 1812.

SINCE I wrote to you from Merida last month, I have collected little military news worth communicating.

For some days previous to our return from the bridge of Almarez, the enemy in front of Sir William Erskine had made some movements, which induced that General to believe, that it was the Count D'Erlon's intention to attack him, before he could be succoured from the force under Sir Rowland Hill. Whether the French General ever had a serious intention of fighting, seems doubtful; one thing is certain, he retired the moment he heard of the arrival of Sir Rowland on the Guadiana.

After spending the 4th of June in a manner worthy of the day, we marched from Merida about one o'clock on the morning of the 5th, and arrived here at ten. The French commandant died a few days before we left Merida, and was buried in the church in the square, with military honours.

Accept of what follows, as a real specimen of Spanish gratitude.—On the evening of the 1st inst., a Portuguese lad, servant to Brevet Lieut.-Colonel M'Donell of the 92d regiment, and a Spaniard, went into a shop close to the square, where they had some wine, for which the lad paid;—they

F

quitted the house arm in arm, in the most friendly manner, and proceeded to the square. When
about 50 yards from the house, and under the
Piazza on the lower part of the square, the cowardly, ungrateful Spaniard plunged a stiletto into
the heart of his friend. I chanced to pass bye
the scene of this horrible murder a few minutes
after it had been committed, and united my efforts to those of many others, in order to find
out the perpetrator of the deed. Two individuals were taken up on suspicion, but the evi-
dence brought against them not being sufficient
to convict them, they were liberated.

On our return to Truxillo from the bridge of
Almarez, we found the inhabitants busily employed in making preparations for a grand bull-fight,
which they intended as a treat to the allied army,
in token of their gratitude for the services rendered to them on the 19th of May. Every street
leading from the great square was barricaded
with waggons, carts, ploughs, &c. to prevent the
escape of the poor bulls ; a small house, in one
corner of the square, was selected by the leading people, as the most convenient prison for
them, till they should be called on to appear before those for whose amusement they were to be
tormented, in every possible manner that the
genius of man could invent.

A few minutes after seven o'clock in the evening,
five Spaniards, who were to fight the bulls, appear-

ed in the square, each provided with a brown cloak in the left hand, and a pike in the right. These having taken their posts, one of the bulls was turned out, who, on making his debût, looked furiously wild, while the air rung with the acclamations of a delighted populace. The honest bull had no idea that such a reception awaited him, as, in all his former perambulations, no one had deigned to notice him.—He gazed on the passing scene with wonder. In a few minutes he became quite furious. Perceiving an opening under one of the waggons at the lower part of the square, he darted towards it, in hopes of obtaining his liberty. The waggon was crowded with men and women, who, at the animal's approach, were precipitated, in curious and truly laughable attitudes, from their exalted station, to the same level with the object of their fears. For a time every eye was turned to the scene of confusion, anxiously awaiting the result of the grand charge of the courageous animal. At this momentous crisis, so big with the fate of many, the Spanish heroes advanced to meet their antagonist, and, with savage bellowings, stopped him short in his victorious career. To one of his tormentors he turned with death-like fury, and on his head seemed determined to wreak his utmost vengeance. The object of his hatred he pursued with such speed, that every one present thought the life of the Spaniard would be forfeit-

ed to his temerity. But well the wily Don knew
that the bull could be deceived; and to show us
that such was the fact, he permitted the mad animal to get so close, as to make an attempt to toss
him on his horns. Thus situated, the Spaniard
had recourse to his cloak, which he threw at the
head of the bull, who, fancying the man in his
power, stopped, and tossed it in the air. The other
four were not idle during this rencontre between
their friend and the bull. Having come to his
assistance, one of them inflicted a wound in the
hip of the poor brute, and made the best of his way
to a place of safety, hotly pursued by his enemy,
till stopped by the cloak of the fugitive, and
the pikes of the others, as before. In this manner the fight continued till the creature was completely exhausted, unable to shake his head or
raise a foot. In this state he was removed to
make room for a second, who afforded no sport
whatever.

The third, when he came forward, appeared
completely out of humour. He scampered round
the square—his eyes sparkling fire, shewed the
state of his incensed feelings. Many a time I
thought I heard him say, " had I the power of
" speech given me, I would this moment pro-
" claim myself the eternal enemy of the human
" race!" To the lovers of this amusement he
furnished a rich treat, till he effected his escape

by a narrow street which had not been very well barricaded.

On the following evening, at the same hour and place, there was a similar exhibition, when the amusements were much the same. Two or three soldiers were, this evening, in consequence of going too near to the bulls, tossed into the air, and severely hurt.

This savage amusement is greatly relished in this country by every class of its inhabitants. The fair, I have been assured, consider it a most refined amusement, and one that reflects the greatest lustre on the Spanish name and character. There are very few of your Scotish ladies, I dare say, will join the Spanish in considering it as such.

Llerena, *July* 11, 1812.

Sir Rowland Hill, having received information that Marshal Soult intended to make an irruption into the province of Estremadura, with a large body of cavalry and infantry, broke up from his cantonments at Almendralejo on the 12th ult., and advanced the same day to Fuento del Maestre, and thence on the 13th to Zafra, Los Santos, and Sancho Perez, where he intended to collect his troops, in proportion as the enemy advanced.

A very severe, gallant, yet unfortunate action, was fought on the 11th June, in front of Ulna, between our heavy brigade of cavalry, under Major-General Slade, and that of the enemy, under General L'Allemand.—Our cavalry made the attack with much spirit, and in a few minutes put the French to flight, leaving in our hands a great many prisoners, besides killed and wounded. The pursuit of the enemy was continued for nearly three leagues with great ardour; during which some prisoners were taken. But the enemy being reinforced by fresh troops, became the assailants in turn; and, after a sanguinary conflict, compelled our brave fellows to quit the field, with the loss of nearly 200 men and horses, killed, wounded, and made prisoners, besides retaking all the prisoners which had fallen into our hands at the commencement of the affair. Sir Rowland Hill was much hurt at the issue of the battle, and, as I have been informed, assembled a Court of Inquiry, to investigate into the cause of the failure.

Sir Rowland having been informed, that a great proportion of the heavy cavalry, taken in the affair of the 11th, had been left in the town of Maguila, sent a party of the same brigade, consisting of 50 men, under Lieutenant Strenuwitz, to bring them off. On his arrival in the vicinity of the place, he fell in with a party of 80 French dragoons, which he attacked, and defeated, with the loss of 20 men and horses, besides a great number killed.

Thus did this little band of heroes wipe away the stain brought on our arms by the unfortunate termination of the affair of the 11th, and fully establish the superiority of our heavy cavalry over those of the enemy.

About this period, the enemy's reinforcements began to show themselves: An advanced corps of cavalry, and the Spaniards, under the Conde de Penne Villamur, retired slowly towards Zafra, and the infantry in Sancho Perez were withdrawn to Los Santos.

The enemy continuing to press forward, as if he intended to bring Sir Rowland Hill to action, the whole of the infantry and artillery began their retreat from Zafra and Los Santos at sunset on the 17th; and by sun-rise, on the 18th, had arrived behind the village of Santa Martha, where they went into bivuoac; and thence, on the 19th, fell back to a wood, near to the small river called the Albuera, where they encamped.

The day after we arrived in the camp at Albuera, we were joined by the 5th, 17th, and 22d Portuguese infantry of the line, and a regiment of caçadores. Our whole force, at that time, amounted to about 21,700 men.

We had scarcely taken our ground on the 19th, before fatigue and working parties were ordered from every regiment in the division, to proceed to the former position of Albuera, and to place themselves under the orders of the officer at the head of the engineer department. From the 19th to the 30th of June, the troops were busily employed, night and day, in strengthening their position, by throwing up works of various kinds. On the extreme right, a redoubt was constructed, which would have rendered the allied army infinite service had it been attacked; as the guns from the fort could have been brought to bear on every other part of the position. This is the height on which the Spaniards were posted at the commencement of the battle of Albuera last year, and which the enemy succeeded in taking from them, by making a movement up a deep ravine on their right. It is in fact the key to the position; and whoever remain masters of that height at the close of an action, must be the conquerors.

The centre and left were also considerably strengthened by redoubts and breast-works. The parapet of the bridge over the Albuera was thrown down. Traverses were thrown up in every street in the village of Albuera, and several of the unoccupied houses were loop-holed.

Aware, that if the Marshal did attack us, it would be with very superior numbers, we made every preparation to give him as warm a reception as we possibly could. In front of the wood in which we lay encamped, strong cavalry picquets were posted, supported by some infantry, placed within an abbatis. An officer from each regiment was sent, with the Quarter-Master General, to the river, and position, who shewed them the fords of the former, by which their respective corps were to cross in case of attack, and the station each was to occupy in the latter.

About nine o'clock in the morning of the 30th, our camp was thrown into a little confusion, on perceiving the baggage-animals of the cavalry flying to the rear. In a few minutes, we were under arms; and in a few more, our brigade moved off for the front, to retard the advance of the enemy through the wood, every inch of which we got orders to dispute with him. At this time, the enemy contented himself with driving in our advanced posts ; having done so, he retired towards Santa Martha. We returned to our camp.

In the afternoon of the same day, the enemy again advanced, and attacked the cavalry picquets of the Conde de Penne Villamur. They being few in number, the Conde was induced to attack them with the whole of his cavalry, who drove them back in excellent style ; but, poor fellows, little did they imagine that the victory which they had just achieved was so soon to be converted into an instrument for their destruction. Having pursued the French farther than prudence dictated, they fell into the snare prepared for them by their enemies. Looking on the whole of the Conde's people as a certain prey, the French rushed from their ambush, to the numer of 1000, and attacked the Spaniards with unmerciful fury, who suffered a terrible loss before they could be succoured from our troops in their rear. I have been told that the Spaniards behaved nobly on that occasion ; and that, although victory was not then within their grasp, they disputed every inch of ground with their foes, in a cool, steady, and soldier-like manner. The first brigade was again ordered to the front, and again retired to their camp at the conclusion of the above affair.

Sir Rowland Hill having at length abundant

proofs before him, that Soult's only object, in driving him back on Albuera, was to give the Marshal time to plunder this fine province of its grain, he resolved to wait no longer for the attack of the enemy, but to become the assailant in turn.

A little after day-break, on the 1st July, we took leave of our camp on the banks of the Albuera, and advanced to Santa Martha, and thence on the 2d, in two columns, towards the enemy.

The left column, consisting of Major-General Long's brigade of light dragoons, Colonel Campbell's brigade of Portuguese cavalry, one brigade of artillery, the first brigade of British, and General Campbell's brigade of Portuguese infantry, was placed under the orders of Lieutenant-General Sir William Erskine, and directed to move against the enemy in Villa-Alba. The remainder of the corps moved on the great road to Zafra, under the command of Lieutenant-General Tilson Chowne.

About ten o'clock in the forenoon, the left column moved from Santa Martha, the advance of which was led by Lieutenant Strenuwitz. The second German hussars, supported by Colonel Campbell's Portuguese cavalry, moved directly on the village, at a time when the enemy were scarcely prepared for such an early visit. Some of them were mounted, but, I believe, the greater part were not. The Germans, with Strenuwitz at their head, dashed into the village, and cut down a few of them in the streets. For some minutes these brave troops carried every thing before them, and would have continued to do so, had the Portuguese behaved with equal spirit. The lukewarm conduct of the Portuguese having given the enemy time to recover from the panic into which this unexpected attack had thrown them, rallied, and, in turn, attacked the Germans, who, being greatly inferior in numbers, were beat back on the village with loss.—The conduct of Colonel Campbell, and that of every *officer* in the brigade, was deserving of the highest praise.

The 9th and 13th light dragoons, and 2d German hussars, continued to skirmish for some time with the enemy;—their loss was very trifling; the infantry took no part in the affair.

The French cavalry having retired from the scene of action about one, we moved across the Guadiana, up the right bank of which we marched about four miles, then crossed to the left bank, and lay down under arms.

Towards evening, and just as we had moved from the bank of the river, to take up our ground for the night, the enemy brought two guns to bear on us from an opposite height. Our artillery was ordered to a hill on our left,—part of the 71st

light infantry was sent to occupy a small eminence on the right bank of the river ; and the rest
of the troops were kept in readiness to act when
they might be wanted. But the enemy, after
firing a few rounds from each gun, retired, and
we went into bivouac. Some of the Portuguese
infantry, and one or two of the artillery-men were
killed or wounded, by the fire of the enemy's artillery. In the afternoon of the 3d we quitted
our camp, on the banks of the Guadiana, and,
after a march of two leagues, across a close
country, we went into bivouac on the left of the
great road leading from Santa Martha to Zafra.
Early next morning we marched to Los Santos,
behind which we bivouacked, and thence, at sun-
set of the same day, continued our route to Bienvenida, which we reached a little after day-light
on the following morning ; and, in the afternoon
of the 6th, we arrived here. We suffered great
inconvenience during this march, from the scorching heat of the sun.

From a convent, on the left of the road by which
we marched into the town, a number of nuns
cheered us through the gratings of their miserable
cells, as we passed under their windows. As long
as any of us were in sight they waved their lily
white handkerchiefs, and hailed us as the deliver-
ers of their country. The poor nuns, I have no
doubt, were sincere, when they expressed their
joy at the appearance of British troops in their

town; but we have been told, by the people in general, in the other towns, that the inhabitants of Llerena have no love for us. From Llerena, the enemy retired towards Cordova, having left a strong rear-guard in Berlenga;—we marched, at day-break on the 8th, to dislodge them.

The Spanish cavalry, who, on this occasion, led the advance, came up with the enemy's picquets two leagues from Llerena, attacked them with spirit, and compelled them to betake themselves for safety to their main body, then posted on a height a little in front of Berlenga, but who, on perceiving our infantry winding along the plain in their front, retired to a height behind the village. From the height on which their cavalry was originally formed, Sir Rowland reconnoitred their rear position, which was very strong; but the enemy, either thinking it or their army too weak to risk a little brush with us, retired, leaving a good many cavalry, and some pieces of artillery, to cover their retreat.

As our brigades of infantry arrived on the height above Berlenga, they were saluted in succession by the French artillery;—our guns, at the same time, returned the salute. The effect produced by this interchange of civilities was truly grand; the only thing we regretted was, that it could not be made more general. During the cannonade, very few of our troops were hurt; our shells, on the contrary, we could distinctly perceive bursting above their cavalry column, dealing destruction to both horses and riders.— We occupied the village during the heat of the day, and in the evening bivouacked in a plain above it. Next morning we returned to Llerena.

A little after the commencement of the action on the 2d instant, at Villa-Alba, one of the 2d German hussars was furiously assailed by a powerful French dragoon;—both being dextrous swordsmen, for some time neither the one nor the other could obtain any advantage. Another French dragoon perceiving the imminent danger of his friend, galloped up to his relief, but his assistance was afforded too late—the German had mastered the arm of his enemy, who then lay at his feet, in the agonies of death. As the German had been long and severely engaged, the Frenchman thought he would have a bout with him ; but the combat did not last long—this Frenchman shared the fate of his companion.—A third advanced, whose sword the German received in his body, at the moment his own had done a similar favour to his second assailant.

One morning, during the time we lay in camp at Albuera, a troop of one of our light dragoon regiments being on out-post duty, were under arms a little before day-break. The enemy being at no great distance, the whole troop remained mounted till after day-light. One of the troop

horses, on which was mounted an honest Hiberni-
an, appearing rather restive, he was desired by one
of the officers to take him to the rear, and endeavour to make him quiet. Pat, more anxious to
get to the front than the rear, replied, " By
" J—s, your honour, if you will let me take him to
" the front, I will show you something that you
" never saw before." Permission having been
obtained, Pat whipped the horse unmercifully,
and gave him the full length of the reins at the
same time, till he got him about one hundred yards
from the troop, when, turning his head towards the
enemy, he set off with all speed, and, in a short
time, was at their advanced post.

Villa Franca, *August* 2, 1812.

Permit me to congratulate you on the glorious victory achieved by the army under Lord Wellington, over that of the enemy commanded by Marshal Marmont, on the plains of Salamanca, on the 22d July. This great victory has made us all frantic with joy. Various letters have been received here from the northern army, all of which represent the army of Marmont as completely disorganized.

Is it not a little singular, that the first intelligence of this victory should have been brought to us by a native, who was an eye-witness of what he stated, and who had travelled the whole distance on the same mule, with no other object in journeying hither, than to be the first to give information of the great event to our gallant General, and the loyal Spaniards in the south.

Having been prepared, by letters from the northern army, to hear of its retreat upon Ciudad Rodrigo, the account of the battle, as given by the peasant, was entirely discredited by almost every body but the Marquis de Almeida, who believed every word of the poor man's story, and at the same time offered to bet thirty dollars to one that a great battle had been fought, and that Lord Wellington had come off victorious.

It having been hinted to the Spaniard that he

G

was suspected of being a spy, he immediately made a voluntary offer of his person to be incarcerated in the common jail of Zafra, till such time as the official account of the battle should be received by Sir Rowland Hill, when, should his information prove false, the British General might order him to be executed as a traitor.

After making such an extraordinary offer, no one for a moment could doubt the truth of all that he had told, unless they believed the man to be insane, and that very few could take upon themselves to do, as he not only appeared perfectly collected, but a most intelligent man for his situation in life. The same evening, Sir Rowland received an account of the battle from Lord Wellington.

The enemy having moved a considerable body of troops towards the right of his position, Sir Rowland Hill found it necessary to make a corresponding movement to his left. On the 18th of July, all the British and Portuguese troops were withdrawn from Llerena to Benvenida, and thence the same evening towards Zafra, where we arrived a little after sun-rise on the 19th.

The enemy continuing to reinforce the troops stationed at Hornachos, the 1st and 2d brigades of British were ordered to Villa Franca to support the cavalry, who were threatened with a visit from General L'Allemand, who commanded the enemy. About one o'clock in the morning of the

29th, we quitted Zafra and arrived near Villa Franca, a little after day-break, where, finding every thing quiet, we went into bivouac.—Sir Rowland, having received the account of the battle of Salamanca before he left Zafra, communicated the contents of the dispatch to the troops as he passed them early in the morning, who received the intelligence with loud and long continued cheering. After we went into bivouac, a copy of the dispatch was given to each regiment, to be inserted in the regimental and companies' orderly books, and ordered to be read at the head of every regiment at the evening parade. A double allowance of grog was issued to every individual, to drink the health of Lord Wellington and his incomparable warriors.

On the 31st, we quitted our bivouac, and marched into Fuento del Maestre.

Yesterday morning the French cavalry, under General L'Allemand, attacked our light dragoons under General Long; a warm brush followed, in which both suffered considerable loss. An officer of the 2d German hussars was killed—he was this forenoon buried with military honours.

On the first alarm, the troops in Fuento del Maestre were ordered to Villa Franca, to support the cavalry and 71st regiment. We had proceeded almost half way, when a counter order was brought to us. We wheeled about, and had marched back a considerable distance, when a

third order arrived for the regiments of the first brigade to march to Villa Franca, where we arrived
about six in the evening. The enemy met with
such a warm reception yesterday, that it is thought
he will not venture out to-day, (now two
o'clock), although he has been showing himself
to our cavalry, in front of his quarters, at Hornachos. My present quarters are the most wretched I have yet occupied. Two of us are stowed
up in one small apartment, a place absolutely not
larger than the houses allotted in your country for
the accommodation of two pigs.

A few days before we left Llerena, an inhabitant of that town, who had acted as a spy of the
enemy, was ordered out to a field in the neighbourhood of the place, and shot by a party of the
Spanish troops under the command of the Conde
de Penne Villamur.

DON BENITO, *September* 7, 1812.

THE fruits of our victory, on the plains of Salamanca, are now shewing themselves in various
parts of Spain. The ci-devant king has been
driven from the seat of his government, and is
now, as it were, an exile in his own country.—
For the present, he has fixed his head-quarters
in the city of Valencia, to which place, it is probable, Marshal Soult intends to march what is called the army of the south, as he raised the siege
of Cadiz on the 25th of August, and retired with
precipitation, leaving a great many cannon, and
a quantity of ammunition in our hands. When this
intelligence was received here yesterday, the joy
of the inhabitants knew no bounds. An illumination is ordered to take place this evening in
honour of the event.

Early in the morning of the 28th ultimo, the
whole of Sir Rowland Hill's corps moved from
their respective cantonments towards Llerena.
That evening the 1st brigade occupied Usagre ;—
next forenoon the whole division assembled in a
field near Villa Garcia, where the troops were
ordered into bivouac. On the 30th, we marched
to our left, and bivouacked in the afternoon on a
height near the village of Llera. On the 31st,
we marched to El Campilo, which we occupied
during the heat of the day, but at sun-set were

ordered into camp about a mile from it. On the 1st instant we quitted our camp before day-light, and after a most fatiguing march of fourteen hours, a great part of it under a scorching sun, and over a parched desert, arrived in Zalamea, where we were received and treated by the inhabitants with the greatest kindness and attention. The enemy left a considerable quantity of corn when they retired from that town, which was immediately given up by the people to those appointed to receive it.

On the 2d, we marched to the village of Quintana, where we were also well received. On the 3d, we occupied the village of Maguela, and on the following morning marched in here.

During our stay in Villa Franca, viz. from the 1st to the 27th of August inclusive, the enemy were not very troublesome, except on one occasion, of which I shall here take the liberty of sending you the particulars.

The out-post duty of the infantry devolved upon the wings of regiments, each regiment taking the duty alternately, commencing with the senior battalion. The troops advanced to a wood about two miles in front of the town, to support the cavalry in case of necessity. We generally moved from our quarters to the out-posts about six in the evening, and were withdrawn on the following morning after sun-rise, if every thing was quiet in front.

The right wing of the 92d regiment, under Colonel Cameron, were on the out-post duty on the evening that the glad tidings of Lord Wellington's entry into Madrid reached that place. Sir William Erskine, who commanded there at the time, gave a splendid ball in honour of the occasion, to which all the officers in the garrison, and the principal inhabitants of the place, were invited. The middling classes of the people were not behind their superiors in testifying their joy at the deliverance of their capital. Every musket and pistol were put in requisition, and an incessant fire was kept up for some time.— Colonel Cameron having had no notice sent him of what was going on, naturally enough concluded that the enemy had penetrated to the village by a circuitous route, and were engaged with the garrison. To ascertain the real cause, an officer was sent by the Colonel to Sir William Erskine, who soon after returned with the pleasing news of Madrid being in our possession.

On the following morning, the enemy advanced with a strong body of cavalry, supported by infantry, and attacked our heavy dragoons, who skirmished with them for two hours, when three of our men falling into their hands, they retired. This circumstance showed clearly that their sole object was to gain information regarding the cause of our rejoicing at Villa Franca the preceding evening.

But I greatly suspect their curiosity on that head remains to be gratified, as, from the united testimony of the inhabitants of every town through which we marched from El Campilo to this place, it appears that these three dragoons were never in the enemy's hands. Behind the village of Hornachos, there runs a very high range of mountains, over which there is a narrow footpath leading to El Campilo and Zalamea. Our poor fellows had ascended the mountain at this place, and pursued the road by El Campilo, Zalamea, Quintana, and Don Benito, in all of which places the enemy were so much alarmed at the sight of the red coats, that before they considered themselves strong enough to engage (as they thought), a great body of British cavalry, of which the three were looked on as the advanced guard, these brave fellows were always out of the reach of pursuit.

We are all distressed for want of money, the army being five months in arrears of pay. Our stock of clothes, particularly socks, shirts, and small-clothes are getting low, and unless an immediate supply of money be granted us, the dress of the whole army, officers and men, will assume somewhat of the appearance of the Highland garb.

ARANJUEZ, *October* 9, 1812.

THE enemy having withdrawn his troops from the province of Estremadura, our services on the banks of the Guadiana were no longer required; but whither we were to bend our steps, was a subject of conjecture. A few days relieved us from this state of suspense.

On the morning of the 13th ultimo, we broke up from our cantonments in Don Benito, crossed that Guadiana at a ford about a mile from that place, and continued our route to the village of Mojaides. On the 14th, our brigade occupied the miserable village of Villa Macia; and, on the 15th, marched into Truxillo.

In the evening, a few pieces of brass cannon were found under a quantity of wood, in a house, the property of the noble family of Conquesta, the lineal descendants of the great Pizarro. This ancient family have resided in Cadiz, since the enemy first over-run this part of the country.

At an early hour, on the morning of the 18th, we marched from Truxillo, and in the afternoon bivouacked on the slope of a steep mountain, a short distance from the village of Jareceijo; and, on the 19th, we crossed the Tagus by a pontoon bridge, thrown over at the same place where the enemy had their bridge of boats on the 19th of May. In the evening, we bivouacked a little in

front of the village of Almarez, situated in a
plain at the distance of five miles from the river.
On the 20th, we bivouacked one league in front of
Naval Moral. On the 21st, we occupied the village
of Calzada de Orepesa; and, on the 22d, our brigade
occupied La Gartera. On the evening of the 25th,
we received from the regimental paymaster 20 dollars, in part payment of our arrears. The same
evening, about 11 o'clock, we marched from La
Gartera, for the city of Talavera de la Reina,
where we arrived about ten on the following
morning. On our march through the different
streets to the great square, we were received by
all classes with every demonstration of joy and respect.

The city is delightfully situated on the right
bank of the Tagus, and surrounded in all directions with most beautiful scenery. Previous to
the memorable year 1808, this was one of the
neatest cities in Spain. Some of the streets have
sustained no injury whatever. Others are partially decayed; but those nearest to the river are
one entire heap of ruins. Those houses that have
been permitted to retain their roofs, have been
so wantonly abused within by the French soldiers,
that till such time as they receive a thorough
scrubbing, no human being whatever can inhabit
them.

Talavera is famous for the victory gained by
Lord Wellington over the French army, on the

27th and 28th of July 1809. The people still
speak in terms of the highest admiration of the
conduct of the British troops on that memorable
occasion; and when we were there, they, with
seeming delight, pointed out the small hill on the
left of the position, which was so ably and suc-
cessfully defended by our present amiable and
gallant General, Sir Rowland Hill. While time
endures, the inhabitants of Talavera will venerate
the name of a British soldier.

With much regret we took leave of the good
people of Talavera, early in the morning of the
27th, and marched to the village of Cybola,
about four leagues from that city, on the road to
Toledo. That little village is completely surrounded with vineyards; the produce of which
sells at a halfpenny farthing a-pound of 14 ounces. On the 28th, our brigade moved from Cybola; and after passing through five towns and
villages, arrived at Torrijos, about mid-day. In
every town we passed through, on that day's
march, the people received us with long and loud
acclamations. The chief magistrates, and other
gentlemen of Torrijos, greeted Sir Rowland Hill
on his arrival at their gates; and in the evening, ordered an illumination in honour of the occasion. On the 29th, we marched to Toledo.
At a little distance from the city, we were met
by the magistrates in scarlet robes, the principal
nobility in the city, and its governor, the cele-

brated guerilla chief El Medico, who gave us
a most hearty welcome within the walls of their
ancient capital.   In the various streets through
which our route led us to the square, the people received us with shouts of joy; everywhere
the cry was heard, of " Long live George the
" Third of England!—long live Wellington!
" —long live Hill!—long live Ferdinand the
" Seventh!"—From the windows and balconies of
every house in the square, were suspended quilts,
sheets, silk-handkerchiefs, and various other articles of the same description, intended to express to us their great joy in having British soldiers within their gates.   In the evening, the
city was illuminated—many of the houses very
tastefully.

Toledo, once the capital of Spain, is situated on
a rock, three sides of which are washed by the
river Tagus; whose stream, murmuring, as it rolls
sullenly over its rugged bed, adds greatly to the
romantic scenery which every where surround
it.   The cathedral is a most splendid edifice ;
from the front of which runs a very handsome
street, all the way to the great square. The spire
is very lofty, and of beautiful workmanship. The
streets are rather narrow ; but, in general, they
are well paved, and very clean. The houses are
from two to five stories in height.

On the morning of the 30th, we crossed the
Tagus by a stone bridge, immediately under the

walls of Toledo; marched about four leagues up the left bank of the river, and near to the ruinous village of Villa Major, went into bivouac. —On the 1st instant, we marched in here.

Aranjuez is situated on the left bank of the Tagus, seven leagues from Toledo, and nine from Madrid. The Palace Royal, in this city, is a most magnificent structure. It is built close to the river, and on the right of the road to Toledo. The apartments are, in general, spacious, and ornamented with every thing princely. Upwards of 1000 oil paintings are distributed with great taste, in the different rooms of the royal residence—many of which are by the first masters, ancient and modern.

The room in which Joseph Bonaparte dined the day before he retired towards Valencia, was shown to us by the keeper of the palace. Every thing was standing in the same state in which he left them—tables, chairs, tumblers, and glasses, in one mass of confusion.

The royal gardens are, perhaps, the prettiest in Europe. By giving the Tagus two courses, the gardens are so inclosed as to bear some resemblance to an island. They are divided into two parts: The first part is that which you enter on crossing the left or artificial branch of the river, and is laid out with excellent taste, in beautiful walks. The rows of trees are so thickly planted along the edge of the walks, that their boughs, coming in contact with each other, form such an impenetrable bower against the rays of the sun, that the finest face in the world might be exposed here for ages, without being in the smallest degree injured by them. The second part is planted with almost every kind of fruit-trees, and is abundantly supplied with hot-houses. Vegetables of every description are to be had in great profusion; and the apples are at this moment lying in hundreds on the ground, and no one paying the least attention to them.

It was currently reported yesterday, that Marshal Soult intends paying us a visit; but none here give the least credit to it. If he should do so, I think we are a match for him. Besides our own corps, we have the 3d, 4th, and light division within a day's march—all of which are now placed under the command of Sir Rowland Hill.

We have been looking for the fall of Burgos every day for the last fortnight; it has been a tough piece of business. Here we have tolerable quarters; but there is a fever raging in the town just now, which renders the place not so pleasant as it would otherwise be.

ROBLEDO, *Nov.* 21, 1812.

LITTLE did I imagine, when I wrote to you from Aranjuez, that my next epistle would be written in this miserable village. But who, at that period, had the most distant idea, that the army then before Burgos, and that under Sir Rowland Hill in Madrid and Aranjuez, should, by the 20th of the following month, be compelled to seek quarters in Portugal? To have hinted at such a terrible reverse of fortune, would have amounted to high treason.

Marshal Soult having collected his troops at Valencia, advanced about the 12th of October, with an army of 50,000 veterans, towards the Tagus. To oppose the Marshal, we had the 2d, 3d, 4th, and light division of infantry, the Conde de Penne Villamur's corps, and that of Don Carlos de Espagna; Major-General Long's, and Major-General Slade's brigades of cavalry, and the cavalry and infantry of the Generals Freyre and Elio.—In all about 40,000 men.

Marshals Soult and Jourdan advanced directly on Madrid; and on the 23d, had arrived within two days march of Aranjuez. Early in the morning of that day, our division crossed the Tagus by a temporary bridge, a little above the Palace; the 1st brigade marched to the town of Colminar de Orejo; and the 2d and 3d brigades received

orders to proceed to several villages on the banks
of the river between Aranjuez and Fuente
Duenna, to guard the different fords on that line
of the river, at which the enemy might cross over
their infantry. The 1st brigade halted in Colminar on the 24th, and on the 25th advanced to
Fuente Duenna, at which place, there being a
good bridge, it was reported the enemy meant
to cross over the greater part of his army.

On taking possession of Duenna, we found the
place had been previously secured against any
sudden attack, by the Spanish Generals Elio and
Freyre, who, on the preceding day, had marched their united forces into it. The former was
second in command under General Liniers at
Buenos Ayres, when it was attacked by General
Whitelock in 1807. The enemy made their appearance on the 27th, and in the afternoon they
sent down a party from the opposite height to reconnoitre, some of whom advanced close to the
river's edge. The 60th rifle company were sent
from the village to line the bank of the river near
the bridge, to prevent them from ascertaining
whether it had been destroyed. Betwixt the
riflemen and the enemy a good many shots were
exchanged, but neither party suffered much in
the business, the enemy having only one man
and two horses wounded.

At the time the enemy made their first appearance on the height, some of our soldiers were

bathing in the river, who, as the French approached them, put themselves into various attitudes, which roused the spirits of the Gallic soldiers to such a degree, that one of them, burning with rage, galloped forward to the bank of the river, levelled his carabine at one of our men, who was in the act of swimming across the river, and would, no doubt, have shot him, had not an instantaneous shout of indignation, which burst forth from every mouth in the brigade, made him ashamed of his intention.

After various movements had been performed by Marshal Soult, his designs were discovered by Sir Rowland Hill, who lost not a moment in preparing to frustrate them. The troops in Madrid were ordered to move forward to the position which he had selected in front of Aranjuez; and those troops that were acting as corps of observation, were withdrawn, to reinforce the main body.

On the evening of the 27th, our brigade quitted Fuente Duenna, and marched all night, and next day, till one o'clock in the afternoon. About that hour, we were ordered to occupy the small village of Villa Conijos. Before seven in the evening we were again under arms; a little after midnight we crossed the Jacama, by the Puento Largo, which the engineers were at that time mining; but, by some mistake, the mine did not take effect. About four in the morning we took up the ground Sir Rowland intended us to occupy, in the position opposite to Aranjuez, and where he had resolved to give King Joseph battle.

The position selected by Sir Rowland Hill, marked, in an eminent degree, the sound judgment of that excellent officer—every part of it was naturally strong ; in short, it was a position of that description, which made us all eager for battle : not that we wished to brave death, but because it was our opinion that a battle was unavoidable, and that on no other ground could we possess such decided advantages over our enemy.

At day-light on the 29th, the enemy seemed to be enjoying themselves in Aranjuez ; but in an hour or two the whole were withdrawn to the neighbourhood of Toledo, a little above which, the Marshal had thrown a bridge over the Tagus, by which he intended to lead over the greater part of his army.

From this moment it became evident, that the Marshal's object was to turn us out of our position, not to attack us in it. Sir Rowland, aware of his intentions, and having received advices from the Marquis of Wellington, that he had been forced to yield to the pressure of the moment on the side of Burgos, ordered an immediate retreat on the metropolis.

About one o'clock on the 29th, the allied army broke up from its position, and marched to the village of Val de Mora, in front of which the 2d division went into bivouac. On the 30th we passed close under the walls of the metropolis; and about three miles from which, on the road to the Escurial, went into bivouac. Our men, having no tents, suffered greatly from the inclemency of the weather. On that day the fall of rain exceeded any thing I had witnessed for a long time.

About nine o'clock on the morning of the 31st we quitted our bivouac near Madrid, and at eight in the evening arrived at the Escurial. Two brigades occupied the palace; the others were quartered in the town. Although a palace was here allotted to us for a night's residence, still our ambition was far from being gratified; many would have cheerfully resigned this magnificent habitation of royalty, to enjoy the quiet of a shepherd's cottage.

On the 1st November we left the Escurial, and marched to the village of Guadarama, near to which we bivouacked. Early next morning we began to ascend the lofty mountain, over which is cut the far-famed Guadarama pass. The summit of that stupendous natural edifice we espied about three hours after we began our march from its base : Here we enjoyed a beautiful view of the surrounding country, in many parts as far as the eye could reach. Descending the mountain at a quick pace, we marched through a large village at the foot of the pass; and at sun-set went into bivouac behind the village of Villa Castine. On the 3d, 4th, and 5th days of November, we continued to retire, passing through the villages of Corde Villar and Flores; and, on the 6th, took up a position one league in front of Penaranda. From a little eminence near to Corde Villar, a person, in a clear day, I am told, can count 48 towns and villages. It being a little hazy at the time we passed that place, 28 only could be distinguished. On the 7th we quitted our position in front of Penaranda, and after crossing the river Tormes, by a bridge, at the town of Alba de Tormes, we went into bivouac at the distance of half a mile from the river.

On our arrival here, we learned that Lord Wellington was in position in front of Salamanca, and that the army of Portugal, under Caffarelli and Souham, had formed a junction with that under Marshal Soult, and were advancing to give us battle. The famed Arepiles was again pitched on as the best spot to meet the united forces of the enemy.

On the 8th, the 1st brigade was thrown into Alba de Tormes, with orders, if attacked, to defend the place to the last extremity. These troops were to be supported by the Portuguese under Lieutenant-General Hamilton, who, for that purpose, were posted on a height on the opposite side of the river.

On the 9th the enemy approached Alba, and drove in the cavalry picquets of Major-General Long's brigade. On the morning of the 10th the whole of the cavalry crossed the river; and about two o'clock the enemy appeared on the heights above the town. Every preparation had been made to give them a warm reception; the Castle was put into a state of defence, and a garrison of 150 men thrown in to defend it. The only defence which the town possesses, is a Moorish wall, which is in many places levelled with the ground. These gaps were filled in the best manner that circumstances would admit of: a certian portion of each regiment lined the walls, and the remainder were under arms in the square, ready to act wherever they might be wanted.

The brigade was formed in this manner when the enemy advanced, about two o'clock on the 10th, to attack the place. Their infantry was supposed to amount to 8000 men, and provided with 21 pieces of artillery. From two till four o'clock, their artillery poured down an incessant shower of shot and shell, from the heights, on the town. Their infantry were repeatedly formed into columns of attack, but never attempted to carry the place by assault. The utmost efforts of the enfuriated Marshal were directed against Alba for more than three hours, but were rendered of no avail, by the intrepidity of the officers commanding corps, seconded by the gallantry of the soldiers. Soult, finding that no impression could be made on the garrison, withdrew the main body of his troops from the heights above Alba, leaving a part of his rifle corps only.

From the 10th to the 14th, the two armies lay in sight of each other, neither of them making any movement of consequence. On the latter day, however, the enemy crossed the Tormes above Alba, with the intention of cutting off Lord Wellington's communication with Ciudad Rodrigo.

Lord Wellington moved, with the 2d division of infantry, to attack the enemy at Mozarles; but on his arrival, found them so strongly posted, that to have attacked them, would have been almost certain destruction.

On the morning of the 15th, finding the enemy still in the same position, and moving strong bodies of troops towards Ciudad Rodrigo, Lord Wellington deemed it most prudent, from the circumstances in which he was placed, to order a retreat on that fortress. The retreat of the army was continued on the 16th, 17th, 18th, and 19th; on the two former the enemy followed us; but gave over the pursuit on the 18th. On the 19th, our division crossed the Agueda, three leagues above Rodrigo, and marched to this place.

It is almost impossible to give you any idea of

our sufferings during the last ten days. Without money, without clothes, and often not well supplied with provisions, our situation, as you may conceive, was not an enviable one.

For some days past, our men have subsisted chiefly on wheat, oak nuts, and tough beef, the very sight of which was often sufficient to satisfy the cravings of hunger. The countenances of the soldiers are sufficient to convince any person who sees them, that the miseries and hardships they have endured in this retreat have been of no ordinary kind. Yesterday morning, no fewer than 60 men of this regiment were entered on the doctor's list, and all of them really ill.—Adieu.

CORIA, *December* 15, 1812.

THE allied army continued its retreat into Portugal, with the exception of the 2d division, which was stationed in Coria, and some other adjoining villages. On the 28th ultimo, we quitted Robledo, and that night occupied the small village of Payo. On the following day we crossed the Sierra de Gate, and in the afternoon marched into Pyrelles. On the 30th we occupied the village of Cases de Don Gomez, and on the 1st instant marched into this town.

Coria is a very ancient town, surrounded by a high wall, in many places flanked by square towers, which, added to its commanding situation, must have rendered it a place of importance before the use of fire-arms. It can boast of four gates; from each of which a narrow dirty street conducts the stranger to the great square, or market-place. Although the wall by which this town is surrounded is yet entire, it could offer little resistance to a besieging army, however poorly that army might be provided with the common implements of destruction.

In the plain between Coria and the river, there stands a most beautiful stone bridge of several arches. The river some years ago forced its way through a different part of the plain, and left its rider a laughing-stock to every person who visits this part of the country.

We are in general poorly quartered here; but having received a great proportion of our arrears of pay, we contrive to make ourselves tolerably comfortable.

Our men have recovered greatly from the fatigues of the late campaign, although there is a great number in general as well as regimental hospitals; still, the proportion of bad cases are few, in comparison to what was at one time anticipated, from the hardships they endured during the latter part of the retreat.

On the 28th of November the Marquis of Wellington addressed a letter to General and other officers commanding divisions and brigades, in which he points out to them the necessity of causing discipline to be observed in the several regiments under their respective commands, from the lieutenant-colonel commanding to the youngest drum-boy. Their attention is particularly called to the captains and subalterns, whose conduct in the late retreat has not given satisfaction. In short, this army, according to the letter, was, latterly, neither more nor less than an armed rabble.

That discipline in some regiments ceased to exist, I have been credibly informed. When that is the case in any corps, numerous irregularities must naturally follow : but that all are equally involved in guilt I can positively deny. It is not my intention to particularise any regiment as failing in duty on this occasion, but merely to do justice to the officers, non-commissioned officers, and privates of our own. From the commanding officer to the youngest ensign, their respective duties were performed with credit to themselves and advantage to their country; and, in regard to the conduct of the non-commissioned officers and privates, I can assert, without fear of contradiction, that throughout the whole of that ill-fated retreat, every man bore his share of privations with manly fortitude, and, on every occasion, obeyed the orders of their superior officers with that cheerful alacrity for which the soldiers of this national corps have ever been remarkable. Although, on many occasions, their spirits were broken by hunger and fatigue, yet, into their gallant breasts, despair never found a passage. With heroic firmness they braved every hardship and every danger, cheerfully submitting to their hard fate without a murmur.

When the regiment marched in here on the 1st instant, I really believe that there was not above one hundred shirts in the possession of the whole private soldiers. Their small-clothes were barely sufficient to cover their nakedness. Their jackets, which had once been scarlet, now possessed almost every colour which I could name; some of them had black sleeves fastened to a red body, others blue, and many of them had brown cloth sleeves to a patched body.—Scarcely any two were mended alike. Their appearance, you may believe, was not very prepossessing—but still their hearts were truly British, and animated with the same ardent love of their country, as on former occasions, when in the arms of victory.

The Spanish ladies are generally handsome and well looked, but the middle class fall off very much, and the lower order are—forgive me—ugly. All the three classes are lazy. The first are well dressed, the second tolerably, and the third miserably. The first class are clean in their persons, the second but so and so, and the third are extremely dirty. They live in the manner of pigs by day, and at night they stow themselves into bed in exact imitation of the swinish multitude. During the time we were quartered in Robledo, I slept in the same apartment with the patron, his wife, and four children. When they went to bed, the patron pulled off his short brown jacket, but the wife and children tumbled in as they were. When they rose in the morning, not one of the family put a drop of water on their hands or face, nor, for the eight days in which I was in the house, did the members of this family wash themselves. When I spoke to them of it, they laughed at my ideas of cleanliness.

The forage being extremely scarce in Robledo about the time we were there, some of the inhabitants, unable to support the number they had on hand, made us accept of a few of their neatest shaped *grey ponies.* But the Commander of the forces having limited the subaltern's allowance of forage to half a ration only, and as that is barely sufficient to support my baggage mule, I endeavoured, on my arrival here, to dispose of mine, which, I am happy to inform you, I have accomplished, but not without a very great deal of trouble, and sustaining considerable loss, notwithstanding I had it for nothing.

MONTE HERMOSA, *February* 3, 1813.

THE 71st having moved some days before, the 50th and 92d regiments quitted Coria on the 7th ultimo, and arrived here in the evening, where they have since remained. The 71st regiment marched from this town on the same day, to a village about three leagues in our front, where they now have their head-quarters. Three companies of that regiment, and 6th Portuguese caçadores, occupy the village of Banos, seven leagues from hence. This part of the country is dreadfully infested by a lawless banditti. Detachments from the partizan corps of Don Julian Sanchez are frequently here in search of them. Of late, these parties have been pretty successful in their operations against the freebooters, several having been taken. One of these parties of guerillas is commanded by a captain of Don Julian's corps, who, from the circumstance of having his upper lip cut by the sword of a Frenchman, is known here by the name of Captain *Hare-lip*. Were I permitted to give an opinion of the discipline of the Don's corps, from the specimen now before me, I would have little hesitation in saying that he ruled his men, not with a rod of iron, but with a rod of steel. If one of his men falls from the ranks one or two paces, without permission, the captain draws his tremendous hanger, and makes a cut at the unfortunate culprit, who, if he has not agility enough to get out of the way, is immediately cut down by his savage commander. Let us hope, however, for the sake of humanity, that the captain's mode of punishing his men has not the sanction of the intrepid Don Julian Sanchez.

A few days after we marched into Coria, an officer was sent to Lisbon, to bring the new cloathing for the regiment, and such other stores as might be wanted for the use of the men. About a week ago, the same officer returned to us with the cloathing, &c. to the unspeakable joy of every half-naked soldier in the regiment. All the tailors in the corps, who can either clip, sow, or cabbage, having been set to work, we expect to have the jackets fitted on in the course of 14 days. Then, my dear friend, the patched and tattered garments of our poor fellows, will no longer point out to the stranger the extreme poverty of the wearer.

Neither the allied army, nor that of the enemy, has made any movement of consequence since the end of November. Both parties appear to have been equally tired of the last campaign—both in great want of repose—and both must receive reinforcements, before they can again resume the offensive.

It is said, that Marshal Soult has been recalled from the command of the French army immediately opposed to us, to assume an important command in the army of Germany. It is also asserted, that a large proportion of the veteran troops in this country has been withdrawn into France, and are to be replaced by an equal number of conscripts.

The people in this village are extremely kind and attentive to us in their own way; but their mode of living is so very different from our's, that we very seldom join them at the festive board. The principal inhabitants are farmers, and the rest are either their immediate dependants, or engaged in commercial pursuits.

BANOS, *March 5*, 1813.

DURING the second week of February, the French General Foy, having collected about 3000 troops in Salamanca, advanced towards the town of Bejer, situated two leagues in front of this village, with the view of securing a large quantity of cloth, then stored in that town, before we could have intimation of his designs. To protect them, the inhabitants made application to Sir Rowland Hill, for a portion of his corps; which being readily granted, the detachment of the 71st regiment, and 6th Portuguese caçadores, then quartered in this place, were ordered to occupy Bejer on the first alarm. The 71st regiment moved to the front on the 12th, (Foy being on his march to Bejer), the 50th marched the same evening from Monte Hermosa, and occupied the village which the 71st had left; and, on the morning of the 13th, the 92d regiment followed the other two.

The enemy had arrived within five miles of Bejer when our troops entered it. On receiving intelligence that we had anticipated him, the French General retired to his former quarters. The 50th and 6th caçadores were ordered to form the garrison of Bejer; the 71st was put into the villages of Puerto de Banos and Candeleiria; and the 92d regiment occupied the village

of Banos. The 60th rifle company was ordered
to Herbas.

About the 20th, information was given to the
officer commanding in Bejer, that the crafty General was again advancing with an increased force,
and intended to surprise the garrison on the following morning. Every preparation was made
for the defence of the place, by Lieutenant-Colonel Harrison of the 50th regiment. The troops
were under arms a little before day-light; and
throughout the greater part of the night, were
kept in readiness to act at a moment's notice.
About day-light, the French attacked the out-
picquets on the Salamanca road; one of which,
composed of the caçadores, had nearly fallen into their hands. In a few minutes, the enemy
was at the gates of the town, into which they
fancied they should be able to penetrate with little
trouble. But, at every one of the gates, there
were parties of the 50th regiment stationed, over
whose lifeless trunks it behoved the foe to march,
before he could attain his object. The attack was
made with great spirit, but the enemy was repulsed
with the undaunted bravery so peculiar to that
excellent corps. Again and again they attempted to force a passage; but these reiterated attempts only served to heighten their disgrace;
for, after a severe conflict, of an hour's duration,
Foy was compelled to withdraw his troops from

the gates of Bejer, with the loss of his aide-de-camp, who was killed, several other officers, and about 100 killed and wounded.

The 71st regiment sent four companies to the assistance of their friends, on receiving the first accounts of Foy's advance ; but these brave fellows arrived just in time to witness the victorious march of their companions, and the disgraceful flight of their enemies from the gates of Bejer.

The 92d regiment marched to the front of the pass of Banos, where they lay, ready to act whenever their services might be wanted. Ever since, we have been busily employed in strengthening our position in front of Banos. Fatigue parties are working every day, throwing up breastworks on the right of the road leading hence to Bejer.

Foy threatens, we are told, to pay us another visit in our present quarters. I can assure the General, that nothing would give us so much pleasure as to see him seated to a little of our salt pork and potatoes, preparatory to his leaving Banos, on his way to a British transport.

The village of Banos is divided into two parts, each governed by its own alcalde. The southern division is seated in the province of Estremadura, and the northern in that of Leon. It lies in a narrow valley, surrounded on every side by rugged mountains, whose summits, one

I

would imagine, reach almost to the sky. To the very top, many of them are cultivated, and produce excellent crops of vines. To wander on these mountains, unarmed, is rather dangerous, from the number of wolves which inhabit them. For the skin of one of these animals, each village, within a certain distance of the spot where the animal is killed, is bound to pay the sum of four dollars to the person who kills it, who has it in his option either to take that sum, or his chance of a collection amongst the people. The skin of one of those ferocious creatures was exhibited here the other day, killed on a hill above the village by two men, who had watched their prey for a considerable number of nights, before they could find an opportunity of killing it. I have been told, that the sum collected by those people was considerable.—Adieu.

EVERY regiment in this brigade has remained
in quiet possession of their respective cantonments since General Foy's last attack on Bejer,
in the month of February last.

In 1809, the Spanish General, Don Carlos de
Espagna, was surprised in this village by the
French under Marshal Ney. The enemy was
conducted hither by a mountain road, on which
the Spanish General had neglected to post a
picquet. The attack was made at two o'clock
in the afternoon. For such a visit the Spaniards
were of course unprepared. The French rushed
into the village thirsting for the blood of their
enemies; but the Spaniards, though surprised,
did not tamely submit to their haughty foe. The
moment the alarm was sounded, every man flew
to arms, and, quitting Banos, scrambled up the
face of a rugged hill, on the north side of it,
from which they kept up a steady and well directed fire on their enemies, and caused them considerable loss in killed and wounded.

The bravery displayed by Don Carlos' division
on this occasion, proved a source of unseasonable
misery to the greater part of the inhabitants of
Banos. Ney, mortified that the Spaniards should
so desperately defend their rugged post, caused
a great part of the village to be burned, in order

to intimidate its inhabitants, and those of the neighbouring villages. Never did a General, in my opinion, put in execution a measure so obviously calculated to injure his own cause, as that adopted by the French Marshal on this occasion; and the issue has shown, in the most striking manner possible, the fallacy of the line of conduct he adopted.

A few days after our arrival in this village, one of our officers asked his patrona, if the inhabitants in general were considered loyal? Pointing to the ruins, she replied, " To these I refer you for " your answer."

Some time ago the French carried away the wife of one of the wealthiest and most respectable inhabitants of Banos, on the pretence that her husband was a patriot. The husband demanded his wife; but the ruthless banditti would not yield her up till they received, by way of ransom, the sum of twelve hundred dollars. In consequence of the barbarous treatment she received from them, she has become quite insane, and is at this moment a living monument of what French immorality has occasioned since their first appearance in this kingdom.

About six weeks ago, a private soldier of the 3d, or Old Buffs, fired at, and mortally wounded one of the officers of that regiment, when standing on parade.

A week or two after that, a corporal of the 42d Highlanders committed a similar crime, and in a similar manner. The officers lived a short while after they received the contents of the assassins' muskets. The two soldiers were tried in a few days after the crimes were committed, condemned, and executed.

A most affecting execution took place in this division a few days ago—the criminal was a young man about twenty-six years of age. He was tried by a general court-martial, held at Coria, found guilty of deserting to the enemy, and attempting to stab the non-commissioned officer who apprehended him. On these charges he was sentenced to suffer death.

On the morning of the execution, the regiment to which this young man belonged was drawn up in a field, and formed three sides of a square. The other face was left open for the place of execution. There being no chaplain present, the poor man was attended by the schoolmaster-serjeant, who continued to read portions of Scripture to him till they arrived at the fatal spot, where they afterwards sung a few verses of a psalm. Having finished his devotions, the cap was pulled over his face, and the provost-marshal was ordered, with his party, to take post in front of the unfortunate culprit, preparatory to carrying the sentence into execution. When the signal dropt from his hand, the whole regiment, officers and men, knelt down, and fervently offered up their prayers to the all-wise Disposer of events, in behalf of him who was about to take a final leave of this transitory world. The whole scene was one of the most awful and affecting I ever witnessed.

You will no doubt be much surprised to find that we are still in comfortable cantonments. I shall endeavour to point out to you the principal cause of our long inactivity.

In a letter I wrote to you from Robledo, I gave you some idea of the privations which this army had suffered, and the wretched situation it was in for want of cloathing. We had not been long in quarters till the hospitals were filled with our soldiers, thousands of whom never again joined, having either paid the debt of nature, or been invalided to Belem or England. To make up the deficiency occasioned by sickness, as well as the field casualties that had occurred from the taking of Badajoz, down to the retreat from Salamanca, required no little time. Our mounted force had suffered severely. The cavalry were rendered very inefficient, from the number of horses which died on the road through fatigue, or had been killed in the various affairs with the enemy. The artillery were nearly in a similar situation; many of the regiments of infantry were almost naked; the military chest was but thinly lined, and our stores of various kinds required to be renewed. Thus situated, what could Lord Wellington do but exercise his patience till men, money, horses, and ammunition, could be transported from England. For the last two months the army has been daily increasing in numbers : every regiment has received one detachment from England, and some two, and our hospitals are now almost empty. Since I came to this country, never did I see the regiments of this division look so well, or appear so well appointed. If all the other regiments of which this army is composed equal those of the 2d division in every respect, I will venture to assert that a finer army was never seen in this or any other country.

The whole army is now in motion, with the exception of this brigade, which also marches on the morning of the 19th. With great regret we quit the good people of Banos—may they be as happy as I wish them. Adieu.

AT the date of my last letter, the enemy occupied a very strong position on the right bank of
the river Douro, extending from Valladolid to
Zamora. King Joseph quitted Madrid about the
beginning of May, with the troops that had win-
tered there, Marshal Jourdan acting as his Major-
General, and assumed the command of the whole
effective disposable force of France in the centre
and north of Spain.

To have attacked him in this position, would,
no doubt, have cost us many valuable lives, without the chance of obtaining us any solid advantage. The prudent plans of our General, not
only prevented the effusion of blood, but caused
the enemy to abandon the whole line of the Douro, and retire with precipitation towards Burgos.

Sir Thomas Graham, with the left wing of the
army, broke up from his cantonments about the
15th of May, crossed the Douro near to Miranda,
marched up the right bank of the river, crossed
the Esla, and advanced towards Zamora, which
the enemy abandoned on his approach, and retired to Toro. About the same time the other divisions began to close to the front. The rear brigades of our division were close up to Banos on
the 18th May, whence our regiment marched on
the following morning to Bejer, and the other

brigades occupied the quarters we had left. On the 20th, the whole corps assembled in a plain near Bejer. On the 23d, we were reviewed by Sir Rowland Hill, who expressed himself highly pleased with the appearance of the different regiments. On the 24th, we advanced from our camp near Bejer, to the small village of Robeira, behind which we went into camp. Next morning we continued our route for Salamanca, and in the afternoon bivouacked near the village of Mattella. On the morning of the 26th we advanced on Salamanca, at that time held by the French General Villate, with a mixed force of 3000 men.

Lord Wellington having joined Sir Rowland Hill with a portion of the cavalry from Ciudad Rodrigo, reconnoitred the enemy from a height on the left of the Tormes, and immediately opposite to the city.

His Lordship no sooner perceived them retreating from the town, than he ordered the cavalry and some horse artillery to cross the Tormes in two columns to attack them. The left column crossed by the bridge at the city, the right by a ford about a mile above it. The two in conjunction moved forward from the river, and attacked Villate with great fury. Their cavalry being inferior in numbers to ours, were, after sustaining considerable loss, compelled to seek for safety around their squares of infantry, which, through-

out the affair, behaved with great coolness and
gallantry.

In this skirmish, which lasted about an hour,
the enemy lost about 300 men, 140 of whom were
prisoners.

The infantry of Sir Rowland Hill's corps crossed the Tormes in the afternoon, and encamped
in a plain about half a mile from Salamanca. In
this camp we were visited by a great number of
very respectable people, who came from the city, to get a view of the interior accommodation of a British tent. At times they astonished
me a good deal, when curiosity led them to draw
the strings of my tent.

Lord Wellington having signified to Sir Rowland Hill his intention of looking at his corps
next morning on their march, notice to that effect was sent to officers commanding regiments,
with a request, that they would have their men
in as good order as circumstances would permit.

We marched from our camp a little after sun-
rise on the 27th, and, about four miles in front
of Salamanca, passed Lord Wellington in review,
who was much pleased with the appearance of
every soldier in the division. The ceremony being over, we continued our route to the village
of Orbada. The Marquis of Wellington and his
staff returned to Salamanca.

At an early hour on the morning of the 3d

June, we quitted our camp at Orbada, and that night bivouacked on the left bank of the Guarena, and at the distance of two leagues from Toro.—Just as we were taking up our ground, 200 French prisoners passed, on their way to the rear. These had all been taken in a skirmish between our hussar brigade, and the rear-guard of the enemy's cavalry, excepting 25, who, I have been informed, were the lawful prize of that enterprising partisan chief, Don Julian Sanchez.

The manner in which this party was taken, may draw your attention, as it speaks more in favour of the military talents of the Don, than volumes written on the subject. This chief was sent to reconnoitre the enemy in front of Toro, with a party of his own cavalry. Coming in sight of one of the enemy's picquets, posted behind a small river, he immediately formed an idea of surprising them, and by a plan exclusively his own. The French picquet consisted of 25 men—the Don's party was 40 strong. One half of the Spaniards were sent unperceived to get into the rear of the enemy; the others were advanced close to the river's edge, and the bridles taken out of their horses' mouths. This little manœuvre tended to lull the enemy into a fatal security: for the French officer, on perceiving Don Julian's party take the bridles out of their horses' mouths, issued a similar order. For a few minutes both parties remained quiet; when the Don seeing that his party had arrived at their post, gave the signal that was agreed on between him and the officer who led them. His faithful followers, on perceiving the signal, rushed from their ambush on the unprepared Frenchmen, who, before they could offer any effectual resistance, were surrounded, and made prisoners. The officer who commanded the French party might be about 32 years of age; he was very handsome, and in height not under six feet six inches. His situation, on passing us, seemed to give him great uneasiness; he walked in front of the whole party, and with his hat under his arm, till fairly out of sight.

On the 4th of June, we crossed the Douro at Toro, and same night encamped about a league and a half in front of that town. On the 5th, we encamped close to a village half way between Toro and Valladolid, where we were under the necessity of pulling down two of the houses, in order to get wood to cook with. Next day we passed Valladolid. Keeping it on our right, we came to the town of Cegales, in the vicinity of which we went into bivouac.

On the 7th, we advanced to Duenas, between which place and the river we encamped. Under the window of a building which the French had converted into an hospital, there were exposed on a dunghill the bodies of two of their soldiers, who had that morning been thrown out of the window

by their *friends*. We were assured by the inhabitants, that one of them was alive at the moment.
Our men were terribly shocked at the sight of
these two Frenchmen. On the 8th we marched
to the town of Torquemada, at a little distance
from which we encamped. During the night
we had a heavy fall of rain. Our men being provided with tents, did not feel it, but the poor
Portuguese soldiers I pitied from the bottom of
my heart, they having nothing but their blankets
to shelter them from the inclemency of the
weather. Lieutenant-General the Honourable
William Stewart being now in command of the
division, ordered an extra allowance of grog to
be issued to the soldiers on the morning of the
9th ; but this order not having been attended to
by the Commissary of Colonel Ashworth's brigade, the said Commissary received a severe re-
primand in division orders. On the 9th we advanced two leagues, up to the knees in mud and
water. On the 10th we crossed the Arlanzon,
two leagues above Torquemada, and encamped
on a small height, at the distance of a league
from the river.

We marched one league only on the morning of the 11th, and encamped in a corn field
near the village of Los Valbasas. On the 12th,
we directed our march on Burgos ; in the afternoon, our light cavalry and horse artillery came
up with the enemy, from whom they took one

piece of cannon, and some prisoners. We had taken up our ground for the night, when the first report from our artillery reached our ears; in an instant we were under arms, and immediately moved forward to support the troops in advance. We had proceeded a very little way indeed, when the rain began to pour with its usual severity, and which, in a few minutes, drenched us most completely. About sun-set we were ordered to retrace our steps to the very spot we had left some hours before.

About five o'clock on the morning of the 13th, the enemy having first removed all the cannon worth carrying away, blew up the Castle of Burgos. Joseph and his Major-General must have been in a state of temporary insanity, when they ordered the destruction of the Castle of Burgos, a place which, with a small garrison, the preceding year, had arrested the progress of our, till then, victorious General. In what light are we to view the conduct of those two great personages on this occasion? Are we to consider them as totally unworthy of the command which the Emperor of the French has bestowed on them? or are we to accept of the destruction of Burgos as a tacit acknowledgement of their own insufficiency to cope with us on this side of the Ebro? If so, a great proportion of their veteran force must have returned into France, to march to the assistance of their brethren in Germany, who are now attempting to stem the all-subduing torrent of Russian patriotism.

A very little time will now decide where the grand struggle for Spanish liberty is to take place; much farther we cannot advance, without coming on French territory. Whenever the mighty conflict shall take place, and whatever may be the issue of the important struggle, you may rely on every thing being done by this army that man can achieve, for a finer army never took the field. Never did an army answer the dread call with greater cheerfulness, nor express more unbounded confidence in their officers.

Adíeu.

CAMP, BEFORE PAMPELUNA, *June* 27, 1813.

THE Marquis of Wellington having received information of the enemy's proceedings at Burgos, and that Joseph Bonaparte had retired with the greater part of his army from that place, in the direction of Pencorbo, gave orders for the whole of his army to make a movement to the left. Sir Thomas Graham, with the left wing, crossed the Ebro on the 14th, at Arenas. The centre crossed on the 15th; and the corps of Sir Rowland Hill, forming the right wing, moved to the left bank on the 16th instant.

We were surprised to find, that the enemy had not occupied the strong natural defences on the left bank of the Ebro. From the bridge at which we crossed, the road for three miles runs up the left bank, close to the river's edge; and for the same distance on the right of the road, there runs a ridge of steep rugged mountains, which is in many places inaccessible. In some parts, too, the road has been cut out of the solid rock; pieces of which still project over the high-way. There is one point, in particular, where the rock not only projects over the road, but absolutely overhangs a part of the river. I am of opinion, that 1000 men would be sufficient to defend this pass against 20,000 for a very long time.

On the 17th, the army moved forward about

three leagues. On the 18th, the light division came in contact with two brigades of French infantry, on the march, which they attacked, and defeated, with the loss of 300 men ;—a considerable quantity of baggage also fell into their hands. On the following day, the same division fell in with another numerous body of infantry, which they also defeated, with loss. In the evening of that day we occupied a height, three leagues above Miranda del Ebro. On the 20th, the whole army advanced towards Vittoria :—the 2d division encamped in a plain, about two leagues from the village of Puebla.

About five o'clock on the morning of the 21st, the rain, which, till then, had fallen in gentle showers, entirely ceased. Soon after the sun burst from behind the gloomy clouds, to spread his cheering rays over fields yet unstained with blood—over rivers, whose streams, meandering through Zadora's vale, were yet undisturbed by the strife of men—over heights, where the best blood of Britain was soon to flow :—to cheer the Sons of Freedom, on their march to the field of honour, hundreds of whom were destined, long before he had finished his daily course, to take their departure for " that bourne whence no traveller returns."

A little after five o'clock we quitted our camp, and about nine arrived at Puebla, through which runs the high road from Burgos to Vittoria.

On the right of the road, and about a quarter of a mile in front of the village, the division halted for a few minutes, to give time to the officers to inspect the arms and ammunition of their men. Our Lieutenant-Colonel gave orders to observe the strictest silence on the march, and in action, excepting when ordered to charge,— the men were then to cheer, but as soon as resistance ceased on the part of the enemy, they were to resume their former silence.

From Puebla the division directed its march along the high road to Vittoria, which, for two miles, runs up the left bank of the Zadora, then turning to the right, leads straight to the village of Sabujana de Alava. On our coming in sight of this village, we first beheld the enemy, drawn up in order of battle, ready to receive us, and at the short distance of a mile.

The left of the French army occupied in force the heights of Puebla. The centre the village of Sabujana de Alava. Their right centre was posted on a height, which commanded the valley of Zadora. That height was crowned with infantry, flanked, and otherwise defended by at least 100 pieces of cannon. A little farther to the right there was a thick wood, the importance of which was not overlooked by the enemy. Some battalions of infantry were posted in it, to keep the line of communication open between the troops of the right centre and right wing, which extended to some distance beyond Vittoria. To the left of the centre there was another wood, the skirts of which were lined with cannon, and numerous bodies of infantry were from time to time thrown into it. In short, their position and numbers were truly formidable; but neither of these circumstances tended to depress the spirits of our soldiers. No: on the contrary, they appeared to be more and more delighted, as the enemy's battalions successively showed themselves from behind their artillery. One heart and one soul animated the whole—all were alike eager for battle. With the fixed resolution to conquer or die, we moved forward, in awful silence, to begin the tremendous conflict.

About fifteen minutes from ten o'clock, the sound of musketry on the heights of Puebla announced that the battle had begun.

The Spanish troops, under General Morillo, began the action, by an attack on the left of the French army, posted on the heights of Puebla. These troops were instantly succoured by the light companies of the division, and the 71st regiment, under the Honourable Colonel Cadogan. After a severe struggle, in which that officer was mortally wounded, and the French commanding officer taken prisoner, the enemy were driven from the heights at the point of the bayonet.

During these operations, the 50th and 92d regiments were ordered to support the attack on the heights. These troops had nearly gained the summit, when they received an order to return. We had descended about half-way, when a third order arrived, for the 50th regiment to proceed to their first destination, and the 92d to attack a French battalion of infantry, posted on a ridge a little in their front, and which acted as a corps of communication between the troops of the left wing and those in the wood to the left of the centre.

Through fields of wheat, which rose above many of the men—over ditches thickly lined on each side with thorns and briers, the 92d regiment marched to meet their foes. Having arrived at the foot of the ridge on which the enemy had been posted, the Highlanders were ordered to load, and prepare to charge. With a firm pace they ascended, every moment expecting to be met by their antagonists :—conceive, then, their surprise, when, on arriving at the top of the ridge, they found that the enemy had precipitately retired to another during their advance.

Two Spanish guns having, by great exertion, been got up to a position on the right of the 92d, that regiment was ordered to form close column, and cover them. These soon drew on the regiment a heavy fire from a battery which the enemy had planted on the left of the wood, and which caused it the loss of a serjeant and several privates.

The enemy, who, till now, had not discovered the importance of the heights they had lost,
detached about 7000 men from their centre to re-
take them. This movement brought on a series
of severe skirmishes, which in the end proved
extremely ruinous to the enemy.

In order to prevent them sending more troops
to the assistance of those engaged in the attack on the heights, Sir Rowland Hill ordered
the 2d and 3d brigades of the 2d division, to attack the enemy in front of the village of Sabujana
de Alava, and possess themselves of that place,
should circumstances prove favourable.

Lieutenant-General Stewart, perceiving the efforts the enemy were making to obtain possession
of the heights, ordered Colonel Cameron to advance
with his Highlanders to the assistance of the
troops already there, and take on himself the
command of the 1st brigade, vacant by the fall of
the Honourable Colonel Cadogan.

With considerable exertion, that regiment succeeded in gaining the summit of the mountain, at a point about half a mile in rear of
that where the 50th and 71st were engaged.
The moment being pressing, the regiment was
hurried along the ridge, at a rapid pace, in open
column of companies, right in front.—We arrived just in time to prevent the heights from becoming the property of the enemy. The 71st
regiment had been ordered to occupy a height

in advance of the one on which the 50th were posted, when, being attacked by numbers four times superior, they were compelled to seek safety with their friends in the rear. A very deep ravine runs between these two heights, from the bottom of which, to where the 50th were posted, the ascent was extremely abrupt.—To this point the 71st were retreating, and the 92d advancing. To this point the march of the enemy's columns was also directed, and they had attained to within a few yards of the summit when the 92d arrived. By their great superiority of numbers, the enemy had succeeded in turning the left wing of the 71st, and had cut off its communication with the 50th. This was the existing state of affairs when the 92d entered the lists, whose presence on the right of the 50th restored every thing to its former state—the united efforts of the three regiments, under the direction of the Highland Chief, compelled the assailants to seek for safety in a precipitate flight.

The enemy formed fresh columns of attack, behind a height immediately opposite us, and, in half an-hour, renewed the conflict :—again they were forced to run. A third time they attempted to dislodge us, but their efforts were attended with no better success. It was now nearly one o'clock. The 3d, 4th, 7th and light divisions had, by this time, crossed from the right to the left bank of the Zadora, and had attacked the heights on which the right centre columns of the enemy were posted. The struggle at this point was short but severe;—the enemy retired in good order towards Vittoria, and, as often as the nature of the ground would admit, turned upon their conquerors. From the summits of Puebla's blood-stained heights, we beheld, with pride and pleasure, the gallant conduct of our friends in the valley.

So close was the terrible conflict, in many parts of the glorious plains of Vittoria, that the hostile combatants were often observed pointing their deadly weapons at each other, when the space between each barely permitted them to do so without crossing the muzzles of their pieces. The courage of the soldiers invariably rose in proportion to the exertions required of them. Wherever the bayonet was directed, there every thing was forced to yield. At times, the fire of our small arms seemed to make but a feeble impression on our enemies; but, as soon as the two armies came close enough to make use of the steel, the French uniformly gave way.

Sir Thomas Graham, with the left wing of the allied army, attacked the right of the enemy, and, after a severe action, which lasted till near night, completely succeeded in cutting off the enemy's retreat, by the direct road into France. These operations were carried on at too great a distance from our position, for me to give you any other account of them than that the success attending them equalled the expectations of the most sanguine individual.

About four o'clock, the troops immediately in our front began to retire towards Vittoria. We pursued them for a considerable distance, but could never get near them, although we ran a great part of the way. We continued to advance till near eleven o'clock at night, when the 2d division went into bivouac, two leagues in front of Vittoria.

Our loss, in this great battle, has been severe—that of the enemy terrible. The killed, wounded, and prisoners of the enemy, it is said, amount to 15,000; 150 pieces of artillery; all their ammunition, money, baggage and provisions, fell into our hands. Joseph succeeded in carrying off two pieces of artillery from Vittoria, one only of which entered Pampeluna, the other was dismounted about four miles from where I now write, and which I passed to-day on my way here.

On the 22d we moved from our bivouac, and same night encamped in a wood near Salvatiera. Lord Wellington pushed rapidly forward, with the 3d, 4th, and light divisions, to Pampeluna, which he invested on the 25th. The 2d division, followed by the 6th and General Hamilton's

Portuguese, continued to advance on the 23d, 24th, 25th, 26th, and this day arrived here.

Sir Thomas Graham is gone in pursuit of the enemy, by the great road into France, with the 1st and 5th divisions of British, and some corps of Spanish troops.

The numerous trophies taken on the plains of Vittoria are the best proof that every man, from the General to the private, performed his duty on that glorious day. The eagle-eye of our great General was directed to every part of the extensive line—every trifling error, committed by the enemy was immediately taken advantage of. His own personal exertions, and those of the other General Officers, were nobly seconded by every regiment in the army.

The battle of Vittoria, whilst it reflects credit on the British General who commanded, and the troops who carried his orders into execution, proves, at the same time, that the French chief is a man totally unfit to command on such an occasion. His arrangements must have been radically bad :—On the most important of the heights of Puebla he had posted a few light troops only, when they ought to have been defended by a division at the least. The consequence of this gross error was, that they became an easy prey to our troops, and ensured us the victory.

CAMP, MAYA HEIGHTS, *July 9, 1813.*

As Sir Rowland Hill approached Pampeluna, the Marquis of Wellington gradually withdrew a portion of his army from before that fortress, with which, and General Mina's corps of Spaniards, he proceeded, on the 27th ultimo, to cut off the retreat of the French General Clausel, who, with a corps of 8000 men, having been too late to take part in the battle of the 21st, was endeavouring to effect his escape into the French territory, by a road to the eastward of Pampeluna. But the enemy having received intelligence of Lord Wellington's movement, retreated towards Sarragosa. On the 1st instant, the Marquis returned to the camp before Pampeluna, and left the pursuit of the enemy to the indefatigable Mina.

Sir Thomas Graham, with the left wing of the allied army, came up with a corps of the French army in the neighbourhood of Tolosa, which he attacked, and defeated with considerable loss. Soon after the enemy retired on the Bidassoa, across which they have since been driven by the gallant Graham, who has also invested the important fortress of San Sebastian.

When the French army, commanded by Joseph Bonaparte, arrived under the walls of Pampelun it was in the greatest distress for want of provisions.

Not having time to collect a sufficient supply from the country, necessity compelled their commander to order a portion of the provisions of the fortress to be issued to his half-starved followers. It is supposed that the French General has committed a most egregious error on this occasion; as it is confidently reported that he has not left the governor of that fortress provisions for a longer period than three months. We are all in hopes that the report may prove correct, as the place is so extremely strong that the chief engineer, (if report speaks truth), has expressed some doubts as to the practicability of taking it by a regular siege.

From Pampeluna, Joseph, with a portion of his army, retired into France, by the pass of Roncesvalles. The remainder, under General Gazan, retired by the valley of Bastan.

Lord Wellington having had some suspicion that the enemy intended to fortify the heights on which we are now encamped, gave orders to Sir Rowland Hill to march with the 1st, 2d, and 4th brigades of the second division, one brigade of General Hamilton's division of Portuguese, (at present commanded by the Conde D'Amarante), a few cavalry, and some pieces of artillery, and approach the enemy by the pass of Lanz; and to the Earl of Dalhousie, to march, with the 7th division, and menace the right of the enemy by a movement on San Estevan.

About seven o'clock on the morning of the

2d instant, Sir Rowland Hill's corps marched from their camp at Pampeluna, and in the afternoon encamped in a wood a little in front of the village of La Zarza. On the 3d, under a dreadful rain, we advanced to a barren heathy mountain, two miles in front of the town of Lanz. At an early hour on the 4th, we were aroused by the bugle's shrill sound, and in a few minutes marched in search of the foe. At noon, we came in sight of their advanced posts, after a long and fatiguing march through the dreary and romantic pass of Lanz.

The necessary dispositions having been made to attack the enemy, our brigade, under Colonel Cameron, and led by Lieutenant-General Stewart in person, marched from the defile in the mountains through the village of Almandos; then turning to the right, we filed by a narrow foot-path to a deep ravine, about 400 yards from the village. The ascent of the right bank of the ravine being very abrupt, and the whole face of it completely covered with loose round stones, we were every moment in danger of having our skulls fractured, by their rolling from beneath the feet of our friends above.

With considerable difficulty, we at length succeeded in gaining the top of the bank. The enemy made no attempt to arrest our progress, although 100 men would have been quite sufficient to have done so for a length of time.

As soon as Sir Rowland Hill perceived that we had established ourselves on the left of the enemy's chain of advanced posts, he gave orders to the other brigades to move through Almandos, and attack the enemy in front. Their picquets retired as we advanced—a few shots only being exchanged between them and our light troops in front.

The main body of the enemy's army was posted in rear of Barrueta; their left rested on a mountain on the left of the village, and their right extended to the river Bidassoa, the right bank of which they had occupied with a few light troops.

The enemy's picquets having retired behind Barrueta, the 50th regiment, from our brigade, was ordered to take possession of it. But the enemy not relishing this movement, brought down a strong body of infantry, and attacked them in the village. At the commencement of the skirmish, the left wing of the 92d regiment was sent to the assistance of their friends; but ere they arrived, an order had been received by the officer commanding the 50th, to evacuate the place, Sir Rowland being afraid that it might lead to a more serious affair than was intended. The Portuguese troops formed the left of our little corps, and, for some time, were rather sharply engaged with the enemy.—Having so far succeeded in our object, the troops were ordered into bivouac about sun-set.

The enemy continuing to occupy the same position on the morning of the 5th, preparations
were made to renew the attack. The arrival of
the Marquis of Wellington, about 11 o'clock,
served as a signal to get under arms. About
12, we began to ascend a tremendous mountain on
our right, in order to turn the enemy's left wing.
After an arduous march, we arrived on its summit a little before one, from which the poor fellows
were gratified with a view of the French territory, and of the ocean, not improperly styled by
them " The high road to England."

For some time, the enemy appeared determined
to check our farther progress ; but no sooner did
they perceive that we were descending the mountain in rear of their left, and that the other brigades
had made a spirited attack on their right and centre,
than the whole gave way, and retired in disorder
towards Elizonda.

From Barrueta, there was only one road by
which the enemy could retire to Elizonda. That
road being narrow, the corps of Gazan could not
retreat so rapidly, as the necessity of the case
required ; two or three of his battalions threw
themselves across the river Bidassoa, followed by
the troops of the Conde d'Amarante—numbers
fled into the corn-fields, and made their escape
in the best manner they could. The road was
literally choked up with the fugitives, many of
whom must have been cut off, as numerous par-

ties of light troops hung on their flanks during the whole of their retreat.

The French soldiers had scarcely quitted Eli-zonda, when the bells were rung by the inhabitants, in token of their joy. These good people, as we marched through their town, hailed us as the champions of liberty, and the liberators of Spain!—About one mile in front of that town, we went into bivouac.

The Marquis Wellington having reconnoitered the enemy's position on the 6th, made his arrangements for a vigorous attack on them next morning, in the only position which the enemy now held in this part of Spain. About ten o'clock in the morning of the 7th, the 2d brigade got orders to ascend a mountain on the right bank of the Bidassoa, across which runs a foot-path from Elizonda to our present encampment. By this road, the brigade was to approach the right of the enemy, posted on the summit of a very high rugged mountain, called the Rock of Maya. This post, after a short resistance, they made themselves masters of.

The better to deceive the enemy with regard to our real intention, the other brigades got orders not to move, till the success of the second brigade was certain. The French General, ashamed of himself, for having so tamely given up a post which he ought to have defended with his whole force, formed his troops into two columns, and made several attempts to wrest it out of our hands. In all his desperate efforts he was repulsed with loss. Once established in a post like this, the British soldier knows how to defend it. He knows what his country expects of him, before it is again surrendered into the hands of his enemies. Well did the soldiers of the second brigade know their duty, and nobly did they perform it! Between one and two o'clock, the other brigades moved from their respective encampments, and advanced by the high-road through the town of Maya, to that part of the position on which the left and centre of the enemy were posted. Our light troops were sent to occupy a small height on the right of the road, and the 50th regiment a height on the left of it, and opposite to the enemy's right centre. The 6th Portuguese caçadores moved along the face of the rock, to keep open the communication between the 50th and the troops on the summit of the mountains. These various movements brought on a very severe skirmish. The enemy made a furious attack on the 50th, which that regiment sustained in a gallant manner. The 92d regiment was sent to their relief, but arrived just in time to witness the retreat of their foes, from before the weapons of their brave comrades.

Along the whole extent of the line, the light troops of both armies were engaged, till the night was so dark, that neither party could distinguish friend from foe. Thus situated, the firing ceased by the mutual consent of parties; for, the moment that the enemy's bugle called in their skirmishers, ours were also ordered to retire. The fog was so thick, and the night so dark, that some of the enemy themselves, when ordered in, did not know which way to turn themselves, to gain their own lines. Two of them past to the rear of our picquets, and were made prisoners.

At day-light on the 8th, the enemy made another unsuccessful effort to get possession of the rock; after which, a loose irregular firing was kept up for some time between our troops on the rock, and the enemy, who at length retired into France, being fully convinced, that without an increase of their numbers, they could not make themselves masters of the rock: They were followed by the Portuguese brigade of Colonel Ashworth, who skirmished with them till late last night. The 7th division moved by the town of San Estevan, and had arrived within a short distance of us, when the enemy retired.

From these heights we have a fine view of Bayonne, St Jean de Luz, and various other places of minor importance.

We are all most anxious to get into France. Although it has rained here, the whole of this morning, the sun has never been obscured.

It has often been alleged that seamen are impressed with very ridiculous superstitions; that the army is not exempt from that weakness, the following will serve as an instance. On the evening of the 7th instant, the enemy made an effort to obtain possession of the height on which the 50th was posted, but were repelled by the gallantry of that corps. One of the wounded passing close to where I was standing, exclaimed, to some questions I put regarding his wound, " I know that I am a dead " man—I have been wounded by a poisoned " ball." It is needless for me to observe, that no assertion was ever more destitute of truth; although an idea prevailed among the private soldiers that the French were guilty of such a practice.

In the attack on the enemy's position on the 7th instant, our light troops were joined by three Spanish peasants, who, eager to revenge their own and their country's wrongs, advanced into the heat of the conflict, and fought with great gallantry, till one of them was killed and another wounded, with whom the third retired to Maya, the place of their abode.

I could not but admire the coolness of a young lad of the name of M'Ewen, in the action of the 7th. Whilst the regiment was standing in close column in rear of the 50th, a musket ball grazed his bonnet. Instead of being put about by this circumstance, he very

coolly, and smiling, said, " O ye coaxing ras-
" cal !"

Lieutenant Masterman, of the 34th regiment,
was killed by lightning, while on the march, on the
24th June. I was about two hundred yards in
rear of him when the accident occurred. On
passing him, he was so dreadfully disfigured, that
I could not recognise a single feature. His clothes
and sword-belt were literally torn to pieces.

Adieu.

CAMP, MAYA HEIGHTS, August 4, 1813.

MARSHAL SOULT arrived at the head-quarters of
the French army about the middle of last month,
and immediately assumed the command. On
hearing of his arrival, we expected that something
decisive would be performed, and that ere long, as
being pretty certain that his first object would be
to attempt to wipe away the stain brought on the
arms of his master by the misconduct of his predecessors. Our opinions respecting the Marshal's
intentions were just. On the 23d July he issued
a proclamation to his army, in which he attributed the loss of the battle of Vittoria, and all
the other losses and reverses which the French
army had sustained in this campaign, to the in-

capacity of those who commanded it. The orders he issued to them were to drive the British beyond the Ebro. How faithfully these orders were per-formed, will be seen in the sequel.

On taking possession of Maya heights, the defence of the pass was entrusted to the first brigade, commanded by Colonel Cameron. The 71st and 92d regiments were encamped on the summit of the ridge, over which runs the road from the valley of Bastan to France. The 92d was posted about 200 yards to the left of the road, and the 71st about 300 yards to the left of the 92d.— The 50th was detached about three-quarters of a mile to the right of the 92d regiment, and was encamped a little under the ridge, on the Spanish side. Three Portuguese guns occupied the space between the road and the 92d regiment.

The 2d brigade was encamped in the valley, one mile from the 50th, having the 34th regiment advanced towards the right of the position, on which that brigade had a strong picquet, and which, in case of an attack, it had orders to defend. This post was about a mile and a half from the pass of Maya. Colonel Ashworth's Portuguese brigade occupied the village of Erraza, and the troops of the Conde de Amarante, a position in the mountain in front of the village. The 82d regiment, from the brigade of Major-General Barnes, in the 7th division, was encamped about

two miles from the left of the 71st regiment.
Such was the disposition of the troops entrusted
with the defence of Maya heights, on the morning of the 25th July.

About ten o'clock in the morning of that day,
the enemy were perceived moving a body of
troops towards our right flank, by a mountain
path which leads from the French village of Espallate, across the ridge to the Spanish village of
Maya. At first, from the smallness of their force,
they were taken for a reconnoitring party, but
towards eleven their numbers appeared to increase rapidly; and about half-past eleven they
filed in columns from behind the mountain, and
attacked the picquets of the second brigade.

At this interesting moment, an unusual sen-
sation pervaded the breast of every soldier. Our
position, to be sure, was strong, but the force appointed to defend it was by no means adequate.
Our soldiers were brave, hardy—every thing but
invincible; our superior officers were brave and
intelligent, worthy in every respect of commanding such troops. The soldiers had unbounded
confidence in their officers, and the officers in
them. Nothing was wanting but a few more
men of the same description to ensure the
most brilliant success—but none were at hand,
and the enemy was at the door, from which it
was our duty to force him, or die in the attempt.

No sooner was it known that the enemy were in motion, than the light companies of the 2d brigade got orders to march to the support of the picquets on the right. The 34th regiment was moved up to the height for the same purpose. The 28th and 39th regiments were ordered to follow the 34th; and the 50th, and right wing of the 92d regiment, were sent from the first brigade to the support of the whole.

The picquets and light companies of the 2d brigade sustained the first onset of the enemy with great gallantry; but their efforts in defence of the post were rendered unavailing, from the overwhelming numbers which the enemy brought against them. The 34th was the first regiment that got up to their assistance, and which, in an attempt to arrest the torrent, was nearly cut off. The 50th having arrived on the heights, that regiment, in conjunction with the 34th, charged the enemy, and gave a temporary check to their career.

The enemy, availing himself of his great numerical superiority, charged these two battalions in front, and at the same time sent large bodies of infantry round their flanks, to surround them. At this crisis the right wing of the 92d regiment was brought into action, and in a few minutes began one of the most severe actions recorded in modern history, if the numbers engaged are taken into the account.

3

From the camp the 92d regiment had moved along the ridge in open column of companies, right in front, but when close to the enemy, the rear companies moved quickly to the front and formed on the grenadiers. Scarcely had the Highlanders formed line when their Colonel ordered them to prepare to charge. On perceiving their intentions, the enemy halted, which gave the 34th and 50th time to form anew.

The right wing of the 92d regiment had now for some time to sustain the brunt of the conflict. Their numbers did not exceed 370 men, whilst that of their enemies could not be fewer than 3000 veterans. Colonel Cameron, on seeing the enemy halt, withdrew his little band about 30 paces, in order to draw them forward, that he might have an opportunity of charging them. They greedily swallowed the bait—they advanced ; but as soon as the 92d halted, the enemy did the same. The French now opened a terrible fire of musketry on the Highlanders, which they returned with admirable effect. For a quarter of an hour the French officers used every means in their power to induce their men to charge us, but their utmost efforts were unavailing. Not one of them could they prevail on to advance in front of their line of slain, which in a few minutes not only covered the field, but in many places lay piled in heaps.

The Highlanders continued to resist the attacks of their numerous and enraged assailants, till their numbers were reduced to 120, and all their officers wounded and borne from the field, except two young lieutenants. The senior of these two, seeing no support at hand, and finding that the ammunition of those with him was nearly expended, conceived that a retreat was the most advisable measure he could adopt. With this handful of men he retired from the bloody field, on which he left 33, that had been killed or mortally wounded during the action. The 50th, and shattered remains of the 92d right wing, retired towards the pass of Maya, where the left wings of the 92d and 71st regiments were posted. The 28th regiment, under Colonel Belson, attacked the advance of the French column, which had so long been opposed by the 92d. The right wing of the 71st was brought forward to the assistance of the 28th, and the 34th and 39th were engaged with the enemy more to the right. The whole of the British troops retired towards the rock of Maya, in hopes of being succoured by the 7th division. The enemy advancing rapidly on us, Lieutenant-General the Honourable William Stewart formed the regiments of the 1st brigade at the pass, and, with the left wings of the 71st and 92d regiments, waited for the enemy. The rest of the troops retiring to take up a position, in order to be ready to repel the assailants the moment that the others retired. For a mile and a half we retired in this manner, the one half of the troops always taking up the ground a little in rear of the others, which being done, those in front instantly retired, and so on, each half retiring alternately till we arrived on a height, rather to the rear of the rock, and on which the 82d regiment had been encamped for some days before. A party of 150 men from the brigade was sent to the summit of the rock, under Captain Campbell, 92d regiment, who poured down a terrible shower of shot on the heads of their assailants. Neither was the party very sparing of the large stones with which the face of the mountain abounds; they rolled them down on the attacking columns, and many of them, I have been informed, took effect.

The 28th, 34th, and 39th regiments having retired by a road to our right, rendered us little service after we retreated from the pass; our force was, therefore, about half-past six, reduced to little more than 2000 men, including the 82d regiment. With faint hopes of receiving help, we continued to dispute every inch of ground with the enemy, till seven, when none having arrived, and as our own numbers were rapidly decreasing, General Stewart gave orders for the whole to retire. But just as the order was about to be carried into effect, General Barnes, with the other regiments of his brigade, arrived to our assistance, when the enemy, although still four to one, retreated as fast as their feet could carry them, hotly pursued by every man in our little corps. Having forced them to retire fully three quarters of a mile, we formed line, and laid ourselves down to rest our wearied limbs. But much of that we could not expect under such circumstances ; about ten o'clock the same evening, we retired from the rock of Maya, and next morning, at seven o'clock, bivouacked in the vicinity of Barrueta. We were there informed, that Marshal Soult had attacked our troops at Roncesvalles, at day-light on the 25th, and had forced them to retire in the direction of Pampeluna. On the 26th, Sir Lowry Cole retired before his powerful antagonist ; and on the 27th, took up a position at the village of Huarte, a little way in front of Pampeluna.

The enemy made no movement in front of Maya on the 26th instant. About two o'clock on the 27th, they began to show themselves in advance of Elizonda, and made some little demonstrations as if they meant to attack us ; but our presence being required in another part of the country, we declined the honour they intended us, and commenced our retreat about five o'clock towards the pass of Lanz.

The 6th, 7th, and light divisions having ascended that mountain before us, we were considerably obstructed on our march across the pass by the baggage of those divisions, which the narrow and broken state of the roads had prevented from getting to the rear so quickly as the occasion required. The night was so extremely dark, that Sir Rowland Hill found it necessary to order a halt at the top of the mountain, least some of us should take a final leave of the division, by tumbling down a tremendous precipice on the right of the road.

At day-light on the 28th, we continued our route towards Pampeluna; passed through the village of Lanz about ten in the forenoon, and arrived at La Zarza about one, where we went into bivouac. Our soup was scarcely ready, when the cry was heard, " to arms." In a few minutes, we were again on our march towards Pampeluna, a few miles in front of which, the two armies were arrayed in order of battle, and at that moment busily employed in the work of mutual destruction.

In hopes of forcing his way to Pampeluna, before the allied army could be concentrated in front of that fortress, Marshal Soult attacked the 3d and 4th divisions at Huarte on the morning of the 28th. Those divisions, assisted by some Spanish troops, and one brigade of the Conde de Amarante's Portuguese, repelled the furious onset of

the enemy with great gallantry. By the numerous attacks of Soult, the numbers of these
corps were rapidly diminishing, and the enemy
had succeeded in getting to the rear of the left
of the 4th division, when the 6th division arrived at the scene of action. The light troops of
this corps were ordered to attack the enemy's
right flank. This unexpected attack made him
retreat, and abandon his march to Pampeluna. Not
satisfied, however, with the blood that had been
spilled, the French Marshal repeatedly attacked
our troops, after every hope of gaining a passage
to Pampeluna had vanished—but in every attempt
to penetrate the allied line, he was unsuccessful;
and was finally driven from the various heights,
with terrible slaughter.

In the evening of the 28th, we took up our
ground on the slope of a steep hill, about four
miles from Pampeluna, and formed the left of the
allied army, concentrated there for the purpose of
frustrating the plans of the Duke of Dalmatia.

In the morning of the 29th, Marshal Soult ordered the greater part of his artillery and cavalry
into France, fully convinced, from what had taken
place on the preceding day, that, by renewing the
assault on the heights of Huarte, he would ex-
pose his army to certain ruin.

Both armies remained very quiet on the 29th;

our brigade advanced about a mile, to a small height, a little to the right of the road from Pampeluna to La Zarza.

Every preparation having been made by the Marquis of Wellington to commence offensive operations against the enemy, the right and centre of the allied army attacked the left and centre of the enemy at day-light on the 30th, and, after a severe conflict of six hours, completely defeated him, with great loss. Soult's only object, after this fatal engagement, was to secure a safe retreat across the frontier. His right wing, under Drouet, was strongly reinforced, in order to drive Sir Rowland Hill from his position behind the village of La Zarza, the possession of which being an object of the very first importance to the French army.

About ten o'clock, the enemy filed about 20,000 men to their right, in order to outflank Sir Rowland's corps, and by penetrating to the rear of his left, compel him to retire, and allow them an open passage into their own country.

The troops which Sir Rowland Hill had under him on that occasion, could not possibly exceed 8000 or 10,000 men. With them he prepared to repel the attacks of the enemy, who, at eleven, advanced towards the heights to begin the conflict.

The 1st brigade was moved up to the summit

of the hill, on the left of the road leading to La Zarza, and as the enemy extended his right, that brigade made a corresponding movement on the ridge. The 2d brigade was ordered to support the 1st, and the Portuguese troops occupied the heights on the right of the road.

The enemy's light troops having arrived within a short distance of our right flank, the 71st regiment was ordered to extend, and skirmish with them. The 50th was left to guard a particular part of the mountain, and the 92d regiment was moved along the ridge, to meet a body of the 'enemy's troops, which had ascended at a distant part of the mountain. The 8th and light companies of the 92d regiment formed a guard to Sir Rowland Hill, who took his station on a height to the left of the road.

The 92d having been formed into two wings, the one in advance was assailed by a French grenadier battalion, who, with drums beating, and cries of " Vive l'Empereur," advanced against the little band. But when the enemy was not more than 30 paces from the Highlanders, the 34th, about 200 strong, arrived to their assistance. These two little corps now charged the enemy, and drove them before them with terrible slaughter.

The enemy, knowing the value of the prize for which he was fighting, renewed his attacks, during two hours, and every time with increased fury, in all of which he was beat back with loss. But the enemy having received such an addition to his original force, as enabled him to outflank us on the left, and we having no reinforcements at hand, orders were sent us to retire to a rugged ridge in our rear, where we might bid defiance to the utmost efforts of our foes.

The second brigade retired by the left of the Portuguese troops, who had also been furiously assailed by the enemy, and compelled to retire, fighting, to the summit of a height, two miles in rear of their original position. But having been reinforced by a brigade of their countrymen, under Brigadier-General Campbell, they became the assailants in turn, and drove the enemy down the hill at the point of the bayonet. This closed the battle. Some loose firing was kept up till dark ; when both armies, being alike in want of repose, consented to a suspension of hostilities for the night. The loss of the enemy on that day was very great—ours was also considerable.

At day-light on the 31st, the enemy began to retire from before us, directing their march towards the pass, called Donna Maria. About seven o'clock, the division moved from their bivouac, and, with a rapid pace, pursued the fugitives. At 11, we came up with about 9000 of them, which we instantly attacked. Having one nine pounder, and one howitzer, with us, these were brought forward, and, at the distance of 300 yards, opened on the enemy, as they retired by three separate roads to the summit of the mountain. These roads being extremely crowded, our guns caused the enemy considerable loss. The 50th regiment got orders to move on the left of the road, and attack the enemy's right flank. The 71st were to skirmish with them along the face of the hill, and the 92d was ordered to advance by the highroad, and attack them in front. These troops were to be supported by the 2d and 4th brigades. The 7th division, under Lord Dalhousie, moved towards the enemy's left flank, by a road that runs parallel to the one by which we advanced. Some of our division having taken the Brunswick for French troops, commenced a spirited fire on them ; but the error having soon been discovered, their united fire was directed against the enemy.

The enemy's light troops were quickly driven in on their main body, posted on the very summit of the mountain. As we ascended, they poured on us one of the heaviest showers of shot I ever witnessed ; under which, we made an attempt to wrest the height from them, but were forced to retire with considerable loss. Again we advanced, and again retired.

The 2d brigade having arrived to our assistance, charged the enemy, in conjunction with the shattered remains of the 1st brigade, and, after a terrible struggle, succeeded in driving them from their strong-hold with dreadful carnage. The enemy having been driven from the pass of Donna Maria, the troops of the 2d division descended, and bivouacked at the foot of the hill, leaving the pursuit of the enemy to the 7th division.— Towards the conclusion of the affair, a musket-ball grazed my head; but I am happy to say has done me no material injury. I hope to be quite well in a few days.

On the first of August we once more crossed the pass of Lanz, and that night encamped about three miles in front of Elizonda. A terrible thunder-storm came on a very short time after we took up our ground. The flashes of lightning were so vivid, and followed each other in such rapid succession, that the whole firmament appeared in one continued blaze. The peals of thunder were much louder than any that I had heard before; and the rain, which fell during the whole time, made such a noise on the canvas roof of my house, that I never closed my eyes.

On the following morning, the first brigade marched into Errazu, and yesterday afternoon again arrived on these heights.

Sir Thomas Graham, on hearing of Soult's advance, withdrew the battering train from before

M

San Sebastian, and sent it on board ship, that he might be ready to move to any part where his services might be required.

On the 2d instant, the allied army resumed possession of every post which it held on the morning of the 25th July.

In order to give you some idea of the fighting we had during the last week of July, I have annexed a list of the casualties in the company I commanded on that occasion.—July 25. Killed, 11; wounded, 35.—July 30. Killed, 5; wounded, 7.—July 31. Wounded, 9.—Total, 16 killed, and 51 wounded.—Take 67 from 82, and there will remain a balance of 15 only. *

Adieu.

* Ten of those returned wounded, died either on their way to, or in the General Hospital.

CAMP, HEIGHTS OF RONCESVALLES, *August* 27, 1813.

EARLY on the 9th instant, the second division quitted Maya, and the same evening bivouacked within the French territory, at Los Alduides. On the following forenoon, we marched to the heights we now occupy, then strewed with the mangled corpses of friends and foes.

Ever since our arrival here, the engineers have been busily employed constructing redoubts, block-houses, and raising breast-works on various parts of the position. Marshal Soult will find us better prepared for his reception the next time he does us the honour of a visit.—As yet, however, he has made no preparations for a journey hither.

The powerful effect of our national music on the minds of the soldiers, was never more conspicuously displayed, than towards the conclusion of the terrible battle of the 25th July. About six o'clock in the evening, the 92d regiment was ordered to take possession of a small height, a little to the left of the rock, whither the enemy bent his course. The piper-major of that regiment viewed the advance of the French with considerable emotion; and conceiving that his countrymen wanted something to stimulate them to deeds of noble daring, he made the hills and valleys ring to the " Gathering of the Camerons." The effect was instantaneous—every Highlander was on his legs in a

M 2

moment; and, with their eyes sparkling fire, only waited for the order to advance. Lieutenant-General Stewart, who was at that time in rear of the regiment, warned the men of the fatal consequences that might follow a movement in advance at that time, and desired the piper not to play again till ordered. But the piper, fancying the danger more imminent than it really was, again favoured his friends with one of his favourite airs, which produced the same effect. The General now forbade him, at the hazard of his life, to play till he was ordered.—Soon after, Major-General Barnes's brigade arrived to the assistance of our corps. As they advanced to the 92d, the piper greeted his friends with the " Haughs of Crom-" dale," in his best style. At the sound of that well-known Scottish air, which recalled to their memory the deeds of their ancestors, the Highlanders rose, and, without waiting for orders, rushed on their numerous foes with the most undaunted courage, who, panic-struck at their audacity, wheeled about, and ran, pursued by the whole corps.

About five o'clock on the same evening, private John Brooks was hit on the throat by a musket-ball, which his leather-stock turned, without doing him any apparent injury. But in a few days, the part was so much inflamed, that he could neither eat nor drink without great pain; and any words he spoke were

3

almost unintelligible. On the morning of the
30th, he was ordered to the rear; but an action
appearing unavoidable, he positively refused.—
With the company he marched into action, performed his duty with the same spirit as on every
former occasion—but, singular to relate, about
the middle of the battle, another ball struck him
on the identical spot that the former one had
done, penetrated his throat, and killed him on
the spot!

Another private soldier, named William Bisket,
had his thigh perforated by a musket-ball during
the dreadful struggle on the right of our position
on the morning of the 25th July. With his musket in his hand, he quitted the field, the blood
flowing from the wound as he passed to the
rear. He had proceeded about 200 yards, when,
turning round, he beheld his companions supporting the conflict with undiminished ardour.
At the sight, his bosom was fired with fresh courage. He returned to the gory field, to assist his
handful of friends against the numerous legions
of their enemies. Being asked, what motive induced him to rejoin his company? He replied—
" To have another shot at the rascals, Sir, before
" I leave you." The gallant soldier fired once,
and was in the act of presenting his piece a second time, when another ball penetrated his arm
above the elbow, shattered the bone, and com-

pelled the hero to retire from the field of honour, regretted by his admiring countrymen.

In the early part of the action of the 25th July, private William Dougald, of the same company, was also hit on the right thigh, by three spent balls, in the course of five minutes; and although all of them were severe in their kind, the poor fellow never quitted the field. An action appearing inevitable on the 30th, and Dougald being so lame as scarce able to walk, he was desired to go to the rear;—" No," said he; " I will rather die " than leave my comrades !" I shall never forget the exertions he made to keep up with the company. He marched—he fought—and, in 15 minutes, the gallant soldier was stretched lifeless on the ground, by one of the enemy's riflemen.

My servant, H—— J——, was ordered, on the morning of the 30th, with some others of the regiment, to proceed to the baggage, and wait the result of the impending battle. They all quitted the regiment about half an hour before the action began; but before it was half finished, who did I see carried to the rear, but poor J——, who had received a desperate wound in the left groin. The force of circumstances having compelled us soon after to abandon that position to the enemy, J—— also fell into their hands. During our advance in pursuit of the foe next morning, I obtained permission from the commanding officer, to send a party of four, to carry him, if alive, into the village of La Zarza. The party found him alive—they offered him something to drink—he accepted of it ;—then, raising himself, he said, " Oh! I would like to see him." His speech then failed him ; he laid back his head on the breast of one of his comrades, and, with a gentle smile on his countenance, took leave of this world ! Such was the fate of as good a man, and brave soldier, as ever graced the ranks of the British army.

In the action between the right wing of the 92d and the enemy, on the 25th July, a French officer of rank rendered himself conspicuous, by various gallant attempts to get his men to charge that little band. The Highlanders, perceiving that their enemies were kept at their posts by the exertions of that officer alone, immediately decreed his death. Numerous ineffectual attempts were made to shoot him. At length, a private soldier, named Archibald Maclean, stepped a few paces in front of his company, and, in a kneeling position, took the fatal aim, which brought the hero low.

To have shot that officer, under any other circumstances than those in which the right wing of the 92d were placed, would, by that gallant corps, have been considered deliberate cruelty ; but when the numbers of the hostile armies on this occasion are kept in view, every impartial man must

admit, (however much he may be inclined to esteem his bravery, and lament his fate), that the
death of the French officer was indispensably
necessary to ensure the safety of the Caledonian
phalanx.

CAMP, HEIGHTS, RONCESVALLES, *October* 1, 1813.

SIR THOMAS GRAHAM having re-landed his battering cannon, re-invested San Sebastian, in the
beginning of August, and prosecuted the siege
with vigour, till the 31st, when, a breach appearing practicable, he ordered the place to be stormed, the same day, about noon.

After a long and murderous conflict, our brave
fellows succeeded in getting possession of the
town; the Governor, retiring into the castle, with
the garrison, defended it with great bravery till
the 9th instant, when the place appearing no
longer tenable, he surrendered at discretion.

On the same day, Marshal Soult advanced
to the relief of San Sebastian, with a part of his
army, amounting to 30,000 men. Crossing the
Bidassoa, he attacked the Spanish troops under
General Giron, and, for some time, drove them
before him. But the whole of the Spanish infantry, in that part of the position, having unit-

ed, and the 4th British division having advanced
to their support, they became the assailants in
their turn ; and, in a short time, and in fine style,
compelled the Marshal to re-cross the Bidassoa,
with the loss of 4000 or 5000 of his followers.
Officers of experience, who were present on
that occasion, declare, that they never saw any
troops conduct themselves with greater gallantry
than the Spaniards did in that battle.

No movement, of any consequence, has taken
place in this part of the position, since I wrote
you. The cannon on the ramparts of Pampeluna have, this moment, informed us that hostilities, in that quarter, still continue. Since the
beginning of July it has been blockaded by a
Spanish force of 15,000 men, under the Conde del
Abisbal. We still continue to strengthen our present position with fresh works of various kinds.—
Redoubts and block-houses crown almost every
height in our possession. On the extreme right
we have a very neat redoubt, not quite finished,
in front of which there is a block-house, where
a part of the inlying picquet is generally sent on
any alarm being given. On the left, there is also
a redoubt, completely finished, and tolerably
strong. On a ridge to the right, and considerably in advance of the redoubt, there is another
block-house, into which a captain's picquet, (always
on duty there), is to throw itself in case of attack. On the ridge of the centre height, there is

another redoubt, and, a little in rear of it, a block-
house :—parties are, at all times, kept in readiness
to move into these places when their services may
be required.—Besides these, there are numerous
breast-works thrown up all along the face of this
extensive range of hills. In short, the Duke of
Dalmatia would find it no easy matter to get to
Pampeluna by this road, should he make the
attempt.

Scarcely a day passes in which the Portuguese
troops, stationed at Los Alduides, have not a
brush, of some kind or other, with those of the
enemy in their front.

Lieutenant-General the Honourable William
Stewart, who has commanded the 2d division
since last May, possesses, in a striking manner,
the esteem and confidence of the soldiers. Having been wounded in the leg, on the 25th July,
he was compelled to leave the division for
a few days. A few minutes after the division
had been put in motion, on the morning of the
31st July, the General made his appearance on
horseback, in rear of the column, with his leg
bandaged, and a pillow fastened between it and
the horse's side. No sooner was he observed a-
mongst us, than one and all testified their joy on
the occasion, by loud and long repeated cheers.
In the action that took place, the same day,
General Stewart was again severely wounded in
the arm. On his return to the division, the other

day, he was repeatedly cheered by every regiment
as he passed their respective encampments. As
he approached the encampment of the 92d Highlanders, he was met by some men of that corps,
who, having procured a little good wine, thought
they could not possibly show a greater mark of
their respect for the General than by presenting
him with a glass of it. Having first testified their joy by three cheers, one of the number
stepped forward and said, " Oh General, ye maun
" drink wi' us !" With considerable emotion, the
General replied, " With all my heart, my man."
Then taking the glass in his hand, and having expressed himself gratified by their attention, and
happy to find them in such health and spirits, he
tasted the wine, and rode towards the encampment. In front of the tents, the men were drawn
up, of their own accord, and received their General with loud acclamations of joy, throwing their
bonnets into the air, as high as they could.

A General Court-Martial was lately assembled
at Roncesvalles, for the trial of a private soldier,
of this division, for deserting to the enemy. The
Court having found him guilty, sentenced him
to suffer death. The punishment was ordered
to be carried into effect a few days ago, at the
head of the regiment to which he belonged, and
as many more of the troops as could convenient-
ly attend. The inlying picquet of our brigade
having been ordered to attend, I, as being the

officer on duty, was compelled to witness the awful ceremony. The troops being formed, the
criminal, attended by Mr Frith, the chaplain to
this division, was brought to the place of execution. The rain was then falling copiously, under
which the clergyman and the criminal kneeled
down, on a spot several inches deep with mud
and water. They had prayed some time, when
an Aide-de-Camp touched the poor fellow on the
shoulder, and desired him to rise. The tears,
which at that time stood in his eyes, were wiped
away, no doubt supposing that mercy had been
extended to him ;—his countenance brightened,
and his eyes, before dim, now sparkled with joy.—
But alas, it was a dream! He was only raised to have
the proceedings and sentence of the Court-Martial read to him,—which having been done, he
again kneeled down, and, in a few minutes, finished his religious duties. The cap being
drawn over his face, and the party having taken
post, a few paces in front of the culprit, the
Provost-Marshal gave the fatal signal, and, in a
moment, he fell, pierced by many balls. The
soldiers were afterwards marched past the corpse,
in slow time. One of them, in passing, disgust-
ingly remarked :—" I think that fellow has got an
" extra allowance of grog this morning."

RONCESVALLES, *November 2, 1813.*

PAMPELUNA was surrendered to Don Carlos de Espagna on the 31st ultimo. The garrison, amounting to 4000 men, of all ranks, are to be prisoners of war. The fall of that important fortress has put us in possession of one of the strongest places in Europe—Gibralter excepted;—it has given a final blow to the power of the French army in Spain, and an accession of strength to the allied army of 15,000 men.

On the 7th October, the left of the allied army crossed the Bidassoa, and drove the French from a strong position which they occupied on the right bank of that river.—Since that period the British standard has waved in triumph over the fields of France.

Every preparation is making to attack the enemy in his strong fortified position, on the frontier; but when, or in what manner the attack will be made, is known only to the General in Chief.

The celebrated guerilla chief, Mina, is in this village at present ; his corps, amounting to a good many thousands, are in bivouac a little behind it. He is a very plain man, and possesses an openness of countenance peculiarly prepossessing ;— he appears to be about five feet seven or eight inches in height, and from 35 to 40 years of age. He is a strict disciplinarian.—His troops are very well drilled, and appear to pay all the attention to their superiors that is required from private soldiers. A few days ago, I saw some of his battalions go through their various evolutions with great accuracy. Mina, before the present war, was a farmer, and rented a small farm in the vicinity of Pampeluna. He is much liked by the people in this part of the country, who always take the liberty of telling you that he is the bravest man in the world.

There was a prodigious fall of snow here on the 28th October. In the valley where we were encamped, it lay eighteen inches deep; and, on the mountains, where drifted, it was fully twelve feet. One of our picquets, on the right of the position, was almost lost;—several of the men were dug out of the snow, some of whom have lost the use of their legs. In the night, the weight of the snow broke my tent-pole in two, by which accident I had nearly been suffocated:—with considerable difficulty, I got myself extricated from beneath the load, about four o'clock in the morning; but where to go I knew not. I groped about for some time without being able to find a place of shelter. At length, however, I poked my foot on the lower part of a tent, which, after some conversation with its inhabitants, I entered, and remained till day-light. The following evening we were ordered into the village of Roncesvalles.

All kinds of provisions are dear in this place;—
potatoes are to be had in abundance, at from three-
pence to sixpence the pound weight.—When our
brigade was encamped on the heights, on the right
of the position, small fish were often brought to
us, from the French side of the mountain, for
which we paid three shillings the pound, of twelve
ounces;—wine is plentiful, and reasonable.

The French General Foy sent in a flag of
truce, the other day, to the officer commanding
on the right, to request the loan of an English
newspaper containing the dispatches of Lord Wellington, detailing the operations of the allied army
on the glorious 21st of June. No account of that
memorable engagement has yet been published in France—nor of the more recent battles on
the Pyrenees, excepting the transient success of
the French Marshal on the 25th July. In return
for the newspapers which we sent him, Foy begged
our acceptance of some Paris Moniteurs. This
little interchange of civilities will tend to show
you that it is the wish of both parties to lessen the
horrors of war, without infringing on the military
duties which each owe to their respective countries.

We have a very fine race-course here, and, now
and then, tolerable races. Sir Rowland Hill
having a pack of hounds with him, those who are
fond of following them have an opportunity afforded them of doing so two or three times in

the week ;—and those who are fond of the amusement afforded by a bull-fight, may have enough
of it every Thursday afternoon, in the village of
Burgueta, about a mile hence.

In this village there is a very neat inn ;—
sometimes we get a snug little dinner, and not a
bad bottle of country wine. Since the arrival
of Mina's guerillas in our neighbourhood, we
are under the necessity, as often as we dine
there, of sending two or three stout fellows
to stand sentry over the dinner, till such time
as it is removed from the fire to be placed
before us.

FRANCE, CAMBO, BANKS OF THE NIVE, *Nov.* 17, 1813.

A LITTLE before day light in the morning of
the 6th November, a picquet of Spanish troops,
part of General Mina's corps, was attacked by a
superior body of French infantry in front of Roncesvalles ; the greater number of both parties were
either killed or wounded. The night was extremely dark, and although the enemy had the
best of it, the advantage was purchased at a high
price.

Early in the morning of the 6th instant, the

2d, 3d, and 4th brigades of this division marched from Roncesvalles for the pass of Maya, preparatory to the general attack meditated on the enemy's position in front of that place.

About one o'clock on the 7th, the enemy having moved a considerable body of troops towards the right and centre of our position, attacked a picquet of the 92d, stationed in a block-house in rear of the centre redoubt. On the first alarm, General Walker called out the 1st brigade and marched it towards the scene of action, and General Mina, with a wing of one of his battalions, ascended the mountain to the relief of the Highlanders. The enemy skirmished with the picquet for some time, but perceiving the preparations making to attack them, they retired before the other troops got up. The picquet had one man wounded.

At four o'clock in the afternoon of the 8th instant, the first brigade left Roncesvalles, and about midnight occupied the village of Los Alduides. At seven o'clock on the morning of the 9th, we marched from Alduides, and arrived at the encampment of the other brigades, near Maya, about four in the afternoon. During the whole of the afternoon troops were moving to the front in every direction. About nine in the evening the first brigade left its bivouac near Maya, and marched across the mountain, where many of our bravest soldiers had fallen on the 25th July. About half past six in the morning of the 10th, when crossing the Nivelle, near to Urdax, the thunder of our artillery on the left announced to us the commencement of the battle.

In a field on the left bank of the river, we joined the other brigades of the division, when beginning to move off to the attack of the enemy's position. As our brigade had been marching for nearly two days, the men were very much fatigued. Sir Rowland, aware of this, sent an order for the men to pile arms and sit down, but to be ready to fall in at a moment's notice.

General Morillo having been sent to cover the advance of the 2d division to the attack of the heights behind Anhoe, our brigade was ordered to support that officer in his operations.

The enemy's position was extremely strong, the left rested on a height in rear, and to the left of Anhoe; thence extended along a ridge of hills which runs across the country in front of the towns of St Pe and St Jean de Luz. On their left the enemy had two redoubts, which they occupied in considerable force. On the ridge behind Anhoe, they had three very strong redoubts, in which were ship guns, 24 and 32 pounders. Towards their left centre they had every little eminence crowned with a field-work of some kind or other, whence to the left the face of the hill was covered by numerous breast-works. Their right was extremely strong. The centre was by far the weakest part of their position; against it, and the right and left centre, the united efforts of the 3d, 4th, 6th, 7th, and light divisions were directed. The 2d division, Sir John Hamilton's division of Portuguese, and Morillo's Spaniards, advanced against the redoubts in rear of the village of Anhoe.

Before nine o'clock the battle had assumed a very serious aspect in the centre. There the enemy's works were attacked and carried at the point of the bayonet;—in one of their redoubts, upwards of 600 men were made prisoners. The operations, in that quarter, having been brought to a successful termination, the 6th division, British, and Sir John Hamilton's Portuguese, were ordered to take the enemy in flank, in their position behind Anhoe, whilst Sir William Stewart, with the 2d division, attacked them in front. The other divisions were to establish themselves in rear of the enemy's right, at the village of St Pe. In the whole of their operations these divisions were warmly opposed, but, by the bravery and perseverance of the troops, their General surmounted every obstacle, and finally succeeded in driving the enemy from the village, and heights in rear of it.

The heights and redoubts behind Anhoe were carried in the handsomest manner, by the troops under Generals Stewart, Clinton, and Hamilton, who, on taking possession of the last redoubt, turned the guns of the place on the fugitives.

During these operations, a detachment of 1500 Spanish troops, from General Mina's division, moved along the heights of Maya, and attacked the advanced post of the enemy in that direction, which they at first forced to retire ; but the enemy having been strongly reinforced, attacked in turn, and beat the Spaniards back almost to the village of Maya.

The enemy being driven from the left of his position, about three o'clock in the afternoon, retired in some confusion towards Cambo. We soon after took possession of their fine huts, constructed during a residence of three months, with much labour, but little expence.

The troops engaged at St Pe kept up the battle with life till dusk. During the night Marshal Soult withdrew the right wing of his army through St Jean de Luz, and retired towards his entrenched camp in front of Bayonne.

Our loss on that occasion is said to amount to 3000 killed and wounded—that of the enemy is estimated at 4000 killed and wounded, and 1500 prisoners ; 51 pieces of cannon fell into our hands.

On the 11th, we pursued the enemy towards this place ; in the evening we took a position in front of the village of Espalette.

2

Sir Rowland Hill having received an order to advance and attack the town of Cambo, the division moved from its bivouac about ten o'clock on the morning of the 12th. The 2d and 3d brigades advanced to the left bank of the Nive, up which they advanced towards the town, driving the enemy's picquets before them. The 1st brigade advanced directly on Cambo, by the high road from Espalette, drove in their picquets, and established itself on an eminence which overlooks the town at the distance of a mile. On reconnoitering the works which the enemy had constructed around the town, Sir Rowland Hill found them to be much stronger than he expected. The idea of taking it by assault was, therefore, abandoned. After a severe skirmish between our light troops and those of the enemy, and a brisk cannonade of several hours, the different brigades were recalled to some distance from the place, leaving strong picquets on the heights above it.

On the same ground we remained till the morning of the 16th, when the enemy having withdrawn his troops to the left bank of the Nive, and blown up the bridge, we advanced and took possession of this village.

The rivers are much swollen just now, the rain having fallen for the last five days without intermission. Adieu.

On board the Britannia Transport,
Passages, *December* 16, 1813.

Marshal Soult, and the French troops under
his command, are using every means in their
power to render the war in the south of France
national. The allied army is accused of every
thing that can rouse the hatred of the people of
one country against the military of another.—
The poor people of Cambo having given a ready
ear to their fabrications, had all emigrated across
the Nive on the 16th November, excepting an old
man and woman, who would also have accompanied their friends, had the health of the latter allowed her to be removed. The articles of household furniture which the emigrants could not remove, were either laid in a bye corner of a field,
or left in their dwellings, a ready prey to the
conquerors.

Opposite to Cambo the enemy began to throw
up works, the day after we took possession of that
place. Their conscripts were drilled every day
within musket-shot of our advanced posts, 20,000
of which joined the army under Soult between
the 10th November and the 1st of the present
month. Their sentries and ours were not more
than thirty paces from each other, during the
period our brigade occupied Cambo. The French
officers very frequently came down to the

river's edge, and conversed with us, but generally avoided military and political topics. One day they asked us, by way of a quiz, " what we " thought of the young ladies of Cambo?" Paris papers were sent to us every second day by the French officer commanding in our front. In re-turn, we sent them the London journals, which were, (as the General acknowledged,) a great treat to him, and every officer under his com-mand. The intelligence conveyed to them by their own papers, the French officers declared to be altogether unintelligible. Those asserted that Bonaparte had gained every battle, al-though he had retired with his victorious army within the French frontier. Notwithstanding the vile imposition practised on the French soldiery, by their leader and his ministers, he possesses their attachment in the same unsha-ken manner which he ever did in the zenith of his glory.

About two hours after our brigade took posses-sion of Cambo on the 11th November, a private of the 66th regiment, who had been made prison-er on the 10th, perceiving British troops in the place, made his escape from a village immediate-ly opposite, and, amidst the fire of numerous sentries, arrived at the further end of the bridge. Finding it destroyed, and seeing the enemy pour-ing down on him from the heights, he leaped into the Nive, which being very much swollen at the

time, and at all times rapid, carried the poor
fellow down the stream for about two hundred
yards, but he sunk close to the river's edge.
Our men, who had by this time lined the bank,
did every thing in their power to save him, by
throwing ropes, and canteen straps buckled together, for him to take hold of. He rose—
and again sunk into the deep! A second time
his hands were above the water—again he rose,
but sunk to rise no more!

When our brigade first went into Cambo,
the salt was so scarce, that one day I was compelled to give 3s. 6d. for a little lump, about a
pound weight.

A strong detachment having arrived at Cambo
on the 27th, from the 2d battalion, Colonel C—
wrote to the Marquis of Wellington on the same
day, requesting permission for the supernumerary
officers of the 1st, to proceed to join the 2d battalion of the regiment in Scotland. An answer
having arrived on the 5th instant, four officers,
of which I was one, received orders to proceed to
Passages, and there embark for England.

On the forenoon of the 8th, my brother officers
took leave of Cambo, and that night slept in
Espalette. Not having all my little affairs settled
till half-past eight in the evening, and as orders
for a general attack on the enemy's position
had been issued, I went to my Colonel, and asked permission to see them across the river in the

morning; to which he sternly replied, " No,
" Sir; you have seen enough." I set about taking leave of my friends. Soon after, he sent the
Adjutant, to say, that if I did not quit Cambo
before morning, I would incur his displeasure.
My commanding officer having at all times
treated me with kindness and attention, I was
well aware that the message proceeded from a
desire, on his part, of doing me a service. Nevertheless, I felt much disappointed; I thought
he might have indulged me.

At three o'clock on the morning of the 9th instant, I took leave of my friends in Cambo—to
some of them it proved an eternal farewell. I
will not attempt to describe the state of my feelings on that occasion—words are inadequate:
You may form an idea of them when I tell you that
they were those of a man taking leave of companions, whose confidence and friendship he possessed—friendship contracted in the haunts of
peace, and cemented in the field of strife. Will
you think the less of me, when I acknowledge, that
the hand of one of those friends I bedewed with
a salt drop, as I shook it and pronounced the
word—Farewell!

Having performed that painful task, I departed from Cambo. I had scarcely proceeded a mile
when I fell in with the advanced guard of the
Portuguese infantry, on their march to the banks

of the Nive. On perceiving these troops, I quitted the road, least they should imagine that I was making the best of my way to the rear, without permission; the consequence was, that I popped into a ditch, nearly to the middle in mud and water. With difficulty I extricated myself, well besmeared with clay.

I arrived in Espalette at day-light, where I found one of my brother officers; we breakfasted, and immediately set out for St Pe. In this village we were kindly entertained by an old gentleman and his wife, in whose house Lord Wellington had lived for some time after the battle of the Nivelle. The old gentleman informed us, that he had a son, an officer in the French army, and now a prisoner of war in Scotland. These kind people gave us a few apples, and requested we would carry some of them to our native homes. Several of the windows and rooms of the house were considerably injured, by the fire of the French troops from a height above the village, on the 10th of November; the marks are still visible. In the afternoon we proceeded to St Jean de Luz. Throughout the whole of the day the firing continued along the line of the Nive; in the evening we could learn no particulars of the action. Next day we crossed the Bidassoa near Irunzun; and that night slept in Renteria. From a height on the right bank of the Bidassoa, we saw the engagement between Sir John Hope and the enemy, in front of their entrenched camp, in which, I am sorry to hear, Sir John was wounded. He is a great favourite with the British army.

We arrived in Passages on the 11th, and embarked on the following day. Before leaving the shore, we had the pleasure of seeing Colonel Kruse, and the regiments of Frankfort and Nassau, march into Passages, and embark in British transports for England. The Colonel and his followers are fine looking men. They left the standard of the enemy on the 10th instant, near Bayonne.

By letters received this morning from the army, we learn, that Marshal Soult, with a corps of 30,000 men, attacked the right of the allied army on the morning of the 13th; but after a terrible conflict of some hours duration, he was signally defeated by the troops of the 2d division, with immense slaughter. As usual, the 1st brigade came in for its full share of what was going. My old corps charged no less than four times, and in every charge maintained its former superiority over the troops of Napoleon.

But to them, and to Spain, I must, for the present, bid adieu. Farewell, ye tented fields— farewell, ye plains and towering heights, stained with the blood of the best and dearest of my friends !—For my native land I leave thy shores; there, in the bosom of my family, 1 hope to spend a few days in peace and domestic felicity.

My gallant friends, of your heroic deeds I will read with delight; and, in the expectation of again joining you at an early period, to share in your dangers and your glory, I bid you all—Farewell !

GHENT, *May* 17, 1815.

THE landing of Bonaparte in France having once more lighted the torch of war, the armies of the European Confederacy are hastening towards the frontiers of that kingdom, where wickedness and perfidy reigns with sovereign sway in the hearts of her inhabitants.

When I parted with you in Edinburgh on the 4th of April, I really did not expect that I was so soon to address you from the ancient capital of Belgium. Our mutual friend J. K. R. and I arrived at Portpatrick on the morning of the 5th, crossed the same day to Donaghadee, and in the evening took the coach to Belfast. An American merchant-ship (being the first since the peace) having arrived in that harbour in the forenoon, bonfires were lighted in every street by the mobility, to testify their joy at the return of peace and amity between the two nations. I was a good deal amused with the crowds around these fires, particularly at the one opposite to the Donegal Arms. At each of the places, there appeared to be one or two individuals, who took the lead in every thing, and whose orders the others implicitly obeyed. Brandishing a large shilella above his head, one of the captains, as they were called, bawled out, " Three cheers for Bonaparte ;" and as soon as that motion had been disposed of, he proposed " Three groans for Louis the Eighteenth." This motion having also been acceded to, the Americans then came in for their share of applause. In this manner they spent the night. The cause of legitimacy appeared to have few advocates in the motley assemblage.

We quitted Belfast early next morning, and posted to Drogheda, where we slept ; we arrived in Dublin about ten on the 7th ; quitted it the same evening by the mail for Cork, where we arrived on the evening of the 8th.

About the 20th, we received an order of readiness, to embark at a moment's notice ; and a few days after, were reviewed by Major-General Forbes, who was much pleased with the general appearance of the regiment.

On the first day of May, we marched to Cove, and embarked in three transports. At nine o'clock in the morning of the 3d, we weighed anchor, and, before 12, had cleared the harbour. With a fine breeze, we scudded along on the 3d and 4th. Early in the morning of the 5th, we passed between the rocks of Scilly and the Land's End. We passed Plymouth on the 6th—Portsmouth on the 7th. During that night, and part of the following morning, we were becalmed off Beachy-head.— About mid-day, on the 8th, we passed Dungeness. At four, becalmed again off Dover. Early

next morning we passed Dunkirk and Nieu-
port; and, at 11 in the forenoon, dropped anchor about two miles from Ostend. In the afternoon, a few of the troops were put on shore; but
the greater part of them remained till the morning of the 10th, when, being removed into smaller
vessels, they were carried into the harbour at
high-water, and landed at the quay on the opposite side of the harbour from the town. At five
in the afternoon, we embarked in large boats on
the canal at Ostend, and the same evening sailed to
Bruges. Next morning, we resumed our voyage
at an early hour, and arrived here about eight in
the evening.

From the Cove of Cork to Ostend, our voyage
was very pleasant, having scarcely been troubled
with what seamen would call a stiff breeze. On
both banks of the canal, all the way from Ostend
to Ghent, the face of the country is every where
extremely beautiful, and almost as level as a bowl-
ing-green. But, on the whole, there is a certain
degree of sameness, which many would not admire, there being fully as much in the scenery of
this country as there is in the New Town of Edinburgh, of which I have heard you so often com-
plain.

When the extraordinary defection of the French
army compelled Louis the Eighteenth to abandon
the French territory, he retired in the first instance
to Ostend; but the King of the Netherlands

having kindly offered the unfortunate monarch an asylum in this city, he quitted the former place some time ago, and is now here with his whole court.

I have seen Louis several times since we arrived here. He is very corpulent; walks extremely ill, being much troubled with the gout. He generally rides out in a coach and four every day about one o'clock, attended by some of his principal officers of state, and a detachment of the Guard du Corps. At any other time, he is seldom to be seen, except during the hour of dinner, when a considerable number of the most respectable part of the community are admitted, by applying to the proper authorities. Before the gates of his present residence, British sentinels are posted night and day. The officer on duty, has, I believe, a general invitation to dine at one of the tables, where a senior officer of the household troops generally presides.

Of officers, who have followed the fortunes of their King, there are here and at Alost about 600. The privates are all quartered at the latter place, and amount to about 1500. Officers and privates are daily coming in, imploring forgiveness from Louis for past offences, and renewing their oath of allegiance to him and his family.

Ghent is situated on the Scheldt, at an equal distance from Brussels and Ostend. Being nearly 30 miles from each, the city covers an amazing

space of ground, fully as great as Glasgow, whose
population is more than double that of this place.
In the centre of the town, there is a very handsome square, which, on the market-days, is so
completely covered with the booths of itinerant
merchants, of almost every sort, that it requires
no little exertion to get from one side to the
other. The streets are spacious, and, in general,
very clean : numerous canals intersect each other
in various parts of the city; so that Ghent is properly neither situated on the main land, nor on
one island, but on many. The bridges over these
canals, I am told, are 328 in number. Some of
them are built of stone, others of wood; some
partly stone, and partly wood.

My landlord, who speaks a little English, told
me to-day, that there are between 4000 and 5000
people employed at present on the works of this
city—the ancient defences having been allowed
to go into complete decay. I have been round
the town three times; and have examined the several works, which are now throwing up for its defence. Considering the circumference of the city,
and the nature of the works, I am of opinion, that
it would require at least 40,000 men to defend
them, and that part of the city which will remain
open after the present defences are completed.

The country around Ghent, for many miles, appears to be in a high state of cultivation; the

crops this season are very fine, and promise an abundant return to the farmers.

In a conversation I had yesterday, my landlord said, that, in 1794, the inhabitants of this city were terrified at the sight of a British soldier. " What a change," said he, " has taken place " in your military system since that period ! We " considered your army as little better than an " armed rabble ; numbers of the soldiers were " daily seen lying in the streets, unable to " walk, from the effect of spiritous liquors. It " was no wonder that your excellent Prince, the " Duke of York, could effect nothing against the " French." He concluded—" There is such a dif- " ference between the troops of 1794, and those " now within our walls, that, had I been impri- " soned at that period in a dungeon, and relieved " this morning, I should have thought myself " conveyed, during my confinement, to another " world." I am of opinion, that this worthy man still looks on us with a suspicious eye ; as, the day before yesterday, he removed his daugh- ter to a convent, till the British troops shall have quitted this part of the country.

Officers and men are treated with the greatest kindness and attention by the inhabitants on whom they are billetted. In fact, they are angry if we do not consent to live with them altogether.

COLONEL CAMERON, of the 92d, having received
orders to march the 3d battalion of the royals,
the 28th, 32d, 42d, 44th, 79th, and 92d regiments, and 3d battalion of the 95th rifle corps,
from Ghent to Brussels, we quitted the former
city at an early hour on the 27th ult., and marched to Alost, where we found the inhabitants as
kind and attentive as those of Ghent. Continuing our route next morning, we arrived here
about one.

At Alost, three of us had some conversation
with a French officer, who, before the peace of last
year, held a commission for 21 years in the British
service. He now holds the rank of Lieutenant-Colonel under Louis, in whose cause he appears to be
a perfect enthusiast. He was present when Marshal
Ney kissed the King's hand, and bedewed it
with tears, upon his leaving Paris to bring the
usurper in an iron cage to his Majesty. He declared to us, that not only the King, but every
other person who witnessed the melting scene,
were sensibly affected. The Marshal is now known
here by the name of " Judas Ney."

We were also informed by that officer, that the
French army, when Bonaparte landed in France,
had been reduced to 110,000 men. By recent
advices from Paris, it appears, that it has been

increased to 250,000 infantry and 35,000 cavalry, all veteran troops, who have served in one or more campaigns, under their present leader. If to these we add the national guards, amounting to 350,000 men, the army which Bonaparte has at this moment under his command, must be reckoned any thing but despicable. If these troops are united in sentiment, much blood will necessarily flow, before the allies can obtain their much wished-for object—the expulsion of Bonaparte.

Every preparation is making by Napoleon to open the campaign with eclat—every allurement is held out to the old soldiers, to join the standards of the usurper. Montmartre, we are informed by the Paris papers, is already almost impregnable. He is endeavouring to render the war national, by disseminating, amongst the inhabitants, the most odious and vile fabrications. He has permitted the raising of free corps in various parts of the country. He has armed the ruffian part of the inhabitants of the Paris fauxbourgs.—In short, the preparations he has made are of the most formidable description, either to repel the allies, if attacked, or act on the offensive, should circumstances prove favourable.

Brussels is a most beautiful city. It is situated on an eminence; the gradual ascent of which, from the plain on the north-west side, bestows on its prospects a delightful variety. The fortifications of this city, once so famous, are now useless;—in many places they are quite decayed. The ramparts have been converted into beautiful walks; the fort, nearest the Park, or grand promenade, is decorated with three rows of trees, and is the part most frequented by the gentry.

The Park is a most delightful place. It is towards the eastern side of the town, and on the summit of the height on which the city stands, It is adorned with beautiful statues, and, excepting a little deep vale at the west end of it, is laid out in very neat walks, and avenues. On each side of the Park, there are rows of houses, forming a charming square. At the south-east corner of the Park, there is a theatre, which of late has been allowed to get into disrepair.

The people here are extremely kind, fully as much so as in any place we have yet been.— Those with whom I am quartered contribute every thing in their power towards my comforts.

Some individuals in England, I perceive, are disposed to lower the exertions of Ministers at this momentous crisis. For my own part, I can see no reason for their so doing. On the contrary, I think them deserving of the thanks of the country. All the disposable force in Scotland, England, and Ireland, has been sent to this country.—They have come forward with money to assist our allies, in order to enable them to ap-

pear on the grand theatre of action by the end of
the present month.

The British army in Belgium is not numerous,
but the men are animated with the best spirit.—
A considerable portion of the army, it is true,
consists of young men, who have seen no service
whatever;—but I have no doubt that they will imi-
tate their more veteran brethren, in deeds of valour and renown, on the day of trial.

Having been favoured with the distribution of
the British and Hanoverian army, I inclose a copy
of it for your perusal.

CAVALRY.

The 1st and 2d life guards, horse guards, (blue), and 1st dragoon
guards, are to be the 1st brigade of cavalry.

The 1st, 2d, (Scots greys), and 6th dragoons, are to be the 2d
brigade of cavalry.

The 1st and 2d light dragoons, King's German legion, and 23d
light British dragoons, are to be the 3d brigade of cavalry.

The 11th, 12th, and 16th light dragoons, are to be the 4th brigade of cavalry.

The 2d, 7th, and 15th hussars, are to be the 5th brigade of cavalry.

The 1st, 10th, and 18th hussars, are to be the 6th brigade of
cavalry.

The 3d hussars and 13th light dragoons, are to be the 7th brigade of cavalry.

2

Major-General Lord Edward Somerset, K. C. B. is to command the 1st brigade of cavalry.

Major-General Sir William Ponsonby, K. C. B. is to command the 2d brigade of cavalry.

Major-General Sir William Dornberg, K. C. B. is to command the 3d brigade of cavalry.

Major-General Sir Ormsby Vandeleur, K. C. B. is to command the 4th brigade of cavalry.

Major-General Sir Colquhoun Grant, K. C. B. is to command the 5th brigade of cavalry.

Major-General Sir Richard Hussey Vivian, K. C. B. is to command the 6th brigade of cavalry.

Colonel Baron Sir F. de Arentschildt, K. C. B. is to command the 7th brigade of cavalry.

Lieutenant-General the Earl of Uxbridge is to command the whole of the cavalry.

INFANTRY.

The 2d and 3d battalions, 1st foot guards, are to be the 1st British brigade of infantry.

The 3d battalion Coldstream, and 2d battalion 3d foot guards, are to be the 2d brigade of infantry.

The 1st battalions 52d and 71st, and 2d battalion 95th, are to be the 3d brigade of infantry.

The 3d battalion 14th, 23d and 51st regiments, are to be the 4th brigade of infantry.

The 2d battalion 30th, 33d regiment, and 2d battalions of the 69th and 73d regiments, are to be the 5th brigade of infantry.

The 2d battalion 35th, 54th, 2d battalion 59th, and 1st battalion 91st regiments, are to be the 6th brigade of infantry.

The 1st, 2d, 3d, and 4th battalions, King's German legion, are to be the 7th brigade of infantry.

The 28th and 32d regiments, 1st battalions of the 79th and 95th regiments, are to be the 8th brigade of infantry.

The 3d battalion royals, 42d, 2d battalion 44th, and 92d regiment, are to be the 9th brigade of infantry.

The 1st battalion 4th, 1st 27th, 40th regiment, and 2d 81st, are to be the 10th brigade of infantry.

Major-General Peregrine Maitland is to command the 1st brigade of infantry.

Major-General Sir John Byng, K. C. B. is to command the 2d brigade of infantry.

Major-General Frederick Adam is to command the 3d brigade of infantry.

Colonel H. Mitchell, 51st regiment, is to command the 4th brigade of infantry.

Major-General Sir C. Halket, K. C. B. is to command the 5th brigade of infantry.

Major-General Johnston is to command the 6th brigade of infantry.

Major-General Du Plat is to command the 7th brigade of infantry.

Major-General Sir James Kempt, K. C. B. is to command the 8th brigade of infantry.

Major-General Sir Denis Pack is to command the 9th brigade of infantry.

Major-General Sir John Lambert, K. C. B. is to command the 10th brigade of infantry.

The 1st division of infantry is to be composed of the 1st and 2d brigades, and is to be commanded by Major-General George Cook.

The 2d division is to be composed of the 3d and 7th brigades, and 3d Hanoverian infantry brigade, and is to be commanded by Lieutenant-General Sir Henry Clinton, K. G. C. B.

The 3d division is to be composed of the 5th British, 1st Brigade King's German legion, and 1st Hanoverian brigade, and is to be commanded by Lieutenant-General Baron Sir Charles Alten, K. C. B.

The 4th division is to be composed of the 4th and 6th brigades, and 6th Hanoverian brigade, and is to be commanded by Lieutenant-General Sir Charles Colville, K. G. C. B.

The 5th division is to be composed of the 8th and 9th brigades of infantry, and 5th Hanoverian brigade, and is to be commanded by Lieutenant-General Sir Thomas Picton, K. G. C. B.

The infantry is divided into two corps. The 1st corps is to be composed of the 1st, 3d, and 5th divisions, and is to be commanded by General his Royal Highness the Prince of Orange, K. G. C. B.

The 2d corps is to be composed of the 2d and 4th divisions, and is to be commanded by Lieutenant-General Lord Hill, K. G. C. B.

The ARTILLERY is placed under the orders of Colonel Sir George Wood, and consists of from 26 to 80 brigades, of 6 guns each—the exact number I cannot ascertain.

The 5th division, of which we form a part,

is composed entirely of veteran regiments, and commanded by a veteran officer, who, with the two Major-Generals in command of brigades, served, with great distinction, in Portugal, Spain, and France, under our present illustrious leader. From those hints, I dare say, you will be expecting great things from us on the day of trial. When that day comes, I hope we will do our duty.

On the 1st day of June, our brigade was inspected by Major-General Pack, who seemed pleased with the appearance of the men.

On the 4th instant, the division was inspected by his Grace the Duke of Wellington, who appeared highly delighted on seeing so many of his old friends again under his command. The Dutchess of Richmond, and some of the Ladies Lennox, rode past us several times, in an open carriage. To those officers whom she knew, the Dutchess bowed with great affability.

I am quartered within one hundred yards of a little image, at a fountain, called the Mannike-Pisse. This little fellow is looked upon as the oldest inhabitant of Brussels; and is elegantly dressed on all solemn occasions.

The regiment was out this morning, firing away some of their practice-ball ammunition:—My landlord thought we should rather hoard it up, in case we should soon have occasion to fire it at real Frenchmen, and not at their painted figures.

BRUSSELS, *June* 22, 1815.

NAPOLEON BONAPARTE, having assembled an army of 165,000 men, on the northern frontier of France, left Paris on the 12th instant, to assume the command of it. This numerous army is composed of veterans, the flower of the French soldiery, are well disciplined, inured to hardship, familiar with danger, eager for battle, and thirsting for revenge. To these troops their leader issued a proclamation, on the 14th, in which he recalled to their remembrance their former deeds of arms. He frankly told them, that they had battles to fight, dangers to encounter—and, in conclusion, he assured them, that, with steadiness, victory would be theirs.

Early in the morning of the 15th, the whole of the French army advanced towards the Sambre, which having crossed at several places, they directed their march on Charleroi, where the first corps of the Prussian army, under General Ziethen, was posted. The enemy attacked the Prussians with spirit, who, after a sharp skirmish, in which they suffered some loss, retired toward Fleurus. Marshal Ney, with the left of the French army, moved along the high-road to Brussels, and, in the evening, attacked the Prince Weimar, in the position of Frasne, and compelled him to retreat to the farm-house called Les Quatre Bras. The right and centre of the French army, under Napoleon's immediate command, pursued the Prussians towards Fleurus, and, subsequently, to the famed position of Brie and Sombref.

About four o'clock in the afternoon of the 15th, it was first whispered, in Brussels, that the French army was in motion; but it was merely a report to which very few gave credit. Two or three of us having proceeded to the Park, after dinner, to take our usual walk, found that the rumour had been considerably strengthened by subsequent reports from the front. A little after seven o'clock, an officer of our acquaintance, who possessed the means of knowing what credit was due to the floating rumours of the day, candidly told us that the Prussian hero had been attacked that morning—that advices to that effect had been received by the Duke of Wellington, during dinner, and that his Grace, (without communicating the contents of the dispatch to any one), on the cloth being removed, desired those at table to fill a bumper to " Prince Marshal Blucher and his gallant army." He advised us to pack our baggage and prepare for a sudden movement, as it was extremely probable that we would leave Brussels during the night. Between nine and ten the order of readiness was issued; and, about half past eleven, the bugles were heard in every corner of Brussels, calling on the warriors, of the four nations, to prepare for battle.

Words are inadequate to describe the scene of confusion which followed. The inhabitants, on hearing of the advance of Napoleon towards Brussels, became greatly alarmed ; and although many of them expressed themselves satisfied with regard to their safety, whilst a Wellington and a Blucher were between them and the enemy; still they could not banish from their countenances the look of despair.

The gentleman under whose roof I then was, on hearing of our intended departure, came into my apartment, and very kindly offered me any thing I might stand in need of. Seeing that I had my baggage packed, he seated himself, when we entered into a serious conversation regarding the advance of the enemy. After some little time he said, with a sigh, " Well, well, Bonaparte is " once more advancing towards Brussels, with a " terrible army. The Duke of Wellington's mili- " tary talents, we are all convinced, are of the " highest order.—The spirit and enterprise of " Prince Blucher is well known even to Napoleon " himself.—In both of those Generals we have " implicit confidence : But, when we compare the " numbers of the hostile armies, the quality of the " troops of which each are composed, we cannot " but look forward to the issue of the approach- " ing conflict with considerable anxiety. The " French troops are all veterans—men of despe- " rate characters, who will undertake to execute

" the most daring and hazardous enterprises ;—to
" them danger has long been familiar—robbery
" and plunder their daily occupation. The Prus-
" sians are brave," said he, " hardy, and inveterate
" enemies of France: But there is a considerable
" portion of them only militia, from whom much
" cannot be expected for some time. The allied
" army, in point of numbers, is, no doubt, respect-
" able; but, when we look to the quality of the
" troops, we have much to fear. The British
" contingent, I have been told, does not exceed
" 33,000. The Hanoverians are very young
" men, and their officers, many of them, mere
" children. The Dutch are good soldiers—so are
" the Belgians ; but," shaking his head, he said,
" they have served one or more campaigns under
" Napoleon." Having thus expressed himself, he
took me by the hand, and with considerable emotion, said :—" Farewell—remember that our sole
" dependence is on the British troops, and their
" unconquered leader."

At the sound of the bugle and bagpipe, all the
soldiers flew to their arms, and in a few minutes had
formed in companies on their private parades,
where six days soft bread and biscuit were issued
to them. Their haversacks proving too small
for such a quantity, a great part of it was left in
the streets. A little after twelve o'clock, the
regiments composing the 5th division had assembled in the Park and Palace Royal, as directed.

The latter was filled principally with the baggage animals of the British officers of the staff, and those of the division. About half-past three o'clock, on the morning of the 16th, we marched out of Brussels by the Namur gate, and were soon after followed by the troops of the Duke of Brunswick, all dressed in black uniforms. It is said, that that Prince and his army has made a vow to wear mourning till the late Duke of Brunswick's death has been amply avenged. Between eight and nine o'clock we passed through the then obscure, but now immortalized village of Waterloo, in a small wood in front of which we were ordered into bivouac. The Duke of Wellington passed us about nine, at full speed, on his way to Quatre Bras. At eleven we quitted our bivouac, and at one halted on a height a mile in rear of Genappe. About a quarter past one we continued our march to the front; descending the height in rear of Genappe, our ears were first saluted with the thunder of the enemy's artillery, within range of which we arrived about half-past two.

Marshal Ney having by that time attacked the Belgians, under the Prince of Orange, we received an order to proceed to the left of the village, or farm of Quatre Bras, and repel the attack of the enemy in that direction, whilst the Prince was to defend the position on the right, till succour should arrive from the other divisions of the British army, on the right.

The highway from Brussels to Charleroi runs through the village of Quatre Bras, where it is intersected by another road which runs from Nivelles to Ligny. The possession of Quatre Bras was of great importance to the ulterior operations of the Duke of Wellington, as, by the highway, he communicated with Brussels, and by the other road with the right wing of the Prussian army. The right of the road from Brussels is skirted by a thick wood, which extends across the plain to a considerable distance between our position and the enemy's. There were numerous fields of wheat and rye, which, for some time after the action began, tended to screen the forces of Ney, not from our fire, but from our sight. The 8th brigade, consisting of the 28th, 32d, 79th, and 95th regiments, under the command of Sir James Kempt, moved down from the height on the left of Quatre Bras, and met the Marshal's advanced columns in the plain below. The numbers of that brigade formed a striking contrast with those of the enemy :—their inequality in point of numerical strength was so striking, that many of our oldest and best officers looked forward with uneasiness to the issue of the conflict. But the 16th of June was not the first time that the gallant Kempt and his brave associates had met their enemies under similar circumstances. With much spirit the two armies advanced to meet each other; a skirmish ensued, which, after a hard struggle, terminated in favour of the thistle, the rose, and the shamrock ; the enemy, having shrunk from our first furious onset, retired a little, and waited the arrival of fresh troops. In a quarter of an hour the battle was resumed with increased fury on both sides. Marshal Ney perceiving his troops again ready to yield the palm to their opponents, sent fresh succours to their relief. The Duke of Wellington, on perceiving the enemy deploy fresh battalions towards our left, gave orders for the 3d battalion royals, 42d regiment, and 2d battalion 44th, to proceed to the assistance of the 8th brigade. The 92d Highlanders were ordered to line a bank on the right of the road leading from Quatre Bras to Ligny, on which the Duke and his staff had taken post,—the right of the regiment to rest on the farm of Quatre Bras. The Hanoverian brigade was formed on the left of the 92d, and the Brunswick cavalry in rear of it. The Brunswick infantry were stationed, partly in rear of the left of the Highlanders, and partly in the wood on the right of the village. The few pieces of artillery we had with us were posted on the highway in front of Quatre Bras. The only cavalry we had were those of the Duke of Brunswick.

Such was the distribution of our little army about three o'clock. The Belgians were then disputing the wood with their enemies on the right.

The French army was drawn up on a ridge which runs parallel to that on which the farm of Quatre Brass is situated, and amounted, according to the testimony of prisoners, to sixty thousand men.

From three o'clock the operations of Marshal Ney were all offensive, and consisted of a multiplicity of attacks of cavalry, of infantry, and often of the two forces united, assisted by a powerful and well served artillery. To detail the numerous conflicts which took place on the left, from three till six, is impossible. All who were engaged, however, conducted themselves throughout with a firmness and gallantry not to be surpassed.

About four o'clock the Duke of Brunswick, with his cavalry, advanced from Quatre Bras to charge a French column of cavalry considerably in advance. Led by their undaunted Prince, the troops charged in gallant style; but the Duke having received a mortal wound in the breast, his troops were seized with a panic, and began to retire from before their numerous foes towards the ground on which they had originally formed. This unfortunate affair gave the enemy a temporary advantage, and inspired his followers with fresh courage. The rear and flanks of the Brunswickers were assailed by their proud enemy, till they arrived almost at the farm of Quatre Bras. The 92d having been ordered to keep themselves hid from the enemy, the French troops no doubt fancied that the day was their own. As the enemy advanced in the direction of the 92d, that regiment was ordered to be in readiness to fire. With their usual coolness and characteristic bravery they prepared to repel their foes. When the fugitives had nearly all passed to the rear of the Highlanders, the French cavalry, who were advancing by the high-way, received a volley from the 92d, which stretched a number of both men and horses lifeless on the ground. A panic seized those who escaped the oblique fire of the 92d. They fled in great confusion, confounded at meeting with such a reception, and at a point where they imagined resistance had ceased.

One of the enemy's officers having advanced to the farm of Quatre Brass before he perceived his danger, attempted to escape by the road on which the 92d regiment was posted. In doing so, however, he was fired at by some of the soldiers, who wounded him in both his feet;—his horse having been killed at the same time, he was made prisoner and sent to the rear.

Disappointed at Quatre Bras, the enemy turned his attention to the troops on the left, who were attacked with a death-like fury by the

French legions. The several regiments having formed themselves into solid squares, presented an impenetrable front to their assailants, who rode up to the very muzzles of our pieces, in order to provoke the soldiers to throw away their fire, that they might, with the greater facility, penetrate our squares. All the attempts of the enemy to induce our soldiers to do so were fruitless; irritated at their obstinacy, the enemy attacked our squares sword in hand, but were always beat back with great loss. By numerous trials of this kind, equally unsuccessful, the enemy lost a number of his bravest soldiers. About half-past five they made a second effort to wrest Quatre Bras out of our possession, but by the steadiness of our soldiers, were again repulsed with loss.

The battle had for some time raged with great fury along the whole extent of our line, and with alternate success, when the hour of six was announced.

At this interesting period of the battle, the brigade of guards, under General Maitland, and third division under Sir Charles Alten, arrived to our assistance. Never did an army receive a more seasonable reinforcement than this was to us. The guards remained in the wood to the right of the farm, and the third division was ordered to the left of the whole line. As the troops passed us on the road we cheered them—tears of joy bade

2

them welcome to share our perils and our glory. Our feelings, on this occasion, were very acute; but they were the feelings of men and of soldiers: we prayed for blessings to be showered down on our friends as they passed, and our best wishes followed them—too many of them to their last and silent abode. As the troops of the third division proceeded from Quatre Brass to their destination, the enemy poured a heavy and destructive fire on them from a numerous artillery, placed in battery on the lower part of the heights of Frasne. Having received but a very few guns in addition to our original stock, we could but feebly return the tremendous vollies of the enemy.

The French had certainly mistaken the movement of the 3d division. They must, I think, have entertained the idea, that the troops of that division were those who had baffled their cavalry in two different attempts to get possession of the village; for no sooner had that corps cleared Quatre Bras, than the enemy made dispositions to renew the attack on that place.

To cover their real design, the enemy opened a tremendous fire from the whole of their artillery, on the troops stationed at the farm, and which lasted without intermission till seven o'clock. By this time, the enemy's infantry had approached very close to the village, by two separate routes; one column advanced by the highway, the other by the hollow, which runs along the edge of the wood, called the Bois de Bossu. The Duke of Wellington, who had all the time been eyeing the French infantry through the clouds of smoke, and was convinced that their object was Quatre Bras, ordered Colonel Cameron to charge them with his Highlanders.

Before the order to charge was given, the enemy had occupied a house of two storeys, which stands on the left of the highway to Charleroi, at the distance of 200 yards from the village. On the opposite side of the road, there was a large garden, surrounded by a thick thorn hedge, having a little gate on the side nearest the road, and another of a similar size immediately opposite to it. Between the two, there was a gravel walk, of about a yard in breadth. On the left of the house, there was another hedge, which the enemy had also taken possession of. The order to charge had scarcely been given, when every man in the regiment appeared in front of the bank, and, amidst one of the heaviest fires of musketry I ever witnessed, advanced to dislodge the enemy from the house, garden, and hedge. Colonel Cameron, with the right companies of the regiment, and accompanied by General Barnes, advanced by the highway, the other companies, by making an oblique movement to their right, threw the whole strength of the regiment against the enemy at the house and garden. The enemy continued to

2

resist the Highlanders for some time with great bravery. Our brave Colonel, Cameron, was mortally wounded close to the garden, and retired from the field, regretted by the whole corps. After a terrible conflict, we succeeded in wresting the house from them. The garden, which had never been occupied by the enemy, was now the only obstacle between us and them. But as they were formed, ready to receive us at a few paces only from the rear hedge, there appeared some little danger in attempting to charge them in that position, as they were greatly superior in numbers to us, and as the space between the garden-hedge and the wood of Bossu would not permit us to advance with the whole of our troops in line. Thus situated, we were under the necessity of hazarding something, or of giving up what we had already gained. As there was little time to be lost, part of the regiment moved round the garden by its right, and another part by the left. It was proposed to enter by the little gate, fronting the road, and, advancing across the garden, break open the one opposite to it, whence the troops, employed on this service, were to sally, and, in conjunction with those on their right and left, attack the enemy with the bayonet. To the centre party I attached myself. We accomplished the task allotted to us, of forcing the gates, with ease, although the enemy kept up a dreadful fire of small

arms during these operations, which, from the
nature of the service, we could not well return.
The rear gate having been speedily opened, we'
moved out of the garden, and quickly formed
in front of the hedge. The right and left columns, seeing us ready, moved round the corners
of the garden, in order to try the metal of the
enemy. The signal having been made, every man
joined in three hearty cheers, and then, with the
irresistible bayonet in their hands, advanced to
the work of death.

For a few seconds, the enemy appeared rather
unwilling to retire; but when they perceived us
to be really in earnest, they wheeled to the right-
about, and attempted to escape by the hollow up
which their left column had advanced. We pursued the fugitives fully half a mile, when the
advance of their cavalry rendered it prudent
for us to retire to the wood of Bossu. The loss
of the enemy in this affair was terrible. At every
step, we found a dead or a wounded Frenchman:
some of them affected to treat the whole business very lightly; whilst others, even in the very
agonies of death, never ceased to echo the cry
of their brethren in the front, of Vive l'Empereur! Our loss was also very great on this occasion, not caused so much by the fire of those
to whom we were more immediately opposed,
as by the fire of their artillery and light troops
on our left flank.

This was the last attempt which the enemy made to gain possession of Quatre Bras, but he still continued to dispute the wood of Bossu with the guards, the 92d, and a corps of Brunswick infantry. At this point, his efforts were attended with no better success than on the left and in the centre. He, nevertheless, continued the conflict till after nine in the evening, when every prospect of victory having entirely vanished, he withdrew his troops, and left us in possession of the ground which they had occupied at the commencement of the battle.

Between two and three o'clock in the afternoon of the 16th, the right wing and centre of the French army, together with all the Imperial guards, under the immediate command of Napoleon, attacked the Prussian army, commanded by Prince Blucher, in its position at Ligny.

From the time we arrived at Quatre Bras on the 16th, till it was almost dark, a terrible cannonade was distinctly heard in the direction of Ligny, and the smoke of the cannon was for a long time visible. The battle proved long and bloody: Both armies fought with the greatest animosity—neither, it is said, gave or asked for quarter. About nine o'clock, Bonaparte ordered one of those desperate charges to be made, with a portion of his guards, which, on many former occasions, had commanded success. It was here also decisive—it gave to Napoleon once more the laurel wreath. The loss which the Prussian army sustained on that day was great; that of the French must also have been very considerable.

The Prussian army had nearly suffered an irreparable loss in the person of their Father and General. This gallant veteran headed numerous charges on that day against the French army. In one of them, he was rather unsuccessful; returning from which, he had the misfortune to have his horse shot under him. His own troops, in their flight, and the French in their advance, passed the hero without observing him. An officer threw himself down beside his General, determined to share his fate. The Prussian cavalry having rallied, returned to the charge, and repulsed the French, who again passed the Marshal, without observing him. On the arrival of the Prussians, he was extricated from his alarming situation, and re-mounted; and in a few minutes was again at the head of his valiant army.

Adieu.

Brussels, *June* 24, 1815.

At the close of the battle of the 16th instant, the 5th division occupied the plain in front of Quatre Bras. The 3d division was formed on the left of the 5th, and the Guards and the foreign troops on the right.

About 10 o'clock, the piper of the 92d took post behind the garden-hedge in front of the village, and, tuning his bag-pipes, attempted to collect the sad remains of his regiment. Long and loud blew Cameron; and although the hills and the vallies echoed the hoarse murmurs of his favourite instrument, his utmost efforts could not produce above one-half of those whom his music had cheered in the morning, on their march to the field of battle. Alas! many of them had taken a final leave of this bustling world. Numbers of them were lying in the fields, and in the woods, and not a few in the farm-yard of Quatre Bras, weltering in their blood.—The yard, I have been assured by a surgeon, who dressed a number of the wounded, at one time contained upwards of 1000 soldiers of the 3d and 5th divisions. The ground, inside of the yard, was literally dyed with blood, and the walls very much stained. In short, the interior of that place presented to the eye a scene of unparalleled horror. From the garden, the 92d regiment retired behind the houses of Quatre Bras, and then bivouacked.

Soon after the last gun was fired, our light cavalry began to arrive in rear of our position; and by eight o'clock next morning, the greatest part of the allied army had approached within call.

On the evening of the 16th, the Duke of Wellington retired to Genappe, to take a little repose. About four in the morning of the 17th, he quitted that village, and arrived at Quatre Bras at five.

The morning being cold, and rather inclined to rain, his Grace, on alighting, came up to some of our men, and said—" Ninety-second, I will " be obliged to you for a little fire." The request had no sooner been made, than every man flew to the village, to procure the necessary materials. In a very short time, they returned, lighted the fire opposite to the door of a small hut, constructed of the boughs of trees, which they repaired in the best manner they could. For their attention, particularly the latter part of it, his Grace expressed himself truly grateful. In this splendid mansion, the Field-Marshal received the Prince of Orange, Lord Hill, and a great many other officers of rank;—in that hut, he received the melancholy tidings from Prince Blucher, communicating the disasters that had befallen his army at Ligny—and in that place, he arranged the order of retreat to the famed position of Waterloo.

Previous to the receipt of Blucher's dispatches, we were all in high spirits, anticipating a splendid victory over the French Marshal before night —never doubting but Blucher would be able to keep Bonaparte at bay, whilst we, having the whole of our army united, amused ourselves with Ney. But the moment that the retreat of Blucher was made known, our spirits were as much depressed as they were elated before. A gloom stole over the countenances of all. Every soldier was more or less affected. The breast of none was more agitated than that of our illustrious General. For some time after he had received the unwelcome news, his Grace remained closely shut up in the hut. Having issued the necessary orders for the retreat of the army, he came out of his airy residence, and for an hour walked alone in front of it. Now and then his meditations were interrupted by a courier with a note, who, the moment he had delivered it, retired to some distance to wait his General's will. The Field-Marshal had a small switch in his right hand, the one end of which he frequently put to his mouth, apparently unconscious that he was doing so. His left hand was thrown carelessly behind his back, and he walked at the rate of three and a half to four miles in the hour. He was dressed in white pantaloons, with half-boots, a military vest, white neckcloth, blue surtout, and cocked hat. He was dressed in a similar manner on the 16th. On the latter day, the telescope was never out of his hand, and very seldom from his eye. He viewed every part of the contested field with a peircing eye—nothing whatever escaped him.

Soon after the allied army began its retreat, the most exaggerated statements were circulated, regarding the defeat of the Prussian army. At one time the loss was rated at 20,000 killed, wounded, and prisoners ; and, at another, it was asserted that they had lost, in prisoners alone, above that number. Every thing wore the gloomiest appearance imaginable. In the full belief, therefore, that the Prussian army had been totally routed, we began our retreat from the scene of our first triumph, towards the glorious plains of Waterloo.

To cover his real design, the Duke of Wellington ordered the troops of the 3d and 5th divisions to remain in front of Quatre Bras, till such time as the artillery, the foreign troops, and those which had arrived in the night, should be considerably advanced on their journey. The manœuvre of the British General completely succeeded ;—the retreat was never observed by the wily Napoleon till his equally sagacious antagonist was out of the reach of pursuit.

As soon as the enemy perceived that we had retreated, he dispatched the greatest part of his cavalry to harass our rear-guard, composed of the British cavalry. A number of very brilliant charges were made, by our heavy dragoons, who succeeded in breaking through columns of the enemy's horse, on whom our light dragoons could make no impression.

The morning of the 17th, which was rather hazy, began to clear up about 10 o'clock, and, before 12, the sun had become very powerful;—about one, the air was extremely sultry;—soon after the clouds began to lower, and, before two, thunder was faintly heard In a few minutes after, the horizon was darkened,—the lightning became vivid, and the thunder rolled in terrible peals over our heads, whilst the rain and the hail fell in such quantities, as if the elements had conspired with men to render the events passing on earth the most important and dreadful recorded in history.

Ascending the heights in rear of Genappe, the body of the gallant Duke of Brunswick passed us. The corpse was laid on a waggon, with the fatal wound, in the breast, exposed to public view. To the wound, the soldiers, guarding the precious relic, frequently pointed, and often swore that they would amply avenge the death of their lamented prince.

On the height above Genappe, the 5th division halted about half an hour. Sir Thomas Picton embraced the opportunity of assembling a Court-Martial for the trial of some men for wantonly firing away their ammunition. This practice is very common among the foreign troops, and is but too much so amongst our own. It cannot be too much reprobated, as it is not only highly detrimental to the service, but endangers the life of many a brave soldier.

During one of the most awful storms of thunder, lightning, hail, rain, and wind, that I ever witnessed, we continued our retreat to Waterloo. Never did I see any thing so appalling as the lightning—the rolling of the thunder was truly terrific.

Five minutes after the rain began to pour, the roads became so deep, that, in many places, we waded through mud and water to the knees. When we took up our ground on the position of Waterloo, not one of us had a dry stitch on our backs, and our baggage was no one knew where. To add to our miseries, we were ordered to bivouac in a newly ploughed field, in no part of which could a person stand in one place, for many minutes, without sinking to the knees in water and clay; and where, notwithstanding the great quantity that had fallen, not one drop of good water could be procured to quench our thirst.

Thus situated, a party on fatigue, under the command of an officer, was ordered to proceed to Waterloo, to bring a supply of water to the regiment. I being the first officer for that duty, was dispatched, at the head of the canteens. We proceeded as directed.—Draw-wells we found in abundance, but not a single rope was there at any of them, to draw up the water. Most of the wells were so deep that 23 canteen straps, buckled together, aided by several fathoms of rope, were not sufficiently long to carry a bucket to the bottom ; in those where they reached the bottom, there was no water. After numerous and fruitless attempts to get our canteens filled with the cooling beverage, we quitted Waterloo, and returned to our camp, where misery, in its most hideous form, stared us in the face. Fancy yourself seated on a few small twigs, or a little straw, in a newly ploughed field, well soaked with six hours heavy rain ;—your feet six or eight inches deep in the mud ;—a thin blanket your only shelter from the surly attacks of the midnight hurricane—cold, wet, and hungry, without a fire, without meat, and without drink.—Imagine yourself placed in such a situation, and you will have a faint idea of what we suffered on the night of the

Q

17th, and morning of the memorable 18th of June. A sound sleep was a luxury which none of us could expect to enjoy. The men were seated in pairs, with their backs to the storm, and their blankets between it and them; some of them were recounting their former sufferings in Portugal, Spain, and France; others their deeds of arms in the same countries; and not a few were humming a verse of some warlike song;—all were attempting to pass away the dreary hours in the best manner they could, in hopes that the morning would present them with something comfortable.

Though the men bore their sufferings with great patience and fortitude; and, at all times, appeared ready to perform their duty when called on, yet it would be in vain to assert, that the spirits of the army were not greatly depressed on that occasion. They certainly were; and, if every thing is taken into account, it is no great wonder that they should be so.—It was a night of horror which hath no parallel. The dreadful tempest continued with unabated violence till eight o'clock in the morning of the 18th; about nine, the clouds began to disperse, and, before ten, the sun burst from behind the gloomy curtain, and shed his fostering rays over the fields which, on that eventful morning, waved with yellow corn.

About nine, the Commissary issued beef to

the division, but very few seemed inclined to eat it. From the hind quarter of a bullock, I cut a steak, which I fastened to a ramrod and held over a fire, till it was tolerably warm; then putting it to my mouth, I swallowed the delicious morsel with more than common avidity. But, to tell you the truth, I was extremely hungry, having had very little of any thing to eat for two days before. Soon after, an allowance of grog was given to each man, which tended to keep our drooping spirits from sinking under our accumulated load of misery.

From our bivouac in the clay puddle, we were moved to a dry one, a little in rear of the other. There we lighted fires, pulled off our jackets, shoes, and stockings, dried them, and endeavoured to make ourselves as comfortable as the existing circumstances would admit. In hopes of getting a little repose, we had begun to construct huts; some, indeed, were finished;—three of us were asleep in one of these, when the bugle's shrill sound called on us to battle.

The memorable engagement of the 18th is known here by three names, viz. Waterloo, Mount St John, and La Belle Alliance. The first is a small village, situated about nine miles from Brussels, on the road to Charleroi. In the approach to Waterloo, the high-way traverses the forest of Soignies, from which it is not more than 300 pa ces. A mile further, on the same road, is situated the village or farm called Mount St John. At that place, the highway branches into two roads; the one leads to Nivelles, and the other to Charleroi, by Genappe and Quatre Bras. On the road to Genappe, at the distance of a mile from Mount St John, and immediately opposite to it, stands the farm called La Belle Alliance.

The following was the disposition of the allied army, when the enemy advanced to give us battle.

The centre of the allied army occupied the farm of Mount St John; the right wing extended along the eminence as far as Braine la Leude, and the left rested on the farm called Ter la Haye. The ground in front of the British position sloped gently towards the valley, and in the same easy manner ascended on the other side. The French army was posted on that ridge which runs parallel to the other, at the distance of 1000 to 1500 yards.

The 1st British division occupied that part of the position denominated the right centre; in front of which was situated a house, called the Chateau of Hougomont. The woods and orchard around the house were occupied by the light companies of the four battalions of guards, some Belgic, and a few Brunswick troops. The chateau and garden were occupied by a part of the

Coldstream regiment of foot guards, and the remaining part of that division was formed in rear of the place, to support their friends in case of necessity.

The 3d division, under Sir Charles Alten, formed the left centre of the army, from which were detached some Hanoverians and light troops from the King's German Legion, to the farmhouse, called La Haye Sainte, situated at the bottom of the hill on the road to Charleroi. The 2d division was formed on the right of the 1st; and the 4th on the right of the 2d. The 4th division, forming the right of the army, had its advanced posts at Braine la Leude.

The 5th division was formed on the left of the 3d division, and occupied a height, which rises gradually from the highway, for nearly half a mile, in the direction of Ter la Haye. Along that ridge runs a hedge, all the way from the centre to the extreme left, behind which our artillery were planted, completely out of the enemy's view. In front of the hedge were posted one brigade of Belgians, whose flanks were protected by two brigades of artillery, and in the rear were supported by the 9th British brigade of infantry, a brigade of Hanoverians, and Sir William Ponsonby's brigade of heavy cavalry. The Belgian infantry, under Prince Weimar, formed the extreme left of the allied army; in rear of which, the 4th British cavalry brigade was posted. The greatest part of the cavalry was posted in rear of the infantry occupying the centre, right, and left centre of the position. The foreign troops were chequered with the British, in as equal proportions as the disposition of the army would admit of.

About 11 o'clock, Napoleon, with a numerous staff, rode along the ridge, in front of the 5th division; but instead of prosecuting his route to La Belle Alliance, he turned to the left, and rode to the rear, the fire of our artillery being rather too hot, a few pieces having been discharged at him from various parts of the line.

At half past eleven, Jerome Bonaparte moved down his division from the heights on the left of La Belle Alliance, and attacked our light troops in front of the Chateau of Hougomont. On descending the heights, the French troops were stopped two or three times by our artillery; almost the first shot from which having killed and wounded several of them. The whole extent of the ridge was at the same time occupied by a numerous and well appointed cavalry, who, proud of their own strength, advanced towards us by the high-way, with all the audacity of soldiers careless of danger. Our cavalry having moved forward to meet them, a terrible conflict appeared inevitable, when the greater part of both was called to another part of the field.

The French troops attacked the post of Hougomont with great spirit, but, for some time, gained very little ground in the wood and orchard. Every moment the conflict became louder, closer, and more murderous. The foreign troops fought gallantly, till the enemy, having nearly surrounded them, they thought it prudent to retire. From that time, the foot-guards had the brunt of the business to bear; and, in the defence of the house and garden, they showed that it could not have fallen into better hands. Attack succeeded attack, without making any impression whatever on the garrison. Round shot, shell, grape, and musketry, were poured into the place in great profusion.

The fire of their artillery was truly terrible.—Their attacks were made with the greatest impetuosity ;—these were met, and repelled by the determined bravery of the British garrison. Every tree was contended for, as if it had been a kingdom. No neutral walls or hedges were allowed ; either the one party or the other behoved to be the absolute possessor ; every avenue to the ancient mansion was contested with an obstinacy seldom equalled. The gates of the place were assailed by the enemy with a bravery bordering on frenzy ;—numbers, in the attempt to force them, fell, pierced with wounds. Our troops having loopholed the court wall, fired thence on their fierce antagonists, whose bodies in a short time covered the ground around the chateau. The enemy continued their attacks for an hour and a half, and every time with increased force.— The furious Napoleon, enraged at this obstinate defence, by the handful of British guards at Hougomont, and seeing that the Field-Marshal was determined to keep possession of it, at whatever cost, turned his attention to the left wing and centre.

About one o'clock, the enemy opened a tremendous fire on us from a numerous artillery, planted along the crest of the ridge on which his infantry were formed. At first we did not mind it much, but in a few minutes it became so terrible, as to strike with awe the oldest veteran in the field. The spirits of our men were very low indeed during the whole of the morning, and although they had been considerably raised before the commencement of the battle, yet there was something wanting to restore their wonted daring, when opposed to the enemies of their country.—That something was at hand. The Duke of Richmond, who had arrived from Brussels a little before the alarm was given, and who had had some conversation with our General-in-Chief on the subject of the impending battle, paid a visit to that part of the position on which we were posted. In the hearing of the men he assured us that the Duke of Wellington calculated on gaining a most complete victory over Napoleon, as Marshal Blucher, with 40,000

Prussians, was advancing by several roads from
Wavre to attack the right flank of the French
army, and of whose movements Napoleon knew
nothing. The effect which the Duke of Richmond's communication produced on the minds of
the soldiers was truly astonishing. But I think it
may fairly be doubted whether the speedy prospect of being succoured by the Prussians, or
the two following verses of Bruce's address, produced the most powerful effect on the hearts of
our brave fellows :—

> Now's the day, and now's the hour,
> See the front of battle lower,
> See approach *Napoleon's* power,—
> His chains and slavery !
> Lay the proud *Usurper* low,
> *Tyrants* fall in every foe,
> *Liberty* in every blow,—
> Let us do or die !

These verses were chaunted by one of their own
number, who altered them a little to suit the occasion.

Under cover of their tremendous cannonade, the
enemy brought forward three columns of infantry,
each from 3000 to 4000 strong, and bore down on
the left and centre of our position. With loud
shouts of " Vive l'Empereur," the left column advanced to the attack of the farm of La Haye Sainte,

and the right, supported by the third, attacked that part of the position where our brigade was posted. The Belgians were assailed with terrible fury; and, for some time, returned the enemy's fire with great spirit. As the French approached them, the Belgians retired behind the hedge, which, although it afforded no shelter to them from the enemy's fire, tended to conceal them from their view. Every moment the battle became more and more animated. By the amazing quantity of shot which the enemy poured on us, our ranks were much thinned—in fact, every thing appeared to warrant the supposition, that nothing short of our final destruction would satisfy the furious assailants.

But the enemy's grand and primary object appeared to be the capture of La Haye Sainte, against which their left column was directed to move. The French troops surrounded the farm, and with loud and horrid bellowing, attempted to force their way into the yard. By the bravery of the little garrison, the enemy were driven back—again they renewed their attack, and again were repulsed with terrible carnage. Between two and three o'clock, the enemy perceiving that the fire of the troops in La Haye Sainte was not so lively as at the commencement of the action, resumed the attack with increased fury. The ammunition of the garrison having been expended, and all communication cut off with the British on the ridge, the brave Germans saw nothing else left them to do, but to sell their lives as dear as they possibly could.'' The gates of the farm-yard were attacked and carried by the enemy :—A dreadful carnage now ensued ;—a fight was maintained for a considerable time with the bayonet alone—it continued indeed while there was one German alive to dispute the possession of the place with their assailants.

The enemy having gained his point at La Haye Sainte, opened a terrible fire from his artillery along the whole extent of the line, but which, to favour the attack he meditated, was hottest from the centre towards our left.

Under cover of his artillery, Napoleon caused the right and left columns, formerly mentioned, supported by the third column, and a numerous artillery, to march forward and attack the heights between the highway, at Mount St John, and that part of the ridge on which the left regiment of our brigade was posted. With their drums beating, colours flying, and eagles soaring above their huge head-dresses, the enemy advanced in solid column, to carry the orders of their master into execution. As they ascended the ridge, the Belgians poured on them a very destructive fire of musketry, and which, with the artillery on their flanks, arrested the enemy's progress for half an hour. About a quarter from three o'clock, the French having almost gained the ridge, the Belgians partially retired from the hedge. These troops were induced to return again, at the entreaty of their officers; but the resistance which the Belgians offered to the enemy, after that period, was feeble indeed. Their whole line began to move—here and there a partial breaking of it took place; some again returned to the crest of the eminence, but it was merely to satisfy their curiosity—for they retired, without firing a shot. At length the whole corps ran as fast as their feet could carry them. Affairs were evidently drawing to an important crisis: A body of the enemy's troops had put to flight between two and three thousand of our allies, although supported by an equal number of British troops in the rear. If 5000 men were not sufficient to arrest the torrent, (which, rolling from the opposite ridge, threatened to sweep every thing before it,) it could scarcely be expected that we could do so with a force considerably less than half of the above number. But such an attempt must be made, or the heights must be yielded, and, with them, the victory to the enemy.

The post abandoned by the Belgians was ordered to be occupied by the 3d battalion royals, and 2d battalion 44th. These two corps retarded the advance of the French, who, although they saw themselves opposed by fresh ad-

versaries, still pressed forward to the object they
had first in view. A sharp conflict took place
between the hostile columns; volley succeeded
volley—neither gave way, each sustained their
respective parts with a firmness worthy the soldiers of the nations to which they belonged. It
was about three o'clock, when the enemy finally
succeeded in establishing themselves close to the
hedge. The two British battalions retired on
the approach of the enemy, who, no doubt,
imagined that they would meet with no farther
opposition at that point—but they were soon un-
deceived : for a conflict, far more terrible, if possible, than any that had preceded it, was about to
take place. Sir Denis Pack, who had remained
with the royals and 44th, till they retired from
the ridge, perceiving the urgent state of affairs,
galloped up to the 92d, and, with a countenance
denoting the importance of the communication
he was about to make, said, " Ninety-second, you
must charge! All the troops in your front have
given way." The regiment answered the call with
cheers. The 92d regiment, reduced to 220 men,
were formed in line, and presented a front nearly
equal to that of the enemy :—But the French were
in close column, and had more than ten such fronts
to support the one in view, forming altogether a
mass of at least 3000 men. The Highlanders
moved forward, and, with cheers, approached
their veteran enemy. For some time they seem-

ed quite determined to meet our assault. But, when we were about 20 paces from them, they, panic-struck, wheeled about, and, in the utmost confusion, attempted to escape. But it was too late. Sir William Ponsonby, perceiving the disorderly manner in which the enemy retired, rushed forward with the 1st, 2d, and 6th regiments of heavy dragoons, and cut his way through them, as far as the valley between the two positions, captured two eagles, and made 2000 prisoners. That they might escape with the greater facility, the French threw away their knapsacks, arms, and accoutrements. For some minutes the carnage was truly dreadful. The French troops, shewing an unwillingness to go to the rear, force was used, and many of them having refused to move one way or other, were cut down without ceremony.—In fact, there was no time to be lost in securing the prisoners, as the wily Napoleon, who witnessed the disgraceful flight of his troops from the heights, near La Belle Alliance, was preparing to attempt a rescue. Nearly one hundred of them fell close to the left flank of our regiment. As the prisoners passed us on their way to the rear, one and all of them declared that we had cut to pieces the flower of the French army. They, no doubt, thought so.

When the Scots Greys charged past the flanks of the 92d, both regiments cheered, and joined in the heart-touching cry of " Scotland for ever !"

2

These words possessed a charm, which none but those ardently attached to their native country ever rightly understood. The mere sound of them, in the ears of every one who was present, will ever recall to their remembrance one of the most interesting and awfully grand scenes which man ever beheld. When we retired behind the hedge on the ridge, it was exactly a quarter past three o'clock. I never saw the soldiers of this regiment so very savage as they were on this occasion; they repeatedly cried to the cavalry to spare none of the French—that they did not deserve mercy at their hands. The British soldiers were, no doubt, much enraged at their opponents, for their extreme cruelty to some of the Prussian and British prisoners, who had the misfortune to fall into their hands on the 16th. Report had, on the 17th, magnified these cruelties into an indiscriminate butchery of all the prisoners who had fallen into their hands. The effect produced by that report was such as might have been expected. The death of their companions, they imagined, called loudly for revenge. Our soldiers no longer looked on those of France as the enemies of their country only, but as a horde of barbarians, let loose upon the inhabitants of every civilized state. I firmly believe, that the soldiers, before the commencement of the battle, had agreed, amongst themselves, to send as many of their enemies into another world as they could.

Whatever may have been the cause, I never saw the same kind of feeling pervade these soldiers in any former battle in which they had been engaged. Towards the close of the battle, when the enemy was more to be pitied than feared, they assumed a very different air, and treated those who were made prisoners with the kindness characteristic of the British soldier.

For nearly 20 minutes after the return of the troops to the ridge, from the charge I have described, there was almost a total suspension of hostilities on the part of the enemy, particularly on their right. The result of the attack of our position, to the left of Mount St John, had dreadfully deranged the plans of Napoleon; so much so, indeed, that to remedy them required fully half an hour. During this time the rocket brigade was busily employed in an attempt to break a mass of French infantry, formed about half way down the opposite ridge, and which had all along acted as a reserve to those troops which assailed the heights. The Scots Greys, at the same time, hovered on their flanks, to take advantage of any opening that might occur. But all the efforts of that brigade, assisted by the few of the artillery in front of the left wing, made no impression on them whatever.

About half-past three, Napoleon ordered an attack on the whole extent of our line. Hougomont was again assailed with increased fury. Numerous attempts were made to wrest it from the gallant spirits who defended it. By the terrible shower of shells which the enemy poured into the chateau, it was set on fire. Numbers of the wounded, who could not be removed from the house, fell a prey to the flames! The fire at Hougomont caused a temporary depression of our spirits, as, in the flames of that ancient edifice, we fancied we beheld the fate of the gallant garrison.

The enemy conceiving, no doubt, that one other effort would make the place their own, surrounded the court-yard and garden, and attempted to carry them at the point of the bayonet. But in that, as in numerous subsequent attempts, the French were driven back, with immense loss. During these important operations, the enemy had penetrated to that part of the ridge on which the 2d division was posted. With a great body of cavalry he attempted to carry the heights; but the infantry battalions having formed themselves into squares, repelled the assailants with great slaughter. The horses of the artillery, attached to that division, were taken from the guns, and sent to the rear of the infantry, and when the enemy came close, the artillerymen took shelter within our squares of infantry. This was a most admirable plan; for the enemy's force being all cavalry, could make no use of the guns when they fell into their hands; and it enabled

R

our gunners to remain at their posts, pouring
destruction on their enemies, till they were
within a few paces of them. The French cavalry were for a long time extremely bold;
they galloped round the British squares, brandishing their swords, and, in several instances, chal-
lenged our officers to single combat ; every where
the enemy fought with great bravery—often, I
thought, it bordered on frenzy.

By four o'clock the battle had become general
throughout every part of the line. Our centre
was furiously assailed by a great body of cavalry,
principally cuirassiers, who were supported in
the attack by a numerous artillery, and a large
force of veteran infantry. The enemy succeeded in penetrating to the crest of the eminence,
but no farther. There they were met by the 3d
division, and right of the 5th, who, in a few
minutes, sent them reeling back on their reserves.

The field of battle now assumed a horrid aspect. The slope in front of our position was so
completely covered with the mangled corpses of
the enemy, that it was scarcely possible for either
man or beast to walk without treading on them.
Their wounded were also extremely numerous ;
those who were unable to remove themselves from
the gory field, were kept in constant terror either
of being shot by the enraged combatants, or trod
to death by their horses. The cries of those poor

creatures were, in part, drowned amidst the clash of arms, and the thunder of 500 pieces of cannon, which spread death in every direction, and absolutely made the earth shake under our feet. The enemy's cry of Vive l'Empereur, which incessantly assailed our ears from every quarter, produced a sound greatly resembling that kind of murmuring noise, which you must have heard when near to a bee-hive.

Marshal Prince Blucher having consented to assist the Duke of Wellington with the greater part of the troops under his command, gave orders for three corps of his army to march from Wavre at four o'clock on the morning of the 18th; two of them by the pass of Saint Lambert, and the other by Ohain. By a road which runs from Ter la Haye to Ohain, the communication between the two armies was kept up. The rest of the Prussian army was left in position at Wavre. Aware that the Prussians were coming to our assistance, we looked for them about three o'clock with much anxiety, but there were none of them in view. Another hour passed away—still there was no appearance of them. But, about half-past four, two Prussian officers passed in front of our line, at full speed, eagerly inquiring for the Duke of Wellington. At the sight of those officers, our hearts leapt with joy; their appearance was an assurance that the intrepid soldiers of the Prussian warrior were at hand. Having delivered

their message, they flew past us in the same manner, all the way cheered by the British line. Soon
after, the fire of the Prussian corps, under General Bulow, was distinctly seen, on the extreme
right of the French army. At first the Prussians
were few in number, and, owing to the bad state
of the roads, were not sufficiently reinforced till
after six, to enable them to make any serious impression on the enemy. As they arrived, however, every Prussian battalion joined in the terrible fray, which, before six, had become pretty
general along the whole of the heights of Aguiers.
Bonaparte, finding himself attacked in a more serious manner than he had anticipated, caused his
right to be reinforced by the reserves of his army;—between them and the troops under Bulow
a tremendous fight continued till near seven
o'clock. By that time the whole of the Prussians,
who had advanced by the pass of Saint Lambert,
had arrived, and entered the lists; and the head
of the other column, commanded by General
Zeithen, and with which the veteran Blucher
moved, made its appearance about the same
time, near Ter la Haye. In order to prevent
the junction of the British and Prussian armies,
Napoleon threw several columns towards the extreme left of the British army. They were attacked with spirit by Blucher, who, from Ohain,
marched directly on Papelotte, leaving Ter la
Haye on his right; by this movement, the junc-

2

tion of the two armies was effected, and the object which Bonaparte had in view completely defeated.

About six o'clock, Napoleon ordered another terrible charge on the centre of our position, the troops, at that point, having suffered more than those to the right. The cannonade, which preceded the march of his infantry, was of the severest kind. The shot fell in such quantities, that many of the balls and shells must have encountered each other before they came to the ground. Under cover of their artillery, the infantry and cavalry columns of the enemy ascended the ridge, where they were met, with firmness, by the allied troops ; and, as before, driven down the slope at the point of the bayonet. From that hour till seven, the battle raged with great fury, from Hougomont to the heights of Aguiers. Every moment the fire of the Prussian artillery became more lively. Although the French troops had been unsuccessful in all their operations against us, still they renewed their attacks with the same spirit which they showed at the commencement of the battle. In many instances, the French cavalry galloped up to our squares of infantry, fired their pistols, and then walked their horses quietly away.—Never did the French troops fight with greater bravery, and never were they so signally defeated.

The hour was now approaching in which the

fate of Napoleon and his army was to be decided. As a final effort to extricate himself from the disagreeable situation in which he found himself placed, he brought forward the reserve of his guard, amounting, it is said, to 15,000 men ; and putting himself at their head, directed them to march to the bottom of the ridge, where he remained to witness the result of the awful struggle.

Their principal efforts were directed against the left centre of the allied position ; but, in fact, it was a general charge of the whole disposable French army, against every part of our line. Under cover of a tremendous cannonade, the Imperial guards ascended the heights. During their march, the cry of Vive l'Empereur resounded from every mouth,—every man of them had sworn to conquer or die. Our bravest officers looked forward to the issue of the conflict with considerable emotion. The effect produced by a similar movement on the 16th, being still fresh in their recollection. The enemy having a superiority of fully 50,000 men at the commencement of the engagement, were, at that moment, notwithstanding their severe losses, still greatly superior to the army under the Duke of Wellington ; and, when we reflected how very small a proportion of that army were British, there seemed to be too much cause for a temporary sinking of the heart. I am aware that many despaired of victory ; but I am as positive that there was not a man who thought of retreating, while one of his companions remained to dispute with the enemy the possession of the field.

Having about this time been wounded in the groin by a musket-ball, I was compelled to make the best of my way to Brussels, leaving my friends, however, firm as the mountain rock, and shewing, by their looks, that every one of them had made up his mind to conquer or die. Knowing how very anxious you will be to hear every particular of that terrible battle, I annex the copy of a letter which I have received from a friend, who was present during the subsequent operations of the allied army. Speaking of the last effort of the French, he says :—" The enemy opened a tre-
" mendous fire on us from every piece of artillery
" he had in the field ; and also from a cloud of
" sharpshooters, who covered the advance of the Im-
" perial guard. The French advanced with great
" intrepidity, and, for some time, carried every
" thing before them :—Our light troops were
" quickly drawn in, who took their station in line,
" and in square, when their services became no
" longer useful in front. As the enemy's troops
" approached the crest of the height, the fire
" from their artillery slackened. The smoke hav-
" ing, in some measure, evaporated, the two
" armies found themselves opposed to each other
" at the distance of twenty paces. For a moment

" the two armies viewed each other with stern
" composure, and then, as if by mutual consent,
" proceeded to decide the important contest.

" The battle raged with violence for a consi-
" derable time; and, till half-past seven, the vic-
" tory was doubtful. About that time, however,
" some little hesitation was observed in their
" movements, and the gallant Blucher was seen
" advancing on the enemy's right, spreading
" death and dismay over that part of the field.
" The Duke, perceiving that all was not right
" with Napoleon, ordered the whole of the allied
" army to advance. The charge was irresistible.
" The enemy fled in confusion, and their flying co-
" lumns were roughly handled by our cavalry and
" artillery. The old guard of Bonaparte attempt-
" ed to stop our progress. The carnage was im-
" mense ;—in many places the enemy lay in
" heaps ;—our artillery made dreadful havock in
" their squares of infantry, and the numerous
" mangled corpses, which every where strewed
" the field, showed, from the nature of their
" wounds, that the cavalry had done their duty.
" After a desperate resistance, on the part of the
" old guard, we drove the enemy past La Belle
" Alliance, a little in front of which we came in
" contact with the Prussians, who halted on our
" approach, and played our national air of ' God
" save the King.' In the vicinity of La Belle

" Alliance, the two great Commanders met, after
" the battle, and congratulated each other on the
" successful termination of their joint labours.

" The French troops fought with great bravery;
" but, on several occasions, with too much feroci-
" ty. They really seemed, at times, to throw
" aside the character of the man, and assume that
" of the tiger. It was a desperate game, to be
" sure, which their leader was playing, and it was,
" no doubt, his best policy to employ men equally
" desperate as himself."

Compelled to retire from the gory heights of Mount St John, I bent my steps towards Waterloo. On my way to the village, the shells and cannon balls of the enemy fell around me in great profusion. A considerable number of the latter skipped along the causeway till their strength was exhausted, or, by coming in contact with some of the poor mutilated soldiers, terminated their own career, and that of the wretched sufferers.

Waterloo was literally filled with the wounded of the allied army—their cries were piercing; every thing was done by the medical people to get them removed—but their numbers far exceeded the means of transport which the chief medical officer had at his command. Without legs, without arms, soldiers were seen lying in every direction; some crying for help, others, who could scarcely articulate, were begging to be placed on a waggon, out of reach of the shot; many were lying horribly disfigured with numerous wounds, and faintly crying Water, water, water! The situation of the wounded was considerably aggravated, by the reports of the runaways, that the French had forced the centre of the allied army, and were on the point of entering Waterloo. On the receipt of that intelligence, a great

proportion of the wounded, who could not be accommodated with seats in the waggons, quitted
the village, and fled into the forest of Soignies.
Many of these poor creatures, unable to proceed
to Brussels, laid themselves down, never to rise
again. Some of them were found three days afterwards, in a state too horrible to describe.

The wounded in the waggons were also doom-
ed to suffer greatly on the occasion. Every one
of the carts was crowded with them; the road
was so completely blocked up, all the way from
Waterloo to Brussels, with baggage and stores of
various kinds, that the carriages with the wounded could not proceed. The consequence was,
that the infamous report which was circulated in
Waterloo, having spread itself in less than an hour
to Brussels, the wounded, thinking themselves in
danger, left the carts, and, like those at Waterloo, sought for safety in the wood, where they
also perished. The foreign cavalry, in their flight
to the rear, threatened to sabre every one who
would not, or rather could not, let them pass.
The greatest part of the Belgians who were driving the waggons, either left them altogether, or
got drunk, and were unable to perform their
duty. In short, the whole scene was one of in-
describable horror and confusion, without a parallel in the annals of our history, ancient or modern.

When the advance of the French was first

known in Brussels, the inhabitants were much
agitated. The 17th was a gloomy day to them;
but the 18th was one of horror. The ramparts
of the city, nearest to Waterloo, were crowded
with people, very soon after the battle began.
After two o'clock, reports from the field were
brought to Brussels every minute. At one time,
the French had been defeated with great loss;—
at another, Napoleon had beat Wellington, and
would make his entry into the city that night.
These contradictory and perplexing rumours
threw the good people into a state of temporary
insanity. The wounded began to arrive about
two, and every moment continued to increase, till
the road was completely covered with them.
About four, the alarm was at its height;—a report
was circulated that a French column was about
to enter the city, but whether as victors or prisoners none ever inquired. Some time after,
the enemy made their entry, about 2000 in
number, guarded by part of Sir William Ponsonby's brigade. These were the prisoners taken
at three o'clock, on the left of our position. Although the people saw, and knew them to be
prisoners of war, still fears continued to haunt
their breasts—still they thought Napoleon must
ultimately be the conqueror.

Nothing could exceed the kindness and attention of the inhabitants to our wounded, on their
arrival in the city. All ranks vied with each

other in their personal acts of kindness. Many
of the most respectable ladies in Brussels stood
all the day at the gate by which the wounded
entered, and to each soldier, as they arrived,
distributed wine, tea, coffee, soup, bread, and
cordials of various kinds; others remained at
their houses, and ministered to the wants of
those who wandered through the streets, many
of whom were taken into the houses of these
humane people, had their wounds dressed, and,
if they were so severely wounded as not to be
able to proceed further to the rear, a bed was
furnished them in the lower flat of the house, on
which they might rest their wearied limbs.

It was past 11 o'clock before I arrived in Brussels. By that time, almost every house in it was filled. I proceeded to an hotel, which I had frequented previous to our late move, but there was no ad-
mission for me. The excuse was, that the French
would enter the city in the morning; and if they
found a British officer in the house, they would
put them all to death. Such an excuse could only proceed from a selfish mind, or one influenced
by French politics. With considerable difficulty,
I procured a billet on one of the principal ho-
tels in the Place-Royal. There every thing was
in confusion, and the people did not know
what to do. A medical officer, and myself, slept
in one apartment. The beds were none of the

best; but any kind of bed was better than the one
on which we slept the preceding night.

We went to bed, expecting to be roused very
soon after day-break by the thundering of Napoleon's cannon under the walls of Brussels.—
Conceive, then, our agreeable disappointment, to
hear from one of the waiters, in the morning, that
the French army had been totally routed!

Those individuals, who assumed such a haughty
demeanour on the evening of the 18th, were now
as humble as you please. Every thing we asked for
was immediately brought to us. Wellington, the
Prince of Orange, and Blucher, were never out
of their mouths. The British, with them, were
all; but they generally reminded us, that the Belgian troops were sharers of the glory of the day,
by putting the question—" The Belgians fought
" very well—Did they not?"

During the whole of the 19th, 20th, and 21st
of the month, the wounded were brought into
Brussels in considerable numbers; and, even so late
as the 23d, they had not all been removed. The
field of Waterloo, on the 19th, presented, I have
been told, one of the most horrid, frightful spec-
tacles ever seen in any age or country. The
wounded covered the field in such a manner, at
the time the last charge was made on the 18th,
that it was found impossible to move the guns
past them. Many of them, therefore, were

either crushed under the wheels of the artillery, or trodden to death by the cavalry. Their mangled corpses, on the 19th, strewed every part of the carnage-covered field, and gave additional horror to the ghastly scene.

A great part of the baggage of the army had arrived at Brussels on the evening of the 17th, and was encamped outside of the walls; but the baggage of some of the divisions having remained near Waterloo till the action began on the 18th, got mixed in the march to the rear, by which means a number of officers have lost every article of their clothes. It is asserted, that a number of the batmen quitted their horses and baggage, and made off to Ghent and Antwerp, as fast as their feet, or canal boats, could carry them.

It is supposed, that upwards of 10,000 of the foreign troops left their standards on the 18th; and, in their disgraceful flight, robbed and plundered a number of the inhabitants of the country, even very close to this city. Surely the conduct of the batmen, who shamefully abandoned their charge, and those soldiers, who committed such enormities, will undergo a strict investigation.

There is scarcely a house in Brussels but what gives shelter to two wounded soldiers. In the greater number, there are not fewer than four, six, or eight. On their doors, or windows, the inhabitants have the number marked on a piece

of paper, distinguishing the number of each nation; as, for instance, " Four wounded English"
—" Four wounded Scotch," &c. To these pa-
tients, the people are uncommonly kind and attentive, allowing them to want for nothing.

The French wounded are almost all quartered
in the city hospitals, or in those houses, whose
owners may have shown a lukewarmness in the
present contest. Their constant cry was, and
still is, " Vive l'Empereur!" Some of them were
brought in from the field the other day, extremely weak, from loss of blood, and want of food—
many of these poor wretches, although scarce able
to lift their head, vented the same exclamation.
Louis XVIII. sent an officer, the other day, to
inquire if they were in want of any thing, and
to afford assistance to those who required it. He
visited every one of the hospitals; but I believe
he could not prevail on one of them to accept of
assistance from him, in the name of his sovereign. They had no king but one, " Vive l'Em-
" pereur!" One of them finding that he had
but a short time to live, converted the cry into
a kind of song, which he continued to chaunt
till he expired.

One of the French Generals, who was made
prisoner on the 18th, having rendered himself
conspicuous on some occasions, by his devotion
to the usurper, was roughly handled on entering
this city. As soon as he had entered the gates,

the General, in a true turn-coat style, cried—
" Vive le Roi!" Indignant at his barefaced
impudence, the populace pelted him with mud,
and every missile weapon they could lay their
hands on, till he cleared the city at the other extremity.

In the house where I am now quartered, there
are three ladies—the mother, and two daughters.
The two latter take the duty of attending the
hospitals with cordials alternately. They pay
their visits at eight in the morning, and the
same hour in the evening. Two days ago, the
youngest of them returned in tears. On inquiring the cause, she said another lady had prevailed on her to visit an artillery officer, who
had lost both his legs, and one of his arms, in
the late dreadful conflict. Having seen a number of very bad cases, in the different hospitals
she had visited, the young lady thought she
would be able to view, without shrinking, the
mangled frame of the unfortunate officer. But,
on entering the cheerless apartment, where the
poor sufferer lay, she found him in the agonies of death. This was more than my young
friend could bear. She burst into tears; and,
quitting the sad scene, with a heavy heart she returned to her home.

Another family, who live in the Rue de l'Empereur, consisting of an aged mother, three daugh-

ters, and a son, have given up the two front
rooms of the street floor, for the accommodation
of the wounded British soldiers. One of the
rooms is fitted up with mattrasses for those men
who are completely disabled; and the other is a
kind of laboratory, cooking, and dressing shop,
where all those who are able to walk about, have
their wounds dressed by the young ladies;—whatever medicines they require are administered;
and the necessary nourishment is distributed with
a bountiful hand.

Yesterday, I asked one of the life-guards-men
what plan his regiment adopted to kill the French
cuirassiers on the 18th? He replied—"At first, Sir,
" we could not kill them at all. Before the battle
" began, our officers gave us orders to cut their
" reins; but we soon found that would not do.
" The next orders we got, were to strike at
" their legs—that would not do either. We
" then received instructions to poke them under
" the arm, and in the groin. We had soon an
" opportunity of trying the new plan, which was
" found to succeed uncommonly well: After
" that we killed them with as much ease as we
" would have done as many rabbits."

During the time that the 92d regiment lined
the bank at Quatre Bras on the 16th, a soldier,
named Milne, while sitting at my right hand,
had his bonnet carried off his head by a can-
non-ball, without injuring his head. For two

days after, however, he appeared in rather low spirits, and not quite so active as he used to be.

Lord Hill having arrived at Quatre Bras on the morning of the 17th, to pay his respects to the Duke of Wellington, the old soldiers of our regiment, who had served under him in Spain, embraced that opportunity of testifying their regard for the character of that truly brave and amiable General:—On leaving the Duke's hut, he was greeted with the loud cheers of every individual in the corps. His Lordship turned round, and, with his hat in his hand, approached his friends, greatly affected—the men still continuing to salute him, with cheers which proceeded from the heart. The Duke came to the door of his wooden house, smiled, and appeared much pleased with this mark of respect paid to his favourite General.

At the conclusion of the memorable charge, made by part of the left wing at three o'clock on the 18th, a friend of mine made lawful prize of a beautiful charger, richly caparisoned. The splendid furniture made him expect a handsome brace of pistols in the holsters. On opening them, however, he was most agreeably disappointed, by finding that a good bottle of Champaigne occupied the one, and the leg of a fowl, and a piece of bread, the other. My friend, being of a very generous disposition, divided the contents of the bottle equally with another officer and myself.

It was certainly the sweetest I ever tasted—
my mouth at the time being much parched with
thirst.

Three of my brother officers, and myself, were
seated behind the farm of Quatre Bras on the morning of the 17th, when I received a message from
a wounded soldier, named Robinson, begging
me to speak with him, as he had in his possession a book which I would like to read. I com-
plied with his request—received the book; and,
on opening it, was truly astonished to find it the
History of Scotland's Champion, Sir William Wallace. It was a very old edition, and, on the morning of the 16th, had been in the possession of
a French soldier, whose name was inscribed on
one of the blank leaves, and who had most probably fallen in the conflict, in the after part of
that day. In France, the histories of Bruce and
Wallace are much read by the soldiers; and it
is a well-authenticated fact, that Bonaparte seldom
went on a campaign without a copy of Ossian's
Poems in his possession.

An officer of the 71st regiment has favoured
me with the two following melancholy anecdotes.

On the morning of the 19th June, the 71st regiment was ordered to cook with as much haste
as they possibly could. In order to obey the
orders of their superiors, two privates of that
corps, and one of the staff corps, proceeded to
break up a French ammunition waggon which was

close to them, thinking, no doubt, that it would make excellent fire-wood. Armed with bill-hooks, they had almost accomplished their purpose, when unluckily the waggon exploded, and carried the poor fellows into the air. Pieces of their jackets, and fragments of their mangled limbs, fell on their comrades, whose feelings on the occasion were of that description which words are inadequate to describe.

About nine o'clock in the morning of the 19th June, the officers of the 71st regiment got orders to inspect the arms of their men, and cause the shot to be drawn from those muskets which they might find loaded. Two corporals, who had for a long time been comrades, and tender friends, happened to be sitting together when the order was issued. On rising from the ground, to draw their ammunition, one took hold of the other's firelock, attempting, in sport, to keep the other down. Whilst engaged in the friendly squabble, the piece of Corporal ——— went off, and lodged its contents in the breast of his friend Corporal Corner, who almost instantly expired.

Bonaparte's carriage was taken by the Prussians at Genappe, a few minutes after he had quitted it. It contains many curiosities, I am informed, well worth seeing; but as yet I have not been so lucky as to see it.

When Colonel Cameron received his wound, he was removed from Quatre Bras to Genappe,

where it was examined, and found to be mortal.
In that village he remained till the following
morning. About nine o'clock, on the 17th, he
was put into a waggon, in which he was to be
conveyed to Brussels. From the moment he was
wounded, he himself declared his wound to be
mortal. He asked " If the enemy had been
" defeated ?"—Having received an answer in
the affirmative, he said—" Then I die hap-
" py !" And a few minutes before his speech
failed him, he said, " I hope my country will think
" that I have served her faithfully." On entering
the village of Waterloo, between one and two o'-
clock, he laid back his head on his servant's arm,
and took leave of this world.

Towards the close of the charge in which
the Duke of Brunswick fell, one of his soldiers was dismounted a little way in front of
the 92d regiment, to which he fled for re-
fuge. But, before he attained his object, the
Highland infantry had got orders to fire on
the enemy's cavalry. Placed between two fires,
and not more than ten yards from us, he naturally enough thought that he was to be blown
to pieces. He screamed dreadfully :—His cries attracted the attention of our men, who called to
him to come behind the bank. Having done so,
his first salutation was—" Oh ! comrades, my
" Prince be killed—my horse be killed, by de
" French devils ; but, (drawing his pistols), G—t

" d—n them, I have my pistols and my sword
" yet !"

The loss of the allied army at Waterloo is not
yet known; but it must have been very great.
It has sustained a severe loss in the fall of these
two distinguished officers, Sir Thomas Picton and
Sir William Ponsonby. The former fell by a musket-ball, which entered at one temple and came
out at the other. The horse of the latter having
stuck in a soft part of the field, he was stabbed
by some of the enemy's cavalry, before he could
be relieved.

Neither the Duke of Wellington, nor Prince
Marshal Blucher, has given the French army one
moment's repose since the memorable 18th. The
latest accounts from the armies are of the most
gratifying description. All the private letters represent the French army as completely disorganized, and in want of every thing. Never was
the rout of any army more complete. The strength
of the French army at Waterloo, on the morning of the battle, was *one hundred and eighteen
thousand men,* and the allied army, under the Duke
of Wellington, *sixty-eight thousand. This information I received from a* FRENCH *General Officer,
in the suite of Louis, on the* 20th, *who stated, that
he had it from the mouth of the Duke of Wellington, on the morning of the* 19th.

On the 20th instant, the Duke of Wellington
issued an order to his army, previous to their

entering the French territory; and, on the following day, he issued a proclamation to the inhabitants of France. The latter is dated from Malplacquet, famous for the victory gained by the
great Marlborough over the French army, commanded by Marshals Villars and Boufflers, in
1709.

I have sent you copies of those two documents,
as they throw a little light on the views of the
allied Sovereigns, regarding the future government of France.

PROCLAMATION.

I announce to the French, that I enter their territory at the
head of an army already victorious—not as an enemy, (except
of the usurper, the enemy of the human race, with whom there
can be neither peace nor truce), but to aid them to shake off the
iron yoke by which they are oppressed. I therefore give to my
army the subjoined orders; and I desire, that every one who
violates them, may be made known to me. The French know,
however, that I have a right to require, that they conduct themselves in such a manner, that I may be able to protect them a-
gainst those who would seek to do them evil. They must, then,
furnish the requisitions that will be made by persons authorised
to make them, taking receipts in due form and order; that they
remain quietly at their houses, and have no correspondence or
communication with the usurper, or with his adherents. All
those who shall absent themselves from their houses, after the
entrance of the army into France, and all those who shall be
absent in the service of the usurper, shall be considered as ene-

mies, and his adherents; and their property shall be appropriated to the subsistence of the army.

Given at Head-Quarters, at Malplacquet, the 21st of June, 1815.

(Signed)   WELLINGTON.

Extract from the Order of the Day, June 20, 1815.

As the army is going to enter the French territory, the troops of the different nations, now under the command of Field-Marshal the Duke of Wellington, are desired to remember, that their respective Sovereigns are the allies of his Majesty the King of France; and that France must, therefore, be considered as a friendly country—It is ordered, that nothing be taken, either by the officers or soldiers, without payment. The Commissaries of the army will provide for the wants of the troops in the usual manner; and it is not permitted to the officers or soldiers of the army to make requisitions. The Commissaries will be authorised by the Field-Marshal, or by the Generals who command the troops of the respective nations, (that is to say, in case their provisions are not regulated by an English Commissary), to make the necessary requisitions, for which they will give regular receipts; and they must perfectly understand, that they will be responsible for all that they receive by requisitions from the inhabitants of France, in the same manner as if they made purchases for the account of their Government, in their own country.

(Signed)   J. WATERS,
                Acting Adjutant-General.

CAMP, NEAR PARIS, *July* 20, 1815.

IN company with a medical officer, I quitted
Brussels on the morning of the 2d instant, dined
at Braine la Compte, and slept at a farm-house
three miles in front of it. I had not been long in
the house before I discovered that at some period
subsequent to their matrimonial union, the farmer
and his wife had changed small-clothes—the original husband appeared to be one of the best-natur-
ed creatures alive, but the wife is one of the
greatest vixens that Belgium or any other country
ever produced. Early on the morning of the
3d, we took leave of these people and rode to
Mons.

The town of Mons stands on an eminence, is
strongly fortified, and the country around it can
be inundated at pleasure. The streets are spacious,
and extremely clean, and the inhabitants are kind
and hospitable.

On the 4th, we crossed the country to Bavay.
The village being full, we were under the necessity
of riding three miles farther, having first procured an order for a billet from the commandant of
Bavay to the mayor of a neighbouring commune.
With some difficulty we found out the mayor in
the person of a respectable farmer, who showed
us every attention in his power ; but the wife was
thrown into hysterics at our appearance ; the salt

tears trickled down her cheeks for nearly two hours after our arrival. Breakfast being almost ready, we asked the mayor for a couple of eggs, and a little milk for our tea. The articles we asked for were brought; but upon their being presented to us, madame tore her hair and wrung her hands in all the bitterness of despair. Her husband endeavoured to pacify her; but all his efforts were fruitless, till she saw us pull a few sous out of our pocket to pay her husband for the trifles we had got from him. The money had a most powerful effect—her tears were instantly dried up —joy beamed in her countenance—and, during our stay, we were furnished with every thing by our hostess, handsome payment, however, being made for the same.

About one o'clock, a party of Prussian troops, headed by an officer, arrived at the mayor's. The officer having alighted to get information respecting the disposition of the people, the soldiers amused themselves with the mayoress during the time their officer was employed. The first thing they did to vex the good woman, was to call for beer, which, being soon produced, part of it they drank and the rest they poured out. The Prussians then requested that a bottle of brandy might be given them. The request being granted, each of the soldiers, in a bumper, wished her long life, and added, that as her brandy was peculiarly well flavoured, it was probable they might repeat their visit next day.

Cateau being the next stage, we departed for that place early on the following morning. Soon after our arrival, the mayor received intelligence that the French army in Paris had consented to evacuate the capital, and retire behind the Loire. The news were received by the inhabitants with rapturous applause, and they seemed to vie with each other in their demonstrations of loyalty and attachment to the Bourbons.

On the 6th, our route led us to La Chatelet. The village being quite full, the mayor gave me a billet on himself. That gentleman lives at a splendid chateau about a mile from the village. From him and his lady I received every attention during my short stay. We sat down to breakfast at two o'clock, and to dinner at ten.

At 11 o'clock on the 7th, we entered Peronne. There being a strong garrison of Belgian troops in the town, we were under the necessity of accepting of an order for a billet on the mayor of a commune three miles in front of it.

Peronne is situated in a marshy plain on the banks of the Somme, and is a place of considerable strength. Had it been furnished with the necessary means of defence, the allied army would have had some difficulty in taking the place; but when the Duke of Wellington made his ap-

pearance before it on the 26th ultimo, there were
only a few guns mounted on the ramparts, and a
very small garrison to defend them.

We arrived in Roye on the 8th, where we
stopped during the 9th; and, on the 10th, we
slept in Gournay, and on the 11th at Pont de
St Maxance. The last town is situated on the
Oise, over which there is a very fine bridge, one
arch of which was lately destroyed by the French
at the close of a sharp engagement with part of
the Prussian army. A number of men are now
busily employed in repairing it. Some of the
houses close to the bridge, which were loop-holed,
and occupied by the French, were either burned
down, or considerably damaged during the battle,
by the enraged combatants.

On the 12th, our route carried us to the village
of Louvre, and on the following day we joined
our respective regiments in camp, behind the village of Clichy, at the distance of one mile from
Paris, and a few yards from the Seine.

From Mons, the allied army, commanded by
the Duke of Wellington, marched to Bavay on
the 21st of June, where his Grace issued the
proclamation to the French people, (a copy of
which I transmitted from Brussels.) On the
22d, the head-quarters were at La Coteau. On
the 24th, the town of Cambray was attacked by
Lieutenant-General Sir Charles Colville, and taken

with little loss. On the 25th, the citadel surrendered to Louis XVIII. who made his entry into Cambray on the following day.—Peronne was
taken on the 26th, by a brigade of guards, under Major-General Maitland.

Prince Blucher, with the Prussian army, entered the French territory by Beaumont, advanced on Saint Quentin, which was abandoned by
the enemy on his approach. The remains of the
French army fled before the veteran Marshal, in
a dreadful state of confusion and wretchedness.

On the 28th, Blucher occupied Senlis and
Villars Coterets; in the latter place, his advanced
guard was attacked by the French troops, under
Marshal Grouchy, who, having effected his escape
from Wavre, was now hastening to assist in
the defence of the capital. The French were
beat off with considerable loss. The same
corps was afterwards attacked by General Bulow, and very roughly handled. On the 30th
June, and 1st instant, Prince Blucher crossed the
Seine, near the town of St Germain; and, on
the 2d, had a very severe action with the enemy,
on the heights above St Cloud. In a village
called Issy, the Marshal was attacked in the morning of the 3d, but repulsed every effort made by
the enemy to dislodge him.

The Duke of Wellington having dispatched a
corps of British troops across the Seine, to co-

2

operate with the Prince Marshal, and the remainder of the allied army being ready to storm
the works of the enemy at St Denis, &c. Marshal
Davoust sent a flag of truce, to request a suspension of hostilities, and stating his readiness to
give up Paris, on certain conditions.

On the same day, Marshal Davoust agreed to
withdraw his army from Paris, and retire behind
the Loire. In conformity with this agreement,
the French troops began their march from the metropolis on the 4th, and finally evacuated the city
on the 6th. The allied army occupied Paris on
the 7th, and Louis XVIII. entered his capital on
the 8th. On the following day, he formed his
ministry; in the list of members composing it you
will find some well-known characters, who have
acted various parts in the tragic drama of the
last five-and-twenty years.

DECREE.

Louis, by the grace of God, King of France and Navarre.
To all, &c. Wishing to give our ministry a character of unity
and solidity, which may inspire our subjects with just confidence, we have decreed as follows :—Prince Talleyrand, Peer
of France, is appointed President of the Council of Ministers,
and Secretary of State for Foreign Affairs ; Baron Louis, Minister Secretary of State for Finances ; (Fouche) Duke of
Otranto, Minister Secretary of State for the Department of General Police ; Baron Pasquier, Minister Secretary of State for
the Department of Justice, and Keeper of the Seals ; Marshal
Gouvion St Cyr, Peer of France, Minister Secretary of State

for the War Department; Count Jaucour, Peer of France, Minister Secretary of State for the Marine Department; the Duke de Richelieu, Minister Secretary of State for the Department of the Household. The Portfolio of the Interior will be provisionally entrusted to the Minister of Justice.—Given at Paris, the 9th of July 1815, in the 21st year of our reign.

(Signed)   LOUIS.

By the King.   PRINCE DE TALLEYRAND.

The royalists are much hurt at the King, for admitting men into his councils, who voted for the death of his brother, the unfortunate Louis XVI.; indeed, it is thought very bad policy of Louis to have Fouche in the ministry at all— a man whose crimes will long be remembered in France.

In Paris, Marshal Ney is charged with all the disasters which have befallen the French army during this short but memorable campaign.— Others are also named as accomplices in his treason. Ney, in a letter to Fouche, attempted to exculpate himself of the foul charge of treason; but his conduct to the King is still so strongly imprinted on the minds of the greater part of the people, that the current report of the day will be believed in opposition to all the epistles which the Marshal may think proper to write on the subject. Ney may be as bad a man as these people attempt to make him; but it is only justice to mention, that there is none in this army who believes the report. Almost every one considers it a patch-

2

ed up story to lessen the glory achieved at
Waterloo by the allied armies.

Since I began to write this letter, a Paris paper
has been put into my hand, containing the following letter from a Captain Bonnefoux, dated

ROCHEFORT, *July* 15, 10 *o'Clock at night.*

To execute the orders of your Excellency, I embarked in
my boat, accompanied by Baron Richard, Prefect of Charente
Inferieure. The reports from the Roads of the 14th had not
yet reached me. I was informed by Captain Philibert, commander of the Amphitrite frigate, that Bonaparte had embarked on board the brig Epervier, armed as a flag of truce, determined to surrender himself to the English cruisers. In fact,
at break of day, we saw him manœuvre to approach the English
ship Bellerophon, commanded by Captain Maitland, who, seeing that Bonaparte was coming towards him, mounted a white
flag at the mizzen-mast. Bonaparte was received on board the
English vessel, as also the persons in his suite. The officer
whom I left in observation, had informed me of this important
news, when General Beker, who arrived a few moments afterwards, confirmed it to me.

(Signed)   BONNEFOUX,
                    Captain of a vessel, and Maritime Prefect.

I beg to congratulate you on the pleasing intelligence contained in the above letter; and,
I may add, on the termination of the present
war. Bonaparte being in the hands of the English, his adherents in France must either fly to
foreign parts, or make another effort to rouse the
people in mass, to drive us out of the country,
as all those who were implicated in the March

T

plot, will, no doubt, be brought to punishment; indeed, the King expressly says so, in his address to the people, of the 28th June.

Since the occupation of Paris by the allied armies, the British officers have, on many occasions, been openly insulted in the streets by the revolutionists. On some they vented their spleen, by spitting on them from the windows; others have been hissed, and called by names that would disgrace the Fauxbourg St Antoine: When it is generally known that Bonaparte is in the hands of the English, they will not be so very bold.

In the mean time, every means of precaution has been adopted to ensure the tranquillity of the city. On the bridges, Prince Blucher has planted cannon, and the artillerymen are standing by them night and day, with their matches lighted, ready to act at a moment's notice. The Prussian army has its advance in front of Paris, on the road to Orleans, the present head-quarters of the French army under Davoust, and denominated the army of the Loire. These troops, with their leaders, have, it is said, submitted to the new order of things, or rather the old order restored. Field-Marshal Blucher's head-quarters are in Paris, which is occupied by a great part of his army. One brigade of British infantry occupies the Champs Elysees, and some regiments are in garrison in Montmartre. The

other divisions of the allied army are encamped in the Bois de Boulogne, and down the right
bank of the Seine, as far as St Ouen. The
greater number of the gates of the capital are
at present held by British, and the rest by the
troops of the other three great Powers.

———

CAMP, CLICHY, *September* 24, 1815.

THE British and Hanoverian troops were reviewed on the 22d by the Emperor of Austria,
in the plain of St Denis. The following particulars of that grand sight may probably amuse
you.

Agreeably to the orders of the Field-Marshal,
the British and Hanoverian army was formed
by nine o'clock on the 22d, with its left resting on the village of La Chapelle, and the right
extending towards St Denis.

From their respective camps and quarters, to
the ground before mentioned, the divisions marched in the following order :

The first corps, consisting of the 1st and 3d
divisions of infantry, formed the left of the line,
and marched from their camp, in the Bois de
Boulogne, by the Port de Neuilly, the triumphal

arch, and by the walls of Paris, leaving Montmartre on their left.

The 2d corps, consisting of the 2d and 4th divisions of infantry, formed the right of the line, and marched from their camp in the Bois de Boulogne, by the Port de Neuilly, leaving Montmartre on their right.

The reserve, consisting of the 5th, 6th, and 7th divisions of infantry, formed the centre, and marched, independently, by divisions, from their respective camps and cantonments : the former from its camp behind the village of Clichy ; the 6th division from Neuilly ; and the 7th from its cantonments at Montmartre and camp of St Denis. The 5th and 6th divisions left Montmartre on their right.

The infantry moved to the ground in column, at quarter distance.

Colonel Estoff's brigade of cavalry followed the 2d corps, and formed in its rear, in close column of regiments, of the front of a squadron.

Lord Edward Somerset's brigade of British cavalry crossed the Seine by the bridges of Anwiers and Neuilly ;—keeping to the left of the infantry, and with the cavalry brigade of Lord George Beresford, which moved by Argenteuil and St Denis, formed in rear of the division, in close column of regiments, of the front of a squadron.

Each division, as it arrived on the ground, was formed in three lines of brigades, in close column of battalions, right in front. The artillery of each division was formed on its right.

The whole army having arrived on the ground, the colours of those regiments forming the front line, and the officers of the leading division, were ordered three paces to the front, as at open order. Formed in this manner, we waited the arrival of the august spectators.

The Duke of Wellington arrived a few minutes after nine; and the Emperors of Austria and Russia, and King of Prussia, about ten. In the suite of the allied Monarchs were Prince Marshal Blucher, Prince Schwartzenberg, Field-Marshal Barclay de Tolly, Platoff, Hetman of the Cossacks, the Archduke Constantine of Russia, two Prussian Princes, sons of the King, and fully 100 others of inferior rank. There was scarcely one of them who had not some decoration or other, and many of them had the whole of their breast covered with them. As they approached the centre of the line, the front companies presented arms, while the music of the whole played our national air of " God save the King." The usual ceremony, of receiving the reviewing General, being over, the Field-Marshal collected the Generals commanding divisions and gave them their final instructions, regarding the operations of the day. The movements were exactly those which were performed by the Field-Marshal on the glorious plains of Salamanca.

The second corps made a movement to its right,
and attacked the supposed left of the enemy, corresponding with that made by the 3d division on
the 22d July 1812. The 5th division marched
to support the 2d corps in the attack, but finding that it had been successful, it was ordered to halt and front. The light troops of the divisions, composing the reserve, were ordered to
cover the advance of their respective divisions to
the attack of the centre of the enemy's position.
On this occasion, the 5th division performed the
same movements as the 6th division did on the
day above-mentioned. As the fifth division was
about to advance, the allied Sovereigns, Princes,
Generals, &c. galloped forward to our brigade,
with which they remained some minutes, admiring the nut-brown knees, and tartan dress of the
hardy Caledonians.

The first corps moved between Montmartre and
Paris, in order to attack the right of the enemy.
The troops kept the walls of Paris on their left till
they arrived at the barrier of Clichy, when, by
debouching on the road to that village, they got
into the supposed rear of the enemy, and conse-
quently gained their object.

The 2d corps, and the corps of reserve, moved
round the northern base of Montmartre, in column, at quarter distance, with their skirmishers in
front, till the former arrived at Clichy, and the
latter within two hundred yards of the road which

leads from that village to Paris. The whole army
was then ordered to halt, and the 5th and 6th divisions to form line ; the front line was dressed
on the 92d. These divisions having formed as
directed, arms were ordered, and the men stood
at ease for twenty minutes.

During this little indulgence, the Archduke
Constantine of Russia rode up to the 92d regiment,
and minutely examined every part of the Highlanders' dress. In a few minutes the Archduke
was joined by his brother the Emperor. To one
of the privates the latter said, " Take off your
" bonnet, my lad, and shew it to this gentleman."
The Archduke having looked at it, returned it to
the owner, when the Emperor remarked to his
brother, " This is a brave regiment." The royal
brothers then rode along the front of the regiment.
Addressing himself to Captain F. the Emperor
said, " This is my brother, Sir : Will you have
the kindness to shew him your sword ?" Having
examined the claymore, the illustrious brothers
left us and joined the other distinguished personages. As soon as they retired, the reserve were
ordered to advance ; the first corps to debouche,
on the road from Paris to Clichy, and the second
corps to turn the village of Clichy, by moving between it and the right of the reserve ; the first
and second corps advanced in column at quarter
distance, and the reserve in line. The 5th and
6th divisions advanced in line about 500 yards,

past whose flanks the heavy cavalry made a very fine charge during the advance. This was the last offensive movement we made on the 22d, against our invisible enemies. The whole army was then ordered to halt, and the battalions in line to form in columns at quarter distance, preparatory to passing the Emperor in review.

The Duke of Wellington and the allied Sovereigns having taken post on the left of the road leading from Clichy to Neuilly, the army marched past in column of companies at quarter distance.

The review was attended by almost all the English nobility and gentry in Paris. Their splendid equipages added much to the magnificence of the scene. Every part of the northern slope of Montmartre was completely covered with them at the commencement of our operations. As the army advanced, the beaux and the belles retired. And when the Emperor of Austria posted himself, as before mentioned, the whole collected round him to witness the novel spectacle, of a British army passing an Emperor of Austria in review, under the walls of the metropolis of France.

It is a curious fact, that there was not above 50 or 100 Frenchmen present on that occasion; and those who did attend, were the very lowest of society.

A few days ago, Sir W—— D—— went out

with his dog and his gun, to pass one or two of those tedious hours which now hang so heavily on our hands. But he had not been long engaged in the amusement, when he received a message from the Duke de B—i, requesting him to leave the royal domains. Sir W. D., a little hurt at the message, proceeding as it did from such a quarter, replied to the bearer—" Pray, Sir, Will " you have the goodness to ask the Duke de B—i, " who was it that gave him these domains ?" The Duke rode off, and Sir W. prosecuted his sport, till the hour of three told him it was time to return to dinner.

CALAIS, *December* 17, 1815.

THIS is the last letter you will receive from me on military matters from this country. By the inclosed copy of a general order, issued by the Duke of Wellington, at Paris, on the 30th November, you will perceive, that your friend's, and a long list of other regiments, are returning home, their services being no longer required in France.

Till the latter end of October, the movements of the allied army were particularly devoid of interest; so much so, indeed, that I did not consider one of them worth sending you.

On the 29th October, the 5th division quitted its camp at Clichy, and that night stopt at St Germain, a town which Bonaparte never honoured with a visit. The reason, it is said, is, that the inhabitants being staunch royalists, the Emperor was afraid to trust himself in the midst of them.

On the 2d November, the 8th brigade occupied Meulan, and villages in the neighbourhood; and the 9th brigade Mountain Ville, Neuf le Veux, Mere, &c. Our regiment removed to Montfort on the 8th.

In these places we remained comfortably cantoned till the following order, issued by Sir Denis Pack, on the 29th, compelled us to leave them on the 30th.

PORT CHARTRAIN, *Nov.* 29, 1815.
BRIGADE ORDERS.

The 4th battalion of the royals, the 42d, and 92d regiments, are to march to-morrow for Meulan, on their route for Boulogne.

The corps are to march independently, under orders from their respective commanding officers, who will please to send forward, very early, an officer to Meulan, to receive directions respecting the quartering of their corps there, and in the vicinity, for the night.

The Staff-Surgeon has been instructed to give directions respecting the sick, and the Commissary of the brigade will afford all the means of transport in his power.

Major-General Sir Denis Pack cannot allow these corps to pass thus from under his command, without expressing his regret at losing them. The conduct of the 4th battalion of the royals, both in camp and quarters, has been like that of the 3d battalion; and that of the two regiments, " orderly and sol- " dier-like ;" and he is confident, from the high state of discipline the corps appear in, they would have imitated their comrades in the 3d battalion, had the same glorious opportunity been afforded them.

The services rendered by the 92d regiment, in the Duke of Wellington's campaigns in the Peninsula, and his Grace's late short and triumphant one in Belgium, are so generally and so highly appreciated, as to make praise from him almost idle ; nevertheless, he cannot help adding his tribute of applause. And to the 42d regiment he really thinks he would seem ungrateful, as well as unmindful of the best feelings of a soldier, did he not, in taking leave, assure them, that he will ever retain, with sentiments of admiration, the remembrance of the invincible valour displayed by the corps on so many memorable and trying occasions.

Agreeably to the above order, we quitted the good people of Montfort, and marched to Meulan. On our arrival at that town, we were informed that the 28th, 42d, and 92d regiments, were to be brigaded, for the march to the coast, under the command of Colonel Sir C. Belson of the 28th regiment. On the 1st instant, these three regiments marched to Pont Oise; thence by Bevais, Abbeville, Montreuil, and Boulogne, to Calais. On our arrival here, this morning, the men were embarked in transports in the harbour.

On our march here from Meulan, the people in general were extremely attentive to us. At the Chateau de Rique, about five miles from Montreuil, I was entertained in the most hospitable manner by the amiable family to which it belongs. The noble proprietor was a captain in the royal army, under Louis the XVIth. At the breaking out of the revolution, he resigned his commission, and retired into private life, where he has since remained, undisturbed by any one of the French rulers, who have governed this unhappy country since the death of that monarch. Marshal Ney was three months in his house, when the Army of England lay encamped in the vicinity of Boulogne; and the ex-queen of Holland was also his guest for a similar period. The entertaining of these individuals, he confessed, cost him a great sum of money. Marshal Soult, he informed me, was a corporal in the company he at one time commanded, and was by him brought to a court-martial, and punished. My noble landlord also told me, that at Montreuil, his own house, and various other parts in the neighbourhood, the cannonade at Waterloo was distinctly heard, by many hundreds of the inhabitants. I was a little incredulous on the occasion; for the distance cannot be less than 90 to 100 miles. He represented the noise as resembling the rolling of distant thunder; and he said, that some of those people who had attentively listened to it, throughout the day, remarked to him, about nine o'clock at night, that the battle was over, and had terminated in favour of the allies.

At dinner, the first day, the Count desired us, and his own friends, to fill a bumper of claret, which, having been done, he gave, as a toast, " The brave Scotch, who so gallantly maintained " their ancient fame on the plains of Waterloo." I quitted that family with much regret. From the Count, and his lady, I had a very pressing invitation to spend a few months with them. They were so very earnest, that on the morning of my departure, they begged that I would apply for leave to return from Boulogne, when the regiment embarked.

A few days after we quitted our camp at Clichy, Captain H. and I were billetted on a chateau, in the vicinity of Mountain Ville. On the evening of the second day, we got orders to march at an early hour, on the following morning, for Neuf le Veux. Before the family retired to rest, they gave orders to the servants to have breakfast ready for us at a given hour. On coming down stairs, in the morning, we found the breakfast table groaning under a load of cold fowls, veal, ham, tea, coffee, wine, &c.— Having finished, the servant began to pack up the veal, fowls, &c.; and in a few minutes presented them to us, saying, " Where shall I put " this parcel?" We told him, that the British officers never carried any thing from the houses on whom they were billetted, and, putting a piece of money into his hand, desired him to express to the family how much we felt ourselves obliged by their kindness and attention.

Astonished at our refusal, and probably more so at what we had given him, the poor fellow stood motionless; then recovering himself, he said, with a vacant smile; " Ah! then, I see you British officers are not Prussians."

GENERAL ORDERS.

HEAD-QUARTERS, PARIS, *Nov.* 30, 1815.

No. 1. The British troops which are to remain in France, are to be formed as follows:—

2. The 1st dragoon guards, 2d dragoon guards, and 3d dragoons are to be the 1st brigade of cavalry.

3. The 7th and 18th hussars, and 12th light dragoons, are to be the 2d brigade of cavalry.

4. The 11th and 13th light dragoons, and 15th hussars, are to be the 3d brigade of cavalry.

5. The 3d battalion, first guards, and 2d battalion Cold-stream guards, are to be the 1st brigade of infantry.

6. The 3d battalion royals, 1st battalion 57th, and 2d battalion 95th, are to be the second brigade of infantry.

7. The 1st battalions of the 3d, 39th, and 91st regiments, are to be the 3d brigade of infantry.

8. The 1st battalions of the 4th, 52d, and 79th regiments, are to be the 4th brigade of infantry.

9. The 1st battalions of the 5th, 9th, and 21st regiments, are to be the 5th brigade of infantry.

10. The 1st battalions 6th, 29th regiment, and 1st battalion 71st, are to be the 6th brigade of infantry.

11. The 1st battalion 7th, 23d regiment, and 1st battalion 43d, are to be the 7th brigade of infantry.

12. The 1st battalions of the 27th, 40th, and 95th regiments, are to be the 8th brigade of infantry.

13. The 1st battalions of the 81st and 88th regiments, are to be the 9th brigade of infantry.

14. Major-General Lord Edward Somerset, is to command the 1st brigade of cavalry.

15. Major-General Sir Hussey Vivian, is to command the 2d brigade of cavalry.

16. Major-General Sir Colquhoun Grant, is to command the 3d brigade of cavalry.

17. Major-General Sir Peregrine Maitland, is to command the 1st brigade of infantry.

18. Major-General Sir Manley Power, is to command the 2d brigade of infantry.

19. Major-General the Hon. Sir R. W. O'Callaghan, is to command the 3d brigade of infantry.

20. Major-General Sir Denis Pack, is to command the 4th brigade of infantry.

21. Major-General Sir Thomas Brisbane, is to command the 5th brigade of infantry.

22. Major-General Sir T. Bradford, is to command the 6th brigade of infantry.

23. Major-General Sir James Kempt, is to command the 7th brigade of infantry.

24. Major-General Sir J. Lambert, is to command the 8th brigade of infantry.

25. Major-General Sir John Keane, is to command the 9th brigade of infantry.

26. The 1st division of infantry is to be composed of the 1st, 7th, and 8th brigades, and is to be commanded by Lieutenant-General the Hon. Sir Lowry Cole.

27. The 2d division of infantry is to be composed of the 3d, 4th, and 6th brigades, and is to be commanded by Lieutenant-General Sir Henry Clinton.

3

28. The 3d division of infantry is to be composed of the 2d, 5th, and 9th brigades, and is to be commanded by Lieutenant-General the Hon. Sir Charles Colville.

29. Lieutenant-General Lord Combermere, will take the command of the cavalry.

30. Lieutenant-General Lord Hill, will take the command . of the infantry.

31. The British troops to return to England, are to be brigaded as follows, for their march :—

.32. The 1st and 2d life guards, royal horse guards, blue, and 3d dragoon guards, under the command of Colonel Athrope, royal horse guards, blue.

33. The 1st, 2d, and 6th dragoons, under the command of Colonel Muter.

34. The 10th hussars, 16th, and 23d light dragoons, under the command of Colonel Quentin.

35. The 2d battalion 1st guards, and 2d battalion 3d guards, under the command of Colonel Askew, 1st guards.

36. The 36th regiment, 38th, 2d 73d, and 3d 95th, under the command of Colonel the Hon. Sir Charles Greville of the 38th regiment.

37. The 2d battalions of the 12th and 30th, and 33d regiment, under the command of Colonel Stirke, of the 12th regiment.

38. The 1st battalions of the 41st and 90th regiments, and a detachment of the royal waggon train, under the command of Lieutenant-Colonel Evans of the 41st regiment.

39. The 3d battalion 14th, 2d 35th, and 51st regiment, under the command of Colonel Mitchell of the 51st.

U

40. The 54th regiment, and second battalions 59th and 69th regiments, under the command of Lieutenant-Colonel Austin, 59th regiment.

41. The 4th battalion royals, the 28th, 42d, and 92d regiments, under the command of Colonel Sir C. Belson, 28th regiment.

42. The 3d battalion 27th, 32d regiment, and detachment of staff corps, under the command of Colonel Sir John M'Lean, 27th regiment.

43. The 16th regiment, 2d 44th, and 1st battalion 82d, under the command of Colonel Tolley, 16th regiment.

44. The 58th regiment, 2d 62d, 64th regiment, and 2d 81st, under the command of Colonel Walker of the 58th regiment.

45. Notwithstanding these orders, the troops are to continue with their divisions, and commanded as at present, till those ordered to England will march; and the Quarter-Master General will, in concert with the General Officers, have assembled those destined by this day's orders to remain in France.

46. When the troops of the German Legion, and the Hanoverian, will march, it will be under the command of the officers commanding the several brigades of infantry and cavalry.

47. Major-General Sir James Lyon will be so kind as to give orders for the formation of the Hanoverian contingent, at a place which will be made known to him by the Chief of the Staff of the Allied Army.

48. Upon breaking up the army, which the Field-Marshal has had the honour of commanding, he begs leave to return thanks to the General Officers, and the

Officers and Troops, for their uniform good conduct.

49. In the late short, but memorable campaign, they have given proofs to the world, that they possess, in an eminent degree, all the good qualities of soldiers ; and the Field-Marshal is happy to be able to applaud their regular good conduct in their camps and cantonments—not less than when engaged with the enemy in the field.

50. Whatever may be the future destination of those brave troops, of which the Field-Marshal now takes his leave, he trusts, that every individual will believe, that he will ever feel the deepest interest in their honour and welfare, and will always be happy to promote either.

——

To-morrow morning, if the wind be fair, we leave this port—" For Old England, ho !"

THE END.

INDEX

(Compiled by editor)

Note:
The following index is divided into the following headings, with further sub-divisions:-
Battles, Campaigns, Wars; Casualties; Ships; Tactics; UNITS AND FORMATIONS; Weapons and Ammunition.

Bagpipes, 12,18,222,235
Bandits, 124
Banos, 124,127,128,129,131,135,136
Barnes, Maj Gen [Sir Edward], 164,
169,180,230
Barrueta, 157,158,170
Bastan (valley), 155,164
Battles, Campaigns, Wars
Alba (1811), 117
Albuera (1811), 64,88
Anhoe (1813), 194-195
Arroya (1811), 41
Badajoz (siege) (1812), 58,59,63,
64, 66,67 [see also under:
Casualties]
Breaches, 64,65
Castle, 65
Barossa (1811), 58
Belgium (1815), 299 [see also
specific battles; ie Quatre Bras,
Waterloo]
Bidassoa (river), 203 [see also in
general section; under
Casualties]
Buenos Aires (1807), 112
Burgos (siege) (1812), 110,111,114
Cadiz (siege), 101
Cuidad Rodrigo (siege) (1812),
51,52,53,55,57,68
Fuentes d'Onor (1811), 9
Ligny (1815), 233,237
Malplaquet (1709), 280
Maya, 159,164-165,168,170-171,
193,196
Nive (river) (1813), 202 [see also:
Nive (river)]
Quatre Bras (1815), 224-233,274
[see also under: **Casualties**;
Quatre Bras in general section]
Peninsula (1809-1814), 299 [see also
individual battles and campaigns; see
also: Spain, Portugal in general
section]
Reconquista (11th-15th Centuries),
105
Salamanca (1812), 97,99,101,293,
294
San Sebastian (siege) (1813), 184
[see also: in general section]
Talavera (1809), 106
Tariffa (siege) (1811-1812), 54
Villa Garcia (1812), 67 [see also
under: **Casualties**]

Vittoria (1813), 147-152,153,163
[see also under: **Casualties**]
Waterloo (1815), 246-265,270,289,
301 [see also: individual place
names; eg Hugomont]
Wounded, 266,267,268,270,
271,272,273,274
Bavay, 282,285
Bayonne, 161,196,203
Beachy-head, 206
Beaumont, 286
Beef, 20,76,119,242
Bejer, 127,128,129,131,136,137 [see
also under: **Casualties**]
Beker, Capt, 289
Belem (fort), 2,37,38,134
Belfast, 205,206
Belle Alliance [see: La Belle Alliance]
Belson, Col Sir C, 168,300,306
Benvenida, 98
Beresford, Lt Gen Sir William Carr,
64,292
Berlenga, 94,95
Berri, Duc de, 297
Bidassoa (river), 154,157,158,159,184,
185,189,202 [see also under: **Battles,
Campaigns, Wars; Casualties**]
Bienvenida, 93
Bill-hooks, 277
Biscuit, 222
Bisket, Pte William, 181-182
Blacier, Capt, 61,62
Black Horse Square, 2,36
Blankets, 141,242
Blockhouses, 179,185,186,193
Blucher, [Field Marshal Gebhard
Leberecht] Prince Marshal,
220,221,233,234,236,237,259,264,
265,270,279,286,287,290,293
Boats, 11,36,39,105
Canal boats, 271
Bois du Bossu (wood), 230,231,232,233
Bonaparte [see: Napoleon]
Bonnefoux, Capt, 289
Bossu [see: Bois du Bossu]
Boufflers, Marshal, 280
Boulogne, 299,300
Bourbons, 284
Bradford, Maj Gen Sir T, 304
Braine la Leude, 244,245
Braine le Compte, 282
Brandy, 76
Bread, 222

Breastworks, 8,89,129,179,186,195
Bridges, 45,60,62,66,67,72,73,74,76,
    77,81,82,89,105,111,112,120,144,
    197,199,209,285,290,292 [see also:
    individual place names; eg Fuente
    Duenna/names of individual
    bridges; eg Puento Largo]
    Pontoon, 105
Brie, 220
Brisbane, Maj Gen Sir Thomas, 304
Britain [see: Great Britain]
British, 36
Brooks, Pte John, 180-181
Bruce, Robert, 276
Bruges, 207
Brune, [Marshall Guillaume-Marie-
    Anne] Gen, 27
Brunswick (Duke of), 223,226,239,
    240,278
Brussels, 208,211,212-213,218,219,
    220,221,223,224,235,243,263,266,
    267,268,269,270,271,278,282,285
    Hospitals, 272,273
Bugles, 220,222,242
Bull fight, 82-85,192
Bulls, 82,83,84,85
Bulow, General [Friedrich Wilhelm],
    260,286
Burgos, 136,141,144,145 [see also
    under: Battles, Campaigns, Wars]
    Castle, 142
Burgueta, 192
Byng, Maj Gen Sir John, 14,216

C

Cacares (province), 15
Cacares (town), 15,22
Cadogan, Col the Hon [Henry],
    147,149
Cadiz, 105 [see also under: Battles,
    Campaigns, Wars]
Caffarelli, General [Louis-Marie-
    Joseph, Maximilian de], 116
Calais, 298,300
Calzada de Orepesa, 106
Cambo, 192,196,197,198,199,200,201
Cambray, 285,286
Cameron, Lt Col, 61,103,149,156,
    164,167,200,210,230,231,277,278
Cameron (Piper), 235

Campbell, Capt, 1
Campbell, Maj Gen [Sir Achibald]
    (also referred to as Brig Gen), 14,
    91,92,175
Camp-kettles, 20
Campo-Major, 30,31,32
Canals, 207,208
Candeleiria, 127
Cano, Aldea del [see: Aldea del Cano]
Canteen, 50
Cantonments, 4,101,105,134,136,
    292,307
Carey, Pte P, 79
Cases de Don Gomes, 120
Castello Branco, 53,55,67
Casualties
    Badajoz
        British, 66,134
        French, 66
    Bejer
        French, 129
    Bidassoa (River)
        French, 185
    Cuidad Rodrigo
        French, 52
    Ebro (mountains)
        French, 145
    Fuento del Maestro
        French, 50
    Maya
        British, 33
    Napoleon (fort)
        Allies, 77
        French, 77
    Quatre Bras
        British, 235
    Ragusa (fort)
        Allies, 77
        French, 77
    Tormes (river)
        French, 138
    Villa Garcia
        French, 67
    Vittoria
        French, 152
Cateau, 284
Cegales, 140
Chamusca, 36
Charleroi, 219,224,230,243,244,245
Chateau de Rique, 300
Chowne, Lt Gen Tilson, 72,91
Churches, 10
Churchill, John (Duke of

Duke of Otranto [see: Otranto (Duke of)]
Duke of Wellington [see: Wellington (Duke of)]
Duke of York [see: York (Duke of)]
Dungeness, 206
Dunkirk, 207
Du Plat, Maj Gen, 216
Dutch, 222

E

Eagles (French standards), 251,254
Earl Dalhousie [see: Dalhousie, Earl]
Earl of Uxbridge [see: Uxbridge, Lt Gen the Earl]
Ebro (mountains), 144 [see also under: **Casualties**]
Ebro (river), 142,144,164
Edinburgh, 205
Edinburgh (New Town), 207
El Campilo, 101,104
Elio, General, 111,112
Elizonda, 158,159,170,177
El Medico, 107
Elsa, 136
Emperor of Austria [see: Francis I]
Emperor of Russia [see: Alexander I]
England/English, 33,134,200,203, 213,289,290
Erraza, 164
Errazu, 177
Erskine, Lt Gen Sir William, 13,25, 28,71,81,91,103
Escurial, 115
Espagna, Don Carlos de, 111,131,189
Espallate, 165,196,197,200,202
Estoff, Col, 292
Estramadura, 15,54,86,105,129
Evans, Lt Col, 305

F

Ferdinand VII (King of Spain), 108
Fires, 23
Fleas, 69
Fleurus, 219,220
Flores, 116
Forage, 123,124
Forbes, Maj Gen, 206
Fortifications, 213 [see also: Abbatis;

Blockhouses; Breastworks; Redoubts; Traverses]
Forts, 77 [see also under: name of fort; eg Ragusa]
Fouche, Joseph, 287,288
Foy, General [Maximilien-Sebastien], 127,128,129,131,191
France, 126,142,143,151,153,154, 155,158,161,164,172,179,189, 191,192,198,207,218,219,222, 242,255,276,280,281,286,289, 298,306
[see also: individual place names; eg Paris]
Royalists, 288,298
Francis I (Emperor of Austria), 291, 293,295,296
Frasne, 219,229
Frederick William III (King of Prussia), 293
French, 7,12,21,27,37,46,49,50,69, 86,90,128,131,132,140,141,162, 179,189,191,210,218,229,232,234, 250,252,255,257,263,276,280,285, 290,296
[see also under: **UNITS AND FORMATIONS** - France]
Freyre, General, 111,112
Friars, 56
Frith, Mr (Chaplain to 2nd Division), 188
Fuente del Maestre, 45,46,50,86,99 [see also under: **Casualties**]
Fuente Duenna, 111,112,113

G

Gaffeta, 34,37
Gallegao, 9,37
Gavao, 11,12,34,37
Gazan, General [Honore-Theodore-Maxime], 155,158,159
Genappe, 223,236,238,239,240, 244,277
George III (King of England), 108
Germany, 142
Ghent, 205,207,208-209,211,271
Gibraltar, 189
Girard, General [Jean-Baptiste], 15,22, 24,26,27
Giron, General [Pedro Agostin], 184

313

T

ERRATA.

Page 58, line 15, *for* 2d, *read* 6th.
   86, line 11, *for* Ulna, *read* Llera.
   88, line 15, *for* former, *read* famed.
   92, line 22, *for* Guadiana, *read* Guadacia.
   93, line 10, *for* Guadiana, *read* Guadacia.
 106, line 22, *for* decayed, *read* destroyed.
 117, line 23, *for* four, *read* five.
 118, line 14, *for* Mozarles, *read* Mozarbes.
 124, line 9, *for* it, *read* them.
 167, line 4, *after* formed, *insert* line.
 219, line 4, *for* is, *read* was.
      line 6, *for* are, *read* were.
 251, line 22, *for* brigade, *read* division.
 256, line 25, *for* few *read* fire.